GROWING
IN THE
SHADOW

CHILDREN OF ALCOHOLICS

EDITED BY Robert J. Ackerman

WITH CONTRIBUTIONS BY 21 LEADING NATIONAL AUTHORITIES

ii

Published by
Health Communications, Inc.
1721 Blount Road, Suite 1
Pompano Beach, Florida 33069

ISBN 0-932194-32-X

Printed in the United States of America

Dedication
To
Kimberly, Jason and Robert

Acknowledgements

Initially, I would like to thank the individual contributors to this book. I am very appreciative of their willingness to share their work and support this collection of writings on children of alcoholics. Not only is their work highly important, but also it is surpassed only by their friendship. Thank you.

I am deeply indebted to Oliver J. Ford III for his editorial assistance and suggestions for cohesiveness and format. To Laurie Brodeur and Sharon Richwine goes my appreciation for their administrative support.

About the Contributors

Robert J. Ackerman, Ph.D., is Associate Professor of Sociology at Indiana University of Pennsylvania, and the Director of Addiction Research & Consulting Services of Indiana, PA. He is an author, lecturer and founding board member of the National Association for Children of Alcoholics. Also, he is a member of the Professional Advisory Board of the Chemical People Institute.

Tim Allen, M.A., is Executive Director of Breakthrough, a program in Costa Mesa, CA, designed to serve the needs of adolescents and their families regarding chemical dependency. He is a founding board member of the National Association for Children of Alcoholics.

Suzanne E. Anderson, M.Ed., is the Family Therapy Supervisor for the Gateway Rehabilitation Center in Aliquippa, PA. She has worked as a therapist and trainer in the chemical dependency field for 11 years.

Claudia Black, Ph.D., M.S.W, is a private practitioner in Laguna Niguel, CA. Her work in the field of children of alcoholics is widely recognized through her writings, and her work as a counsutant. She is chairperson for the National Association for Children of Alcoholics, and winner of the 1985 Marty Mann Award.

Julie D. Bowden, M.S., is a licensed marriage and family therapist in private practice in Santa Barbara, CA. She is an author and consultant, and is a founding board member of the National Association for Children of Alcoholics.

Gael Lanier Caution, Ph.D., is Chief of Psychology at Morris Village Alcohol and Drug Addiction Treatment Center in Columbia, South Carolina. Her major area of research is in mental health issues facing black Americans. Additionally, she has served as a White House fellow.

Timmen L. Cermak, M.D., is a psychiatrist and co-founder of Genesis, a treatment program for adult children of alcoholics in San Francisco, CA. He is an author and consultant. A founding member of the National Association for Children of Alcoholics, he currently chairs that organization.

Sharon Wegscheider-Cruse, M.A., C.A.C., is President of ONSITE Training & Consulting, Inc., Sioux Falls, SD, and Director of The Caron Foundation Training Institute, Wernersville, PA. She is a past recipient of the Marty Mann Award, and is the founding board chairperson of the National Association for Children of Alcoholics.

Philip Oliver-Diaz, M.S.W., is the Director of the Division of Alcohol and Substance Abuse for the Rockland County Mental Health Center, Pomona, NY. He is co-founder and co-chair of the Black and Hispanic Alcohol and Substance Abuse Network, and is a co-founder and past president of the New York State Coalition for Children of Alcoholics. Currently, he serves as vice-chairperson of the National Association for Children of Alcoholics.

Lorie Dwinell, M.S.W., is in private psychotherapy practice in Seattle, WA. She specializes in the treatment of alcoholism, children of alcoholics, grief, loss, depression, and the treatment of alcoholic women.

Ronald Figueroa, M.S., is the Administrator for Project Rainbow in Pomona, NY. He is the author of a bilingual children's book on alcoholism, and is currently lecturing nationally on Hispanic family alcoholism, outreach strategies, and ethnotherapeutic treatment.

Jerry P. Flanzer, D.S.W., is Professor and Chairperson of the Department of Social Work at the University of Arkansas at Little Rock, AK. He is the Director of the Mid-America Institute on Violence in Families, and is well noted for his work on alcoholism and family violence.

Herbert L. Gravitz, Ph.D., is a licensed clinical psychologist in private practice in Santa Barbara, CA. He is an author, consultant and the former Program Director of the UC-Santa Barbara Counseling Center. He is a founding board member of the National Association for Children of Alcoholics.

Joseph C. Kern, Ph.D., is the Director of the Department of Drugs and Alcohol Addiction, County of Nassau, Hempstead, NY. He is the author of numerous research articles on children of alcoholics, and currently serves on the board of directors for both the National Association for Children of Alcoholics and the Children of Alcoholics Foundation. Joe would like to thank Miriam Solomon of the Alcoholism Services for Nassau County for her comments and contributions to his chapter.

Rokeller Lerner is co-founder and co-director of Children Are People, Inc., St. Paul, MN. She is an author and a consultant and a founding board member of the National Association for Children of Alcoholics. Additionally, she is the co-author of a chemical abuse curriculum for elementary schools.

Ellen R. Morehouse, M.S.W., is the Executive Director for Student Assistance Services, White Plains, NY. She is an author and consultant and the creator of the Student Assistance Program model which has been adopted nationally. She is an adjunct faculty member to Fordham University, and a founding board member of the National Association for Children of Alcoholics.

Jane Middleton-Moz, M.S., is the Clinical Director of the Seattle Mental Health Institute. She is on the faculty of Seattle University and a family therapist on the Tulalip Reservation. Jane would like to thank Mr. Wayne Williams and Ms. Juanita Morales, Tulalip Tribes, Tulalip, WA, for their contributions in the chapter, "The Wisdom of Elders."

Barbara Naiditch is co-founder and co-director of Children Are People, Inc., St. Paul, MN. She has co-authored a chemical abuse curriculum for elementary schools, and specializes in establishing support groups for children of alcoholics ages 5-12. She was a founding board member for the National Association for Children of Alcoholics.

Patricia O'Gorman, Ph.D., is a psychologist in private practice in East Greenbush, NY, and Vice-President of O'Gorman and Diaz, Inc., a training and consulting firm. She is former director of the Division of Prevention for the National Institute on Alcohol Abuse and Alcoholism, and a founding board member of the National Association for Children of Alcoholics.

Tarpley Richards, M.S.W., is a private practitioner and is affiliated with Counseling Associates, Washington, DC. She is an author and consultant, and a board member of the National Association for Children of Alcoholics.

Robert A. Ross is the former executive deputy director of the New York State Division of Alcoholism and Alcohol Abuse. He is an author and currently works as an independent consultant to substance abuse and health care agencies at the national level.

Janet Geringer Woititz, Ed.D., is a human relations counselor in private practice, and president of the Institute for Counseling and Training in Verona, NJ. She is an instructor at the Rutgers Summer School of Alcohol Studies and lectures at the national level. She specializes in adult children of alcoholics, and has published extensively in this area.

Introduction

Only recently have the effects of parental alcoholism on children been accorded the serious attention due a social problem of such large dimensions. The problems of children of alcoholics have been addressed in much the same fashion as other problems of children, such as children's rights under the law, and child abuse and neglect. They have been considered to be derivative from and secondary to the problems of their parents. Typically, the focus of intervention strategies has been on addressing the problems of the primary person impaired, then on addressing the needs of the non-impaired spouse, and finally on addressing the needs of their children. The priorities of intervention have been reflected in the creation of organizations to meet the needs as they were understood to exist. Alcoholics Anonymous was founded more than fifty years ago to assist alcoholics, and Al-Anon was founded some years later to assist spouses of alcoholics. It was not until the late 1960s that all states even passed laws regarding the reporting of suspected cases of child abuse, however, and it was the 1970s before a national center for the study of child abuse and neglect was established.

The movement to address the specific needs of children of alcoholics has evolved only recently. In retrospect, it seems rather curious that the needs of the children of alcoholics should have been assigned the lowest priority in receiving treatment, moreso in light of the fact that there are far more children of alcoholics than there are alcoholics. Estimates of the prevalence of alcoholism indicate that there are approximately 10 million alcoholics in the United States today, 73% of them married. It is estimated that there are more than 28 million children of alcoholics, however, a ration that may well have been greater when larger families were the norm. Recognition of the need to address the problems of children of alcoholics may have been delayed by the failure to recognize their problems as being apart from those of the alcoholic parent(s), as noted above. This situation doubtless was exacerbated by the lack of societal understanding of, or resources to, address any further problems, and by the fact that the children had little choice but to endure much of their conditions, lacking any legal standing or power to change them. Although the effects of parental alcoholism on children had been addressed throughout the history of Al-Anon, it was not until the 1980s that there was sufficient recognition of the individual nature of the concerns of children of alcoholics that formal organizations were created to address their concerns. The Children of Alcoholics Foundation was founded in 1982, and the National Association for Children of Alcoholics was founded in 1983.

With the formation of these two organizations, which represent and bring together much of the research, observations, efforts, and energy of the past 30 years, the issues confronting children of alcoholics have finally been recognized as needing to be addressed in their own right, rather than as an aspect of the problem of parental alcoholism. Treatment, support, recovery, and growth are now possible for children of alcoholics, if concerned and informed citizens, some of whom may be adult children of alcoholics themselves, will advocate and implement services for children of alcoholics. Much of this advocacy already has begun, as is evident in the efforts to increase public awareness of the problems of children of alcoholics of all ages chronicled in many of the essays in this collection. The authors of these essays are many of the modern "pioneers" in the field, who have, and continue to create, informed awareness about the needs of children of alcoholics. In their contributions, they offer a diversity of insights, opinions, and perspectives on the many issues related to children of alcoholics gained in their collectively broad experience in this comparatively recent field of study.

This book is divided into four parts and addresses children of alcoholics from childhood through adulthood. The first part considers the most immediate and most powerful influence on children of alcoholics—the family. The second part concerns the impact of parental alcoholism on young children during their formative years. The period of adolescence and the difficulty adolescents experience in establishing a consistent identity in a dysfunctional alcoholic family is the focus of part three. Part four is about adult children of alcoholics, who comprise the largest age group of children of alcoholics today. Finally, this book has been written for anyone with an interest in, or who currently is working with children of alcoholics, and especially for those children of alcoholics who want to better understand and to accept themselves and want to live their lives to the fullest.

—*Robert J. Ackerman*

CONTENTS

Part One
Family: The Museum of Memories

Central to understanding the impact of parental alcoholism is understanding that it affects each individual in the entire family, perhaps in very
different ways. In the first chapter, Robert Ackerman offers an overview
of alcoholism, and examines how families evolve through different
phases of adjustment to alcoholism and the effects on children during
each phase are discussed. In chapter two, Timmen Cermak offers a new
category of diagnosis of chemical dependency and children of alcoholics.
In chapter three, Jerry Flanzer addresses the relationship between parental alcoholism and family violence and describes how many children of
alcoholics must endure not only parental alcoholism, but also domestic
violence. Sharon Wegshgeider-Cruse, in chapter four, discusses working with members of the alcoholic family and helping them to recovery
for exposure to dysfunctional family dynamics. Chapters five, six and
seven are concerned with the effects of parental alcoholism in minority
families in our society. In chapter five, Philip Oliver-Diaz and Ronald
Figueroa offer a treatment approach for working with Hispanic families.
Jane Middelton-Moz, in chapter six, addresses alcoholism in Native
American and Native Alaskan families. Finally, in chapter seven, Gael
Caution considers the dynamics involved in alcoholism and the black
family.

Chapter One
Alcoholism and the Family

Robert J. Ackerman

Living with an alcoholic is a family affair. Because it subjects all members of a household to constant stress and fears of various kinds, it has often been referred to as a "family illness." To one degree or another, all members of the family are affected. However, not all alcoholic families, nor all members of the same family, are affected in a similar manner.

The Collective Mind

Not all alcoholic families, nor all members of the family, are affected in the same way. To assume that all family members are equally and identically affected is to assume that the family possesses a "collective mind." The "collective mind" assumes that the entire family shares the same feelings about the alcoholic and alcoholism. Additionally, this would mean that all alcoholic families are alike. This is not true. To understand the effects of alcoholism on the family, we need to look at the individual members of the family. The individual is the beginning unit of analysis to understanding family dynamics in an alcoholic home. This is true for the alcoholic as well as the non-alcoholic family members.

Why are individual members of the alcoholic family affected differently? To answer this question, three variables should be considered. These are the degree of alcoholism, the type of alcoholic in the home, and the individual perception of potential harm from living with an alcoholic.

The degree of alcoholism refers to the severity of the problem. How

---

This chapter is based on works from the book, *Children of Alcoholics*, by Robert J. Ackerman, Learning Publications, 1983.

often does the drinking occur? Is the alcoholic a binge drinker once a month, intoxicated daily, or totally unpredictable? Can the alcoholic be relied upon to function socially and for performance of his or her normal duties? Is the alcoholic employed or capable of working in and outside the home?

Closely related to the degree of alcoholism is the type of alcoholic that lives with the family. One type of alcoholic is the belligerent type who is verbally abusive and is consistently looking for an argument. The recipient of these attacks is exposed to high degrees of verbal and emotional abuse.

Another type of alcoholic may be jovial after drinking. This person likes to laugh a lot and is preoccupied with entertaining. Being around this alcoholic, although not physically or verbally harmful, may be emotionally stressful, due to inappropriate joking, or the inability to express himself or herself seriously.

These are a few examples of the many different types of alcoholics. Obviously, these differences can be manifested in a variety of forms for non-alcoholic family members. A child growing up with a physically abusive alcoholic parent may have a very different perspective on alcoholism, as opposed to a child living with a highly passive alcoholic.

The variables of degree and type relate to the alcoholic. The third variable—and perhaps the most important for non-alcoholic family members—is their perception of the situation.

Does the non-alcoholic family member perceive the situation as harmful? Often, our perception dictates our reactions. Whatever we perceive to be real, we react to it as if it is. Reality may be secondary to perception. In an alcoholic home, some non-alcoholic members may feel minimally affected, because they perceive that the alcoholism is not harmful to them. However, in the same family, others may be totally devastated because they feel that they are living in a crisis situation.

In summary, although we are concerned with alcoholism in the family, we need to be even more concerned with the effects of alcoholism on the individual members of a family. Each family member requires his or her own individual analysis of the situation. To understand the individual situation, the degree of alcoholism, the type of alcoholic in the family, and the non-alcoholic's individual perceptions must be considered.

Which Parent Is Addicted?

Do we have a higher probability that the father is alcoholic or that the mother is alcoholic in a family? To answer this question, we must consider several factors.

In our society today, if a woman is married to a male alcoholic and there are children under the age of 18 in the family, nine out of ten women will stay with the alcoholic. However, if the situation is reversed, and she is the alcoholic, only one out of ten males will stay. Many of the women's reasons for staying range from a lack of viable alternatives to denial. Additionally, the norms of society must be considered. For example, a male can become inebriated and engage in drunken behavior, and still be permitted to feel masculine. It is difficult for a woman to become inebriated and engage in drunken behavior and feel feminine. For the male, there exists a complementary norm of excessive drinking and masculinity. However, for the female, there exists a conflicting norm regarding excessive drinking and femininity. Where a complementary norm exists, there is a higher probability of its continual occurrence and a higher level of societal acceptance.

Another factor may be that if a woman has children, and she is suspected of having a drinking problem, one of the first things that may be said about her is that she is an "unfit" mother. It is unlikely that the male will stay in this situation. However, how long does male alcoholism continue before we hear that he is an "unfit" father? The woman has traditionally remained in this situation.

Finally, there simply is a greater number of male alcoholics than female alcoholics in our society. Some estimates indicate that 76% of problem drinkers are men, and only 24% are women (NIAAA, 1980). Although we are currently discovering female alcoholics at a faster rate than male alcoholics, it is doubtful that given societal values and socialization patterns, alcoholism will become an "equal opportunity" destroyer (Ackerman 1978).

In summary, if the alcoholic family is physically residing in the same house, there is a higher probability that the alcoholic in the family is the father. The percentage of cases where both spouses are alcoholics represents only 20% of the alcoholic homes in America. The majority of alcoholic homes, therefore, have a higher probability of only one spouse being alcoholic, and this spouse is usually the father.

Family Responses to the Alcoholic Parent

Responses to alcoholism in the family can be divided into four phases. These are called reactive, active, alternative and family unity phases. These different periods are distinguished by several characteristics which dominate the particular phase. Not all alcoholic families experience these conditions similarly, however, nor are these universally progressive: that is, not all families will progress from one phase to the next. Many families, unfortunately, remain in the first phase and never reach the fourth state of sobriety and family growth.

Phase I — The Reactive Phase

The reactive phase is characterized by the behavior of non-alcoholic family members reacting to the alcoholic's behavior. During this time, most family members become extremely cautious in their behavior, in order to avoid further complicating the existing problems of alcoholism. However, by being reactive, they are constantly adapting their behavior in order to minimize or survive an unhealthy situation. Much of this adaptation will not only have detrimental effects on those who are adjusting, but also indirectly allows and supports the continuing alcoholism. During the reactive phase, three typical family characteristics emerge: family denial, coping strategies, and social disengagement.

Family Denial

It is ironic that family members deny a drinking problem in their family, because this is exactly what the alcoholic does. We know that, for the alcoholic, denial is functional for the continuation of drinking. As long as the alcoholic denies that he/she has a problem, there is no reason to seek a solution. Non-alcoholic family members also deny, but their denial is totally dysfunctional to meeting their needs. Everyone in the family denies that anything is wrong, yet no one feels right. Family denial of alcoholism occurs in at least three ways: as systemic denial; as protection against exposure; and, as the primary patient philosophy.

1. *Systemic Denial*

Systemic denial means that the entire system denies the existence of a problem. Certainly the family is analogous to a system which is a pattern of inter-relationships. Within the family system, denial usually occurs when family members do not want to admit that one of them is an alcoholic, or because they perceive alcoholism as some sort of reflection upon themselves. This is particularly true in the case of non-alcoholic spouses who are women. For example, in American society, if the husband has a drinking problem, often there is a connotation that the wife is partly responsible. Statements such as "she drove him to drink" are typical. Even though these statements are not empirically correct, the woman may perceive them as true, and that she may be somehow responsible for the development of his alcoholism. Therefore, as long as she denies that her husband has a drinking problem, she can deny that she had anything to do with causing the problem.

An additional form of systemic denial occurs at the societal level. The family itself is also part of a larger system, which is the community or society in which it resides. Our society does not readily admit to alcohol problems. Although we accept alcoholism as a disease, there still are many who attach a moral stigma or deviancy status to alcoholism. Consequently, we cannot blame a family for covering up a condition that is not understood by society.

Another consideration is that the family is in an unfortunate position of "negative anonymity;" that is, being anonymous has a negative implication for the family. They are in a "no win" situation. To deny, on the one hand, keeps others from knowing or judging, but, on the other hand, keeps the family from getting help. This situation is similar to the alcoholic who covers up his or her drinking, but is also different if getting help is considered. For example, the alcoholic who wants help may join Alcoholics Anonymous. In this instance, his anonymity works for him, but for the non-alcoholic family members, their anonymity works against them. One of the paramount problems for families of alcoholics is in being recognized as individuals in need of assistance. If they are to overcome denial, they must overcome anonymity.

2. *Protection Against Exposure*

A second form of family denial is protection against exposure. Protection means not talking about the problem as a method of sheltering oneself from the situation. Exposure means not only experiencing the problem, but recognizing it, discussing it, and overcoming any effects. In the alcoholic home, the non-alcoholic spouse will often attempt to protect the children from exposure. A common mode of protection is to treat the situation as if it does not exist. This is impossible in an alcoholic home, but it is not uncommon for the non-alcoholic parent to say, "I have to cover up because I want to protect my children." Usually this means that the situation is never discussed, particularly with the chidren. This would be fine if protection were the problem, but trying to protect the children when they are exposed continually is a form of denial. In essence, the exposure is denied, any effects from the exposure are denied, and, more importantly, their need for help is denied. If we are going to help non-alcoholic family members, we must concentrate our efforts not on protection, but on overcoming the effects from exposure. To assume that children in an alcoholic home do not know and feel the effects of alcoholism is naive. They know. They may not understand, but they know. Living in an alcoholic home is not a "spectator sport." Everyone is involved to one degree or another, including the passive participants. This cannot be denied away.

3. *Primary Patient Philosophy*

The third form of denial is the "primary patient philosophy." In the past, when alcoholism existed in a family, it was assumed that the alcoholic was the primary concern. The alcoholic was to be helped first. The majority of alcoholics do not quit drinking, however, and while we are waiting for sobriety to occur, families fall apart, marriages may collapse, and children grow up and leave home As long as we consider the alcoholic the primary concern, we again deny intervention for the non-alcoholic family members. Non-alcoholic family members should be considered the primary interest, not the alcoholic. This is not to ignore the alcoholic, but to insure that we do not ignore the effects of alcoholism on the family while drinking is occurring. Additionally, as mentioned earlier, there are far more non-alcoholic family members than alcoholics, and their needs cannot be denied.

Coping Strategies

The key to surviving in an alcoholic home is adaptation. You learn to adapt your behavior in order to minimize the effects of alcoholism. A method of adaptation is to develop coping strategies. In the alcoholic home, these strategies are developed, even though the family denies the existence of alcoholism. The denial within the home is no longer as strong perhaps, but it is maintained outside of the household. For this reason, coping strategies are "home remedies." They are efforts by non-alcoholic family members to survive a situation while denying its existence to others. These strategies are severely limited, and seldom work. Coping strategies can be either verbal or behavioral attempts, and at best they provide a brief, but anxious, respite.

1. *Verbal Coping Strategies*

Verbal strategies are efforts by non-alcoholic family members to communicate effectively with the alcoholic about alcoholism—efforts which are usually interpreted by the alcoholic as "nagging" or persecution. As a response, the non-alcoholic resorts to morality lectures, pleas for self-respect, threats, promises, and statements such as "How could you do this to us?" Unfortunately, most verbal strategies do little to motivate the alcoholic, but do a lot to increase everyone's anxiety.

Verbal communication between non-alcoholic family members may be helpful, though in most homes no one wants to talk about the addiction, hoping the silence means non-existence. Although it is true that the problem cannot be talked away, discussing verbally and sharing the "family secret" is a positive beginning for non-alcoholic family members in their attempts for recovery. Family members often develop verbal strategies in only one direction, which is from the non-alcoholic to the alcoholic. Thus, there is no possible positive reciprocal effect for them. Verbal interaction among non-alcoholic family members is an available strategy, if they are willing to risk the sharing of information and feelings with each other.

2. *Behavioral Coping Strategies*

The second type of coping strategy is behavioral. The behavioral strategies are behaviors that non-alcoholic families knowingly—or unknowingly—adopt to cope with their situation. Typical behavioral strategies are hiding alcohol, refusing to buy alcohol, marking bottles, avoiding the alcoholic or other family members, staying away from home, and isolating oneself. Many families deny that they have developed coping strategies, but it is difficult to deny their unusual behavior. In a home where drinking is permitted, and is within normal acceptable limits, family members do not engage in this unusual behavior. Where drinking is abnormal, there exists abnormal non-alcoholic behavior as coping mechanisms. As a result of these coping strategies, non-alcoholic family members become socially disengaged from friends, family, community, and themselves.

As stated earlier, many non-alcoholic family members deny—or are unaware of—their participation in coping strategies. The following questionnaire has been developed for non-alcoholic family members to help to overcome their denial of the effects of alcoholism on their lives.

Note that most of these questions pertain to the behavior of non-alcoholic family members.

These questions should be answered by family members with as much honesty as possible. The questions were developed by Betty Reddy, Program Specialist, Alcoholism Treatment Center, Lutheran General Hospital, Park Ridge, Illinois.

1. Do you lose sleep because of a problem drinker?
2. Do most of your thoughts revolve around the problem drinker or problems that arise because of him or her?
3. Do you exact promises about the drinking which are not kept?
4. Do you make threats or decisions and not follow through on them?
5. Has your attitude changed toward this problem drinker (alternating between love and hate)?
6. Do you mark, hide, dilute, and/or empty bottles of liquor or medication?
7. Do you think that everything would be O.K., if only the problem drinker would stop or control the drinking?
8. Do you feel alone, fearful, anxious, angry, and frustrated most of the time? Are you beginning to feel dislike for yourself, and to wonder about your sanity?
9. Do you find your moods fluctuating wildly as a direct result of the problem drinker's moods and actions?
10. Do you feel responsible and guilty about the drinking problem?
11. Do you try to conceal, deny, or protect the problem drinker?
12. Have you withdrawn from outside activities and friends because of embarrassment and shame over the drinking problem?
13. Have you taken over many chores and duties that you would normally expect the problem drinker to assume—or that were formerly his or hers?
14. Do you feel forced to try to exert tight control over the family expenditures with less and less success—and are financial problems increasing?
15. Do you feel the need to justify your actions and attitudes and, at the same time, feel somewhat smug and self-righteous compared to the drinker?
16. If there are children in the house, do they often take sides with either the problem drinker or the spouse?
17. Are the children showing signs of emotional stress, such as

withdrawing, having trouble with authority figures, rebelling, acting-out sexually?

18. Have you noticed physical symptoms in yourself, such as nausea, a "knot" in the stomach, ulcers, shakiness, sweating palms, bitten fingernails?

19. Do you feel utterly defeated—that nothing you say or do will move the problem drinker? Do you believe that he or she can't get better?

20. Where this applies, is your sexual relationship with a problem drinker affected by feelings of revulsion; do you "use" sex to manipulate—or refuse sex to punish him or her?

Here are some additional questions specifically for children of alcoholics to help assess their feelings about parental alcoholism (Brooks, 1981).

1. Do your worry about your mom or dad's drinking?

2. Do you sometimes feel that you are the reason your parents drink so much?

3. Are you ashamed to have your friends come to your house, and are you finding more and more excuses to stay away from home?

4. Do you sometimes feel that you hate your parents when they are drinking, and then feel guilty for hating them?

5. Have you been watching how much your parent drinks?

6. Do you try to make your parents happy so they won't get upset and drink more?

7. Do you feel you can't talk about the drinking in your home—or even how you feel inside?

8. Do you sometimes drink or take drugs to forget about things at home?

9. Do you feel if your parents really loved you, they wouldn't drink so much?

10. Do you sometimes wish you had never been born?

11. Do you want to start feeling better?

Social Disengagements

Social disengagement is the withdrawing of family members from interaction with others. The family literally denies itself the support structure that it needs. This withdrawal is exacerbated because the family feels that it must protect itself, has been embarrassed, or fears future encounters with others where the alcoholic is present. The family becomes isolated and, at this point, feels there is a lack of available alternatives. The home becomes a "habit cage." Families of alcoholics need not become isolated if they do not choose to be. Most families rarely feel that they have a choice, however; they see their only response as withdrawal. This social disengagement can occur as either physical or emotional withdrawal.

1. *Physical Disengagement*

Physical disengagement occurs when the family stops receiving and giving invitations for social interaction. The family is pulled back from physical contact with others. Children, for example, no longer invite their friends to their homes. Non-alcoholic spouses hide invitations to functions involving alcohol to avoid any confrontations or embarrassment. Fewer people stop by to visit because of the unpleasantness or tension from a previous visit. The family becomes significantly separated as a unit from others. This physical isolation can lead to emotional disengagement.

2. *Emotional Disengagement*

Emotional disengagement is a decline in positive emotional relationships. In the alcoholic home, this decline is replaced with an increase in negative emotions. The longer the alcoholism continues, and the more the family withdraws, the greater the probability of negative emotions such as tension, anxiety, despair, and powerlessness emerging. One method of handling these negative emotions is to attempt to become "non-feeling," that is, to deny and minimize negative feelings to prevent further pain. Thus, avoidance becomes the norm for handling negative emotions, even though avoidance can lead to the denial of benefits of positive relationships which could be offsetting factors for the negative ones. The goals of positive relationships are sacrificed for the "comfortableness" of isolation within the family. As stated earlier, not all family members are affected equally; however, some members are able to overcome the internal negative emotions by outside non-family relationships. In research with children of alcoholics, it was found that children who were able to establish primary relationships outside the home were not as likely to become alcoholic in their adult lives as children who did not establish these relationships (Ackerman, 1978).

This is particularly relevant, considering that approximately 50% of alcoholics come from an alcoholic home.

Of all the problems encountered by non-alcoholic family members, emotional isolation may be the greatest. It affects not only the non-alcoholic life within the family, but also outside the family. Healthy relationships are denied or postponed to survive an unhealthy situation. Most non-alcoholic family members never assess the negative impact of this approach; they do what they believe makes the most sense at the time. The real impact may be found outside the family or for children in their adult lives. This is particularly true when considering that the children of alcoholics are disproportionately represented in juvenile courts, family courts, spouse and child abuse cases, divorce, and within populations plagued with psychological or emotional problems as adults.

Unfortunately, many families of alcoholics do not go beyond the reactive phase. They deny that the problem drinker is alcoholic, they helplessly hope for recovery, or they passively participate in the alcoholism syndrome. This stagnation at the reactive phase is likely to lead to these common effects on the alcoholic, the non-alcoholic spouse, and the children (Coates, 1979).

During the Reactive Phase, the alcoholic:
—Denies the alcohol problem, blames others, forgets and tells stories to defend and protest against humiliation, attack, and criticism from others in the family:
—Spends money for day-to-day needs on alcohol;
—Becomes unpredictable and impulsive in behavior;
—Resorts to verbal and physical abuse in place of honest, open talk;
—Loses the trust of family, relatives, and friends;
—Shows deterioration of physical health;
—Experiences a diminishing sexual drive;
—Has feelings of despair and hopelessness; and,
—Thinks about suicide, and possibly makes an attempt.

The spouse:
—Often tries to hide and deny the existing problem of the alcoholic;
—Takes on the responsibilities of the other person, carrying the load of two and perpetrating the spouse dependence;
—Takes a job to get away from the problem and/or maintain financial security;
—Finds it difficult to be open and honest because of resentment, anger,

and hurt feelings;

—Avoids sexual contact;

—May over-protect the children, neglect them, and/or use them for emotional support;

—Shows gradual social withdrawal and isolation;

—May lose feelings of self-respect and self-worth;

—May use alcohol or prescription drugs in an effort to cope.

The children:

—May be victims of birth defects;

—May be torn between parents; being loyal to one, they arouse and feel the anger of the other;

—May be deprived of emotional and physical support;

—Avoid peer activities, especially in the home out of fear and shame;

—Learn destructive and negative ways of dealing with problems and getting attention;

—Lack trust in anyone;

—May lose sight of values, standards and goals because of the absence of consistent, strong parenting;

—Suffer a diminishing sense of self-worth as a significant member of the family.

Phase II — The Active Phase

The main difference between the active and reactive phases are the responses of the non-alcoholic family members, even though the alcoholic is still drinking. Rather than being passive to the effects on themselves from the alcoholism, they begin to take an active interest in themselves. No longer do they perceive themselves as totally under the alcoholic's control, and they attempt to gain some control over their own lives. In this manner, the family begins to "de-center" itself from alcoholism. In addition, family denial of alcoholism is not as strong. A major step into the active phase is the overcoming of denial by family members. They begin to realize that the problem cannot be denied away. Likewise, they are willing to abandon their anonymity in exchange for help and a viable alternative to the way they have been existing. The two predominant characteristics of the active phase are awareness and being normal.

Awareness

During the active phase, the family develops a growing awareness

about alcoholism, their family, and themselves. Some of the awareness that develops is:
—they are not responsible for causing the alcoholism;
—they do not have to live like this, that alternatives are available;
—they recognize the need for help;
—they realize that help is available; and,
—they are not alone and do not have to be alone.
Much of this active time for non-alcoholic family members is becoming involved in their own recovery. They begin to become involved in various educational, counseling, and self-help groups that are available to them. During this time, they may begin to realize that they, too, are important, and that even the failure of the alcoholic to stop drinking should not necessarily prevent them from getting help. During the reactive phase, they may have assumed that nothing could be done until the alcoholic received help. Now, in the active phase, they realize that to wait may be futile, denies their own needs, and only perpetuates and reinforces the impact of alcoholism on their lives.

Being Normal

During this period, the non-alcoholic family members, particularly the non-alcoholic spouse, attempt to stabilize the alcoholic home. Despite active alcoholism, i.e., the alcoholic is still drinking, it is decided to "get on with" normal family activities as much as possible. Even though it is desirable for the alcoholic to quit drinking, and become a part of the normalizing process, sobriety is not a prerequisite. True, it will impede the process, but what is actually happening during the normal stage is an open and honest attempt to make the best of a negative situation inside and outside of the home, in order to overcome the negative impacts of alcoholism. The idea that families can begin their recovery process and become involved in normal activities that once were avoided, begins to take hold.

These activities may include supporting children to become involved in school and group activities, joining self-help groups, encouraging family conversations, and the sharing of feelings. These endeavors do not necessarily pertain to alcoholism and recovery, which is significant in itself, but also, and perhaps more important, is that they pertain to the normal activities of children who are not in alcoholic homes. These "other" activities have their benefits, not only in the activities themselves, but also in the separation from alcoholism. These can serve as positive, outside factors offsetting to a negative home environment, as well as contribute to building better family interaction patterns. Again, paramount to this phase is overcoming denial, risking the loss of anonymity, and once again taking an active interest in their lives by the non-alcoholic family members. These steps begin with awareness of the desire to feel normal.

Phase III — The Alternative Phase

The alternative phase now begins, when all else has failed. The family now faces the painful question of whether or not separation is the only viable alternative to survive alcoholism. It is not necessary that a family progress through both of the previous phases. Some families will go directly from the reactive phase into the alternative phase, while others will attempt the active phase before making the decision to separate. The characteristics of the alternative phase are polarization, separation, change, and family re-organization.

Polarization

Prior to separation, many alcoholic families go through a process of polarization, that is, family members begin to withdraw from each other, and are often forced into "choosing sides." Parents may begin to make threats to each other, or statements to the children that they are considering a legal separation or divorce. For the children, this means many things, but ultimately it means that they will not be living with both parents. The effects of alcoholism on their lives now have become even greater; it has now led to a divorce. Unfortunately, alcoholism contributes to approximately 40% of family court cases, and thus, many children of alcoholics experience the "double jeopardy" of being not only children of alcoholics, but also children of divorce. Polarization is also the process leading up to a separation. In many cases, this time of decision is long and painful, and in some cases may be more traumatic than the actual separation. For children, it is a time of impending change, and is often accompanied by feelings of confusion, torn loyalties, fear, resentment, anger, and increased isolation.

Separation

For some families, the only viable alternative left to them will be family separation. For others, the separation will only compound existing problems, and still others will only exchange one set of problems for a new set of problems. In short, for some life will get better, for others it will be about the same, and for still others it will get worse. For many children, separation will be life without daily contact with the alcoholic. Even within the same family, this change may be greeted with different feelings. For younger children, the loss of the parental role is of more concern than the loss of the alcoholic parent, but for older children it may be the opposite. They may perceive that although they may be losing the parental role, it was lost anyhow for all intents and purposes, and that they will no longer be affected by all of the family alcoholic problems. Much of their reaction will depend upon how the individual family members perceive this change in their lives.

Change

There is a belief that change is, in and of itself, always traumatic. What should be considered when assessing the impact of change, however, are the rates and the directions of change. If the rate of change occurs too rapidly, it can be traumatic, because of the inability to adjust quickly enough. On the other hand, change that occurs too slowly can also be anxiety-producing. For example, not only may the separation be painful, but also the manner in which the separation has occurred. In some alcoholic families, the process of polarization may have been a long and tedious affair, whereas, in other families, polarization occurred too rapidly, and the decision to separate was made in haste. In some instances, however, it may be that the family members perceived that it was time for a much-needed change, and that the time was now. Thus, the rate of change can help or hinder the alternative phase.

Additionally, the direction of change becomes critical for each family member. Individual family members see the new change to their advantage or disadvantage. If a child perceives that he or she will be worse off after separation, then the child views the change as undesirable, and is opposed to it. If the child perceives that his or her life will improve, however, then the change is not problematic. Life without the alcoholic is seen as better than life with the alcoholic. In reality, for some members of the alcoholic family this will be true, and for others it will not. Much depends upon how the new family grows and is re-organized.

Family Re-Organization

For alcoholic families that have chosen the alternative phase, several things can occur when re-organization takes place. The family begins to re-organize, pull together, and grow. In these families, family members may begin to seek help for themselves, or become further involved in their recovery process. Family members will begin to feel good about themselves, and establish healthy relationships within and outside of their family.

For other families, re-organization will involve new and additional roles. The custodial spouse now faces the single-parent role alone, whereas in the past, even though the alcoholic parent was often absent at times, he/she helped in parenting. In addition, children may find themselves in roles with added responsibilities. All of the family members' new roles can, however, be impeded by old feelings and behavior, such as their feelings of resentment, anger, guilt, abandonment, failure, and doubt about alcoholism, and about being the child or the spouse of an alcoholic. These feelings can be coupled with the old behavior of continually talking about the alcoholic, blaming problems on alcoholism, or holding the alcoholic solely responsible for their lives.

Re-organization can be complicated further by the recurring visits of the alcoholic parent, particularly if the alcoholic is still drinking. For example, the alcoholic can use the children to "get at" the non-alcoholic spouse. The children may become pawns between the spouses, a situation which can be further complicated by the alcoholic's seeking support from the children for a reconciliation. Even within the same family, however, this idea can receive mixed reactions. Younger children, again, may favor the idea more than the older children, because they may not have been exposed to the longevity of the alcoholism. One of the main problems of re-organization will be the tendency to fall back into many of the patterns of the reactive phase. A family will need to be supported during the alternative phase, if the alternatives are to become viable solutions.

Phase IV — Family Unity Phase

Unfortunately, many alcoholic families never reach the family unity phase, because of continuing alcoholism. There are no definitive progressive patterns that lead to the unity phase. Some families will proceed directly from phase one to phase four, others will go through the first two phases and then on to four, and still others may go through all the phases on their way to family unity. When they arrive, however, the family will face at least three concerns which are characteristic of this phase: sobriety, the "dry drunk," and family growth.

Sobriety

Central to the family unity phase is the maintaining of sobriety by the alcoholic, but sobriety alone may not be enough. Certainly, it is superior to inebriation, but acceptance of the sober alcoholic back into the mainstream of the family is not automatic. Sobriety does not guarantee family growth, it only makes it possible. Just as the family does not cause alcoholism, sobriety does not cause an immediately healthy family. The initial stages of sobriety may contain some pitfalls. For example, the family probably has waited a long time for sobriety to occur, and now that it has, they expect to enter "paradise." The longer the alcoholism continues, in many alcoholic families, the higher the probability that all family problems are blamed on the bottle. Therefore, the family expects other problems to end when the drinking ends, but difficulties continue to exist, as they do in all families. Difficulties which were formerly believed to be related to alcoholism surface as ordinary, normal, family disagreements. In the past, these problems may have been denied, as was the alcoholism, but now new ways of dealing with normal family problems will be needed. Some families have heard promises of sobriety before, and adapt a "wait and see" attitude before committing themselves to the family recovery process. Other families, however, will be more active and supportive of the new-found sobriety, and will be eager for many of the normal family behaviors that have been missing.

The Dry Drunk

For those families who are not able to join in the recovery process from alcoholism, much of their lives will remain the same. That is, even though sobriety has occurred, no other changes in the family are taking place, because the results of the previous breakdown in family communications continue to take their toll on the emotions of family members. Unless the family is able to adapt to the sober alcoholic and themselves, and can establish and grow as a unit, the family may find itself on a "dry drunk." In such cases, tension, anxiety and conflict persist, because other problems have not been solved. The family needs to understand that throughout the drinking period, family relationships were deteriorating, and were never sufficiently established. Some children in the "dry drunk" situation are unable to remember anything but drinking behavior on the part of one or both parents. The recovering alcoholic may, in fact, be trying to parent properly, but since this is a new or strange behavior, it may not be entirely trusted within the family when the drinking stops. The family must be incorporated in a new adaptive process. To ignore the role of the family in helping the recovering alcoholic support his or her sobriety, is to ignore the emotional impact that alcoholism has had on the family.

Family Growth

For those family members who can integrate the alcoholic back into the family, and emotionally integrate themselves, their lives will get better. With this integration comes the potential for family growth. This family growth will mean that the family does not dwell on the past, nor hide the past, but has learned from it. The growing family is one that goes beyond the past. It continues to change and improve, moving toward the goal of healthy family relationships. It is a family that is overcoming the negative influences of alcoholism, and is united. Unfortunately, this does not happen often enough, as was noted earlier.

Family Interrelationships

What are the effects of all this adaptation and change? Many alcoholics are not aware of the emotional hazards they unthinkingly cause for their young. These effects, if considered at all, are seen as latent in the home, but may be seen as manifest by others outside the home. In order to consider the impact of these effects, some of the dynamics occurring in the home should be noted. It is critical to consider whether or not both parents are alcoholic. In cases where both parents are involved in alcoholism, physical as well as emotional needs of the children may be unmet. When parents are unable or unwilling to assist in the home, their children consistently may be forced to organize and run the household. They may be picking up after parents, and assuming extremely mature roles for their ages.

The time of the onset of parental alcoholism is also an important consideration. Were the children born into an alcoholic home, or did parental addiction occur later in their lives, and at what age? It is fairly well agreed upon in various educational studies that the impact of emotional crises upon children are more detrimental at some ages than at others. Many children will experience an emotional separation from their parents, often feeling rejected by both parents, even though only one is alcoholic. The inability to discriminate between love as a noun and love as a verb, and the lack of emotional security take their toll on many children of irresponsible parents. Alcoholic behavior in the family can prohibit intimate involvement and clearly impede the development of essential family bonds. When children's emotional needs have been stunted by neglect or destroyed by cruelty, the traditional function of parents as mentors and guides for their offspring becomes a farce. Clearly, the generally agreed upon effect of the positive influence of parents in the early education of children becomes questionable (Brookover and Erickson, 1975). It cannot be assumed that the proper parental roles toward education are being met, let alone attempted, in the alcoholic home.

The roles their parents play in the family are of critical importance in the development of children. When a parent is alcoholic, his or her parental roles too often are marked by inconsistency, and inconsistency is exhibited by both the alcoholic and the non-alcoholic parent. The alcoholic parent behaves like several different individuals, with conflicting reactions and unpredictable attitudes. Often his or her role performance is dictated by successive periods of drunken behavior, remorse, or guilt, followed by high degrees of anxiety, tension, and finally, complete sobriety. Children may learn through experience to adapt themselves to such inconsistency in roles, and even to develop some form of predictability, but they develop very little emotional security. What emotional security is attained is usually attained only during periods of sobriety, and then only if other family issues are not producing tension.

A typical example of this kind of cycle goes as follows. On Friday night, and all day Saturday, the alcoholic is drunk. Sunday and Monday are hangover or recovery days, commonly marked by some degree of guilt or remorse. The middle of the week is the most normal. As the next weekend approaches, the alcoholic is being dominated by increasing anxiety and tension, precipitating another drinking episode. The children in such a situation learn that whatever is needed, physically or emotionally, must be obtained in the middle of the week. These become the "getting" days, when the getting may be optimal, because it is at this time, if any, that parenting or positive stroking by the alcoholic will occur. This is also the time when many unrealistic, as well as realistic, promises are made, which may or may not be kept. Normal promises made on good days may go unfulfilled because the collection day is one of inebriation. Sometimes this results in the making of still bigger and more elaborate promises, which are, in turn, broken. Occasions when promises are kept are sporadic, and thus cannot be relied upon, again adding to the inconsistency. The alcoholic may show exaggerated concern or love one day, and mistreat the child the next. It is little wonder that a major problem for such children is a lack of trust and security in relationships with an alcoholic parent.

The non-alcoholic parent is hampered in attempting to fulfill the needs of the children, because he or she is usually under constant tension over what is happening, or may happen. Even when the alcoholic is sober, the spouse tends to suspect that the situation is tenuous, and consequently cannot support the alcoholic's attempt to win respect and approval—knowing that the probability of consistency is low. The non-alcoholic parent, who is subjected to, and controlled by, the inconsistent nature of the alcoholic, may become so engrossed in trying to fulfill two roles, that he or she is unable to fulfill one role adequately and consistently. Just as the alcoholic fluctuates between different levels of sobriety and emotionalism, so does the non-alcoholic parent react to these positions. As a result, the non-alcoholic parent may be just as guilty as the alcoholic in showing too much concern for the children at times, and too little at other times. In addition, the non-alcoholic spouse, worried about the effects of alcoholic behavior in the family situation, is apt to become too protective or fearful for the children. This protection is often misunderstood by the children, especially when it is negatively administered in the form of unexplained warnings against certain places or people.

Perhaps, most of the non-alcoholic spouse's parental concern is justified by the fact that as many as 40 to 60% of the children of alcoholic parents become alcoholic themselves (Hindman, 1975). Much has been written about the causal factors for this phenomenon. The question is centered around the nature-nuture controversy surrounding alcoholism. Is alcoholism genetically based, or are other factors present? This author believes that the nurturing aspects play the more prominent role, and that the damage inflicted on the child is not limited to preadolescence or adolescence, but has long-range implications. Although not directly related to drinking practices, additional evidence that the nuture impact is the stronger influence is shown by the fact that children of alcoholic parents are more affected by the disharmony and rejection in the home life than by the drinking. They see that drinking stops once in a while, although the fighting and tension continue. This constant state of agitation affects personality development. More particularly, children observe the use of alcohol as a method of dealing with uncomfortable situations. Although the children may vow not to drink, and are cognizant of the potential harm of alcohol abuse, this position may give way to use of drinking as a means of escape during real or perceived crises in later life.

The two-parent family in which alcoholism affects one or both partners, cannot provide a healthy parental relationship. A single, non-alcoholic parent can give children a healthier atmosphere. In a family where one of the parents is alcoholic, the other parent will not be able singly to overcome all of the impacts of the other's drinking; he or she cannot provide a separate environment because both parental roles are distorted or inconsistent. The non-alcoholic parent devotes energy in trying to deal with the alcoholic at various phases of adaptation, leaving little energy for the needs of the offspring. Often, the children are forced into a position of increased responsibilities and unfamiliar roles. The eldest child may be put in charge of smaller children, or be drawn into the role of confidant for the non-alcoholic spouse.

Sometimes children find themselves abandoned in the middle, or forced to choose sides, either of which can lead to withdrawal and a preference to be left alone. It was earlier mentioned that family disengagement from contact with others is a form of adapting behavior to the alcoholic problem. Disengagement can also occur within the family itself. The children avoid family contact as often as possible, having learned that minimal contact may also mean minimal discomfort. Such children want only to be left alone, and no longer feel close to either parent. The need to be isolated from their parents' conflicts may carry over to their attitudes toward other adults. Such children associate solitude with the absence of conflict. Thus, being alone is not always as feared as one might expect; it may be viewed as a pleasant time of relaxation. Affection or emotional support outside the home is a vital aspect in helping such children, a topic which will be considered in subsequent chapters.

Many families can become recovered, or recovering families, but not without assistance from others. Outside support is critical to this process, especially when we remember that there may be no support from within the family. Often children need help in acquiring or regaining a sense of trust in their parents and others. Also vital to the children is the acquisition of self-awareness and self-esteem. Basic to a family recovery program is the question of whether the children can grow up to face life successfully. Will they be able to achieve a sense of security, to be able to grow while accepting their circumstances, and, more importantly, to feel good about themselves? When working with the children of alcoholic parents, we must remember to address the many manifestations of alcoholism, not just those directly related to the alcoholic. We must bring the entire picture into focus, and examine and address the not-so-visible symptoms as well as the easily visible ones, with concern for how they manifest themselves in each individual in the family.

REFERENCES

Ackerman, R.J. *Children of Alcoholics.* 2nd Ed., Learning Publications, Inc., Holmes Beach, FL, 1983.

Ackerman, R.J. "Socio-Cultural Aspects of Substance Abuse." *Competency-Based Training Manual for Substance Abuse Counselors,* Office of Substance Abuse Services, Department of Health, Michigan, 1978.

Brookover, W., and Edsel L. Erickson. *Sociology of Education.* Dorsey Press, Illinois, 1975.

Brooks, C. *The Secret Everyone Knows.* Operation Cork, CA., 1981.

Coates, M. and Gail Paech. *Alcohol and Your Patient: A Nurse's Handbook.* Addiction Research Foundation, Canada, 1979.

Hindman, M. "Children of Alcoholic Parents." In: *Alcohol World Health and Research.* NIAAA, Rockville, MD, Winter, 1975-76.

National Institute on Alcohol Abuse and Alcoholism. *Facts About Alcohol and Alcoholism,* Rockville, MD, 1980.

Reddy, B. "Alcoholism, A Family Illness." Lutheran General Hospital, Park Ridge, Illinois.

Chapter Two

Children of Alcoholics and the Case For a New Diagnostic Category of Co-Dependency

Timmen L. Cermak

It has been recognized, at least since Al-Anon's founding in 1951, that the Twelve Steps of Alcoholics Anonymous are of value to both alcoholics and their spouses. The recent growth in Twelve Step meetings for adult children of alcoholics (ACoAs) attests to the value of this traditional pathway to recovery for yet another group. At the beginning of 1982, there were 14 registered adult children groups in Al-Anon. By December 1983, the number had risen to 194. The following chapter explores parallels in the recovery process for alcoholics and ACoAs, and proposes a new diagnostic category of co-dependency, in recognition of the fact that ACoAs are suffering from the same disorder as are alcoholics. This discussion is based on the author's clinical experience in counseling both alcoholics and adult children of alcoholics.

Co-Dependency

The concept of co-dependency has been applied almost exclusively to people (mostly spouses) who knowingly or unknowingly cooperate in an alcoholic's denial. Traditionally, therapists have tended to label behavior—such as placing greater importance on another person's feelings than one's own—as "alcoholic thinking" when seen in the alcoholic. However, such behavior is also characteristic of spouses and children of alcoholics. Although the word "co-dependency" is likely to be improved upon in the future, the concept has already become a valuable tool for

Printed with the author's permission from *Alcohol Health & Research World*, Vol. 8, No. 4., Summer 1984.

describing a recognizable and treatable personality disorder seen in people with a spectrum of stressful life experiences, and perhaps most reliably seen in those who have been touched directly or indirectly by alcoholism.

Difficulty in achieving a clear definition of co-dependency is probably more a reflection of our conceptual inadequacy than a reflection of its reality as a concrete entity. On the one hand, co-dependency seems to qualify as a Personality Disorder under Axis II of DSM III (*Diagnostic and Statistical Manual of Mental Disorders*). It is certainly a deeply ingrained, inflexible, maladaptive pattern "of relating to, perceiving, and thinking about oneself ..." of sufficient severity to cause either significant impairment in adaptive functioning or subjective distress." Furthermore, Dependent Personality Disorder describes many prominent features of co-dependency, such as getting others to assume responsibility for major areas of one's life, subordinating one's own needs to those of others, and a lack of self-confidence. Anxiety and depression are features of both co-dependency and Dependent Personality Disorder, as are the tendency to have one's relationships dominated by the needs of others upon whom one is dependent and the invariable preoccupation with abandonment whenever dependency needs are not being satisfied by a secure relationship.

On the other hand, the concept of co-dependency differs from Dependent Personality Disorder in at least two major ways. Whereas dependency/autonomy are the central issues in Dependent Personality Disorders, issues of control are at the core of co-dependency. People who exhibit co-dependent personality disorders share an overwhelming devotion to will power as the preferable avenue to achieving self-worth. Control of self and others, feelings, and things is blindly pursued as an antidote to free-floating anxiety. As in alcoholism, the means (i.e., will power) becomes more highly valued than effective attainment of the end (i.e., sobriety). For the co-dependent, loss of control is phobically avoided, and both dependent and autonomous behaviors are pursued in an effort to maximize security.

On a more fundamental level, co-dependency differs from the general class of personality disorders constituting Axis II by being a diagnosis that exists on the individual level and the systems level simultaneously. Family therapists recognize that co-dependency is embodied in and transmitted by the interactions of a dysfunctional family system. On this level, co-dependency exists independently within the individual members of that system, and each individual ultimately is responsible for his or her own recovery.

I suspect that difficulty in achieving a concise definition of co-dependency stems in part from the fact that it is the first of a new class of diagnoses. The concept of co-dependency speaks simultaneously to both intrapsychic and interpersonal dynamics. It proposes that a single process of distortion underlies all the co-dependent's relationships, both those with other people and those among the parts of the self.

Alcoholics usually face a lengthy recovery after withdrawing from alcohol. Unfortunately, abstinent alcoholics are not universally successful in entering into an effective process of psychological convalescence. Instead, many abstinent alcoholics stubbornly maintain the same pattern of distorted beliefs and generally immature defenses that are more consistent with active alcoholism than with active recovery. Conventional wisdom recognizes that recovery involves an attitudinal shift of far deeper significance than simply abstaining from ingesting alcohol. This is expressed in the distinction between being "dry" (i.e., merely abstinent) and being "sober" (i.e., recovering emotionally and spiritually). In a similar vein, co-dependency parallels the psychological aspects of alcohol and the non-recovered, abstinent alcoholics, and that progressively wane in recovery.

These psychological aspects of addiction in the alcoholic can be described in terms of Vaillant's hierarchy of adaptive ego mechanisms (1977). In his investigation of adaptive styles, Vaillant found that among nonpsychotic adults, denial of external reality is most often encountered in addiction. More precisely, projection, fantasy, hypochondriasis, passive-aggressive behavior, and acting out are noted to be the adaptive mechanisms that underlie chemical addiction. Because such defenses are normal in adolescents, Vaillant chose to call them "immature mechanisms." Immature adaptive mechanisms represent efforts to cope with unbearable interpersonal events. Their effect is a merging of personal boundaries and a breakdown of the distinction between what is the responsibility of the alcoholic and what is the responsibility of those around the alcoholic.

Chronic alcohol ingestion simultaneously bolsters immature mechanisms of adaption, and makes more sophisticated defenses less likely to occur. Once a person has begun to counteract psychological threats by mechanisms of denial, the pharmacologic effects of alcohol work synergistically with one's defenses. Whenever immature defenses become inadequate, they tend to be temporarily shored up by alcohol ingestion, which decrease general awareness of the threatening reality one needs to deny. At the same time, an alcohol-affected brain becomes less capable of supporting more mature adaptive mechanisms—such as intellectualization, reaction formation, sublimation, and suppression.

Abstinence is often attempted in an atmosphere of magical thinking, rather than a sober assessment of psychological realities. The situation could not be otherwise, since the choice to enter abstinence is generally made by someone with an alcohol-affected brain and firmly ensconced in a co-dependent family system. Such a person is still locked into an adaptive strategy based on denial, although alcohol has been ruled out as a permissible reinforcement.

In distinction from the above, the truly recovering alcoholic has entered into a therapeutic alliance with hitherto unavailable parts of himself or herself, often referred to as the Higher Power, in a conscious effort to develop more mature adaptive mechanisms. This person begins to use defenses that acknowledge more realistic personal limitation. Perhaps most important, the recovering alcoholic begins to base strategies of adaptation on the reality, rather than the denial, of illness.

Of particular importance to the concept of co-dependency is the fact that it exists within members of an alcoholic's family and social circle independently of the alcoholic's drinking behavior. Indeed, many spouses and children continue to suffer from co-dependency for decades after an alcoholic's death or recovery.

A person is prone to become co-dependent when he or she responds to the alcoholic with an increased reliance on immature adaptive mechanisms, when a pattern of immature defenses crystalizes around the alcoholic's behavior, the non-alcoholic has begun to suffer from co-dependency. The alcoholic and the co-dependent non-alcoholic lock into supporting each others' denial systems. The effect is that each independently displays the psychological aspect of addiction to alcohol.

Why would anyone enter into a dynamic mutual reinforcement of immature defenses with an alcoholic? The basis for answering this question lies within each of us, since it is a nearly universal human characteristic to react personally when being confronted by immature defenses. Furthermore, our own less mature adaptive mechanisms are a powerful "means of making a painful truce with people whom we can live neither with nor without ..." (Vaillant 1977). Co-dependent interactions permit an illusion of constancy in relationships with people who are too important for us to acknowledge the truth about their behavior, or our own.

Two distinct categories of people come into sufficient contact with alcoholics to begin suffering from co-dependency—spouses or other significant adults and children. Greenleaf (1981) argues that an important distinction exists between the adult who marries an alcoholic (or someone who later becomes alcoholic), and a child who is born to an alcoholic parent. In the latter case, personality development occurs within a context of immature adaptive mechanisms, and leads to distortions of interpersonal reality. Greenleaf suggests that the prefix "co" be reserved for adults who enter into mutually destructive relationships with an alcoholic, and the prefix "para" be used to refer to the child who grows up in an alcoholic family. Such a distinction highlights the unique problems that may occur in a child raised in an atmosphere of blurred personal boundaries, pervasive denial, and unrestrained projection. The result may be that immature adaptive mechanisms come to be perceived as normal adult behavior and as the standard by which to measure interpersonal reality.

Adult Children of Alcoholics

Definitive data on the prevalance and nature of problems affecting children of alcoholics are not available, but clinical observations by those who work with children of alcoholics give cause for serious concern. Half of all alcoholics may themselves be children of alcoholics (Miller 1977). Genetic factors alone can cause a four-fold increase in the risk of alcoholism in some populations (Goodwin 1973). Half of the referrals to employee assistance programs may be adult children of alcoholics (Lavino 1982). A review of the literature indicates that adult children of alcoholics are at increased risk for most of the serious psychosocial illnesses of adulthood (El-Gueboly and Offord 1977), yet less than five percent are being appropriately treated (Whitfield 1980).

While it seems clear that they are at increased risk for many problems, further research and clinical descriptions are required to establish the presence of common characteristics. In an article reporting on interactional group therapy with adult children of alcoholics, Cermak and Brown (1982) identified issues of control as a dominant dynamic. On an interpersonal level, ACoAs tend to be exquisitely attuned to how each nuance of interaction shifts the balance of control within any system. They remain hypervigilant in order to detect change before it gets out of control, and they value highly the ability to maintain a controlled facade despite whatever turmoil might exist within themselves or the family. On an intrapsychic level, chronic stress is created by an expectation that feelings themselves ought to be under conscious control. Spontaneity and intense affect are both desired as a release, and yet feared as a potential Achilles heel, leading to irreparable loss of control. As long as a facade can be maintained to oneself as well as to others, the ultimate catastrophe of "loss of control" is being staved off successfully. Other issues commonly contain a special emotional charge of ACoAs by virtue of tapping into the overarching control issue. These include difficulty in trusting, unclear boundaries of responsibility, suppressed expression of personal needs, and rigid control of emotional spontaneity.

The author hypothesized that ACoAs can best be understood as suffering from a variety of post-traumatic stress disorder (PTSD) in combination with co-dependency. The symptoms of PTSD relevant to ACoAs are: (1) a tendency to re-experience the trauma through obsessive thoughts about the family and compulsive reemergence of behavior and feelings in response to symbolic equivalents of the trauma; (2) psychic numbing, with a sense of isolation; (3) hypervigilance (anxiety); (4) survivor guilt (depression); and, (5) intensification of symptoms by exposure to events that resemble the original trauma, such as withdrawal by others.

Compounding these symptoms of PTSD is the ACoA's co-dependent dedication to flawed beliefs about will power and control. In essence, the adult children of alcoholics are engaged in a struggle to build their self-esteem based on their ability to exert will power, a struggle in which their alcoholic parent failed. Unfortunately, failure is guaranteed as long as success is based on the ability to control one's own feelings, to control the actions and feelings of others, or to control the effects of alcohol in themselves or another person.

Recovery

Because co-dependency has not yet received the same diagnostic legitimacy as alcoholism, the resources devoted to its treatment remain inadequate. As a result, recovery is probably not the norm. However, this norm may be changing, as the explosion of interest in Twelve Step programs for ACoAs testifies. A clinical description of recovery for ACoAs has been advanced by Gravitz and Bowden, whose stages of recovery parallel the continuum model of alcoholism suggested by Stephanie Brown (in preparation). The continuum model emphasizes that the recovery process for alcoholics follows a dynamic of its own, distinctly different from a mere reversal of the addictive process. During the addictive process, an alcoholic feels ever more deeply that alcohol enables normal functioning, and eventually survival itself. Increasing energy is put into denial, rationalization, and projection, in order to keep the alcoholic's cherished belief system regarding control and willpower intact.

The moment when recovery begins is heralded by an acknowledgment that one is alcoholic, in a way that simultaneously calls into question the ability to control the disease. This emerging awareness is quite tenuous at first, and requires considerable consolidation. Only after an alcoholic has firmly accepted the reality of his or her illness, and the total inability to control it, is he or she able to explore the core issues. Traditional psychotherapy eventually begins to proceed in response to its own momentum once the alcoholic begins integrating the experience of recovery. At that point, the alcoholic understands the processes of dismantling denial, re-evaluating basic principles, relinquishing illusions (such as that of control), and accepting a more realistic identity.

Striking parallels between the recovery process for alcoholics and for adult children of alcoholics strongly suggest that a common process is occurring. Both alcoholics and ACoAs must recover from the pattern of immature coping mechanisms characteristic of psychological addiction — to alcohol or to other people. These immature defenses confuse denial with willpower, and distort both interpersonal and intrapsychic realities.

Therapeutic Implications

Many lessons that were painstakingly learned over years of treating alcoholism can be transferred directly into the developing field of treatment for adult children of alcoholics. As with alcoholics, the first task to be undertaken in treating ACoAs is evaluation of the stage of recovery from their co-dependency. If significant amounts of denial prevail, the client is probably involved in what is subjectively perceived as a battle for survival. Self-identification as an ACoA is likely to be primarily intellectual, if present at all. Dealing with issues of control still lies in the future. The therapeutic goal at this point is to bring denial into conscious awareness and to draw connection between this denial and the client's inability to alter his or her painful patterns of feelings and behavior. Referral to Twelve Step meetings for ACoAs and educational, time-limited groups is often helpful.

As the ACoA client moves from survival to emerging awareness, therapists must be prepared to modify their techniques accordingly. Much supportive work is required as ACoAs first identify their parents' alcoholism. Direct education regarding alcoholism and alcoholic family systems may be required. Therapists may have to be the first to validate their client's perceptions regarding the parents' alcoholism, and directly reassure clients that abandoning denial is not a betrayal of the family. Referral to a time-limited, topic-oriented ACoA discussion group may be useful.

As ACoAs enter into the stage when issues of control are faced directly, group therapy probably becomes more the treatment of choice, although individual work remains a useful adjunct. If feelings are highly rigid and inaccessible, experiential Gestalt-oriented groups are useful. Ultimately, long-term interactional group psychotherapy provides the optimum environment for completing work in resolving core issues. Once these issues are addressed, active steps may be taken to change relationships with others. A group permits this integration to be experienced more fully than is possible in individual therapy.

Individual therapy with ACoAs can be conceptualized as occurring along two parallel tracks. One track relates to PTSD-like symptoms; the other track deals more with co-dependent personality structure. The author begins track one with clarification of the ACoAs current feelings. In the process, confounded feelings such as love and pity are identified and accurately labeled. Subjective physical sensations can often be associated with separate feelings in order to make them more fully concrete. The author then introduces Gestalt techniques to facilitate the client's experience of each feeling's full intensity. By asking clients to report on how old they feel during different states of feeling they can be brought to recover lost memories through free association. In this way, a more realistic assessment of alcohol's effect on their family and their own early efforts to cope with these effects can gradually be made.

Simultaneously, the author works along track two, which is an exploration of the client's current relationship with family, self, others, and alcohol. Eventually, the two tracks coalesce as the client becomes aware that current patterns of feelings and coping mechanisms are persisting from the past and creating difficulties because of their inappropriateness in the present situation.

Summary

Co-dependency is a pattern of immature adaptive mechanisms that exist in alcoholics, many spouses of alcoholics, and many children of alcoholics. In all cases, recovery from co-dependency involves a similar sequence of stages. The initial stage of denial, motivated by survival instincts, can be transformed by a conscious and more realistic identification of one's self and its powers. A context then exists for reexamining core issues of control. The generalization of this process of acceptance may lead to a personal integration supportive of more mature adaptive mechanisms.

In the case of both the alcoholic and the adult children of alcoholics, recovery is dependent throughout one's lifetime on a continual recognition of one's vulnerability to dependency or co-dependency. As soon as such vulnerability is forgotten or denied, recovery can collapse like a house of cards.

REFERENCES

Cermak, T.L., and Brown, S. Interactional group therapy with the adult children of alcoholics, *International Journal of Group Psycho-therapy*, 32(3): 375-389, 1982.

El-Gueboly, N. and Offord, D. The offspring of alcoholics: A critical review. *American Journal of Psychiatry*, 134:4, April 1977.

Goodwin, D., Schulsinger, E., Hermansen, L., Guze, S.B., and Winokur, G. Alcohol in adoptees raised apart from alcoholic biological parents. *Archives of General Psychiatry*, 28:238-243, 1973.

Greenleaf, J. "Co-Alcoholic/Para-Alcoholic." Paper presented at the National Council on Alcoholism National Forum, New Orleans, 1981. Available from Health Communications, Pompano Beach, FL.

Lavino, J. "Children of alcoholics in the workplace." Paper presented at Governor Carey's Conference on Children of Alcoholics, New York, 1982.

Miller, D. Children of alcoholics: A twenty-year longitudinal study. San Francisco: Institute of Scientific Analysis, 1977.

Vaillant, G.E. *Adaption of Life.* Boston: Little, Brown and Company, 1977.

Whitfield, C.L. Children of alcoholics: Treatment issues. *Maryland State Medical Journal*, June, 1980.

Chapter Three
Double Trouble: Alcoholism and Family Violence

Jerry P. Flanzer

Alcohol abuse and family abuse often intensify one another in a deadly spiral. This interacting double trouble is well known, but not as well known is how both these diseases are similar and overlapping. For, like the disease of alcoholism, whose pathology it so closely follows, intra-family violence impairs the development of each family member and tears at the very fabric of society. Initially, as with alcoholism, family violence represents a way for the abuser to gain mastery over his/her world. It may take many forms: sexual abuse and incest, child abuse and neglect, and spouse abuse (primarily wife abuse) are the most widely known. Sibling abuse and abuse of the elderly (so-called granny-bashing) are more hidden forms.

Alcohol is almost always involved in family violence. Some forms of family violence seem more linked to alcohol than others, especially child sexual abuse, spouse abuse and severe child neglect. If moderate and severe drinkers are added to the alcoholics, and we also included children of alcoholics, then we may say: Up to 80% of all cases involve drinking, whether before, during, after, or instead of, the critical incident. Moderate and problem drinkers are more frequently involved than light drinkers and abstainers. A moderate drinker or heavy drinker is more likely to be the aggressor; certainly he or she is more likely to neglect his or her family. As a whole, men and women seem equally likely to be abusers; until alcohol is involved, then the heavier drinker (usually the man) is more likely to be the perpetrator. Available statistics point to drinking women as child abusers, drinking men as wife abusers and sexual

This chapter is based on the article "The Vicious Circle of Alcoholism & Family Violence" by J. Flanzer, *Alcoholism,* 1981.

molesters. Women get "hurt more," show up more frequently in emergency rooms, etc. Women are ten times more likely to be the victim. (Our society does not allow men to admit their abuse—men show up more frequently in the morgue. The folklore is that the woman must "shore-up" her deficit in strength with weapons and is more likely to strike when the man does not suspect her.)

Three patterns often are seen. In one pattern, the family seems to alternate between alcohol and aggression, drinking to avoid hitting, hitting perhaps to avoid drinking. In another family pattern, violence appears only when alcohol is imbibed. This style takes two forms. In Form A, the Abuser Form, the drinker has a few drinks and seems to feel licensed to hit. In Form B, the Victim Form, the drinker imbibes until he/she is in a helpless stupor and becomes an easy target for abuse. In the third pattern, the heavy drinker becomes so preoccupied with the habit, that family members are severely neglected and many family roles impaired. This pattern refers to an incipient form of violence—extreme passive aggression. Thus, the timing between the two is not clear cut: Alcohol may be before, during, after or instead of family violence. Drinkers who have stopped when treated for their alcoholism alone continue to abuse physically, and vice versa, physical abusers who have stopped their abuses after being treated for the abuse alone, are found to continue their drinking.

Family violence works! It is initially a very effective form of conflict resolution. The abuser uses it to reinstate the "steady state," i.e., to

Table I INTERMESHED FACTORS		
SHARED CHARACTERISTICS	**DIFFERENT CHARACTERISTICS**	
Alcoholism & Family Violence	**Alcoholism**	**Family Violence**

Resolves conflict
Forces reaction
Tolerated, learned
Blocks feelings, intimacy
Masks depression, pain
Different baseline/limit
Sexual stereotyping
Economic frustrations
Rigid family patterns
	Different locations
	Act affects others
	  secondarily
	Building level
	  of incidence
	Physical safety
	  impaired
		Privacy of home
		Act affects others pri-
		  marily & secondarily
		Quick, high level
		  of incidence
		Physical safety
		  endangered

ward off any attempt at change taking place within the family. It feels good! The aggression itself causes a physical "rush," much like the alcoholic's euphoric state. Depression is masked, pain thwarted. The tolerance to pain rises, and correspondingly, the level of abuse is raised: all is tolerated. Often the aggression helps to reinstate control and feelings of mastery over others. A common situation is for the aggressor to feel emasculated at work or under some other severe external duress, but to re-establish his or her sense of dominance by aggression within the family.

As the alcoholic incident forces reaction, so does the family violence incident. The "problem at hand" must be dealt with, if only to be hushed and buried. Family members begin "walking on egg shells," lest Mt. Vesuvius erupt again. Structure becomes necessary between and among other family members in order to obtain some stability and "save needed energy." Family patterns and roles rigidify or reverse; children take on parental roles, in order that they and the family can survive. Doesn't this sound like the description of an alcoholic family?

Children pick up drinking styles from parents, though not all alcoholics learn their drinking at their parents' knees. Similarly, not all family abusers learn their behavior at their parents' homes, but we tend to punish as we were punished. We tend to construct our marriages as our parents did. We tolerate levels of abuse as learned in the home of our childhood. Typically, this is where we learn to cast women as deserving victims and to accept as "macho" for males to drink and hit (but for a woman, such behavior is inappropriate). Society in general has tolerated family violence. What goes on in the family castle is private and sacrosanct. Our laws reflect it; our values of privacy protect it. So similar is it to the alcohol case, that one might believe it is the same, but it is not. They are overlapping diseases, overlapping societal problems and issues, but they differ in a number of ways.

The first difference, of course, is that the act is different. Alcoholism affects the entire family, but it initially affects only the alcoholic, and subsequently it victimizes the family. Family violence initially affects at least one family member as the initial victim, the recipient of the assault, and another as the aggressor. The second difference is that family violence, by definition, must occur between family members and most often occurs in the privacy of the home. Alcoholics behave drunkenly everywhere. The family need not be involved, at least during "the actual event." Third, the alcoholic slowly increases his drinking before he/she crosses the "alcoholic" line; frequency of drinking slowly curves upward. The alcoholic must drink more and more to achieve the same effect. Similarly, the frequency of intrafamilial aggression curves rapidly upward after the initial series of incidents. The abuser quickly reaches a high plateau, where the abuse is frequent and less and less is needed to set off more and more to achieve the same effect.

And finally, the alcoholic may be slowly committing suicide. He/she may indirectly endanger others in the family, while physical safety, including imminent death, is more immediately at stake in the family violence picture.

Table Two

The Abusing Triangle

ALL RESCUERS
Have good intentions
Have strong need to control others
Get "triangulated"—asked to take sides,
to collude, to pair against the other,
and thus become the victim/persecutor

ALL ABUSERS	ALL VICTIMS
Learn behavior during childhood	Socially isolated
Project blame	Internalize blame
Possessive and jealous of their victims	Loyal to abuser and family
Have inappropriate role expectations	Not victim all the time
Have questionable judgment	Don't reveal plight to others
(during event)	Maintains family secrets—
Not abusive all the time	"blood is thicker ..."

Common Family Dynamics

The dynamics of abusing families and drinking families may best be viewed through the classic pathological triangle of interchangeable roles. Once a part of the triagle, a family member finds him/herself constantly rotating from one role to another, stuck on the merry-go-round.

The Abuser: Abusers/persecutors tend to have learned their behavior by observing their parents' violent relationships. Children learn to hit from the same ones who teach how to love. The message is clear: hitting and loving go together. If you don't hit, you don't love. If they themselves were hit as children, they learn that parenting equals hitting. They also yearn to be an adult to have the increased size and strength to hit. THEY

LEARN TO DRINK TO RESOLVE PROBLEMS, TO HIT TO RESOLVE PROBLEMS AND REASSERT CONTROL.

Universally, all abusers, whether hitters or drinkers, project blame onto others. "It's not my fault that ... " "She deserved that ... "Universally, all abusers tend to be jealous and possessive of their victims. The slightest suspicion of a spouse's relationship with another, for example, produces tirades and recriminations. Often, the abuser expects the child to behave like his/her parents or expects the spouse to take care of everything—role expectations that are impossible to meet.

If you question the abuser about the critical incident, you find that he/she doesn't always remember the details and may even "black out" the incident all together. Furthermore, the abuser is not abusive all the time. In fact, he/she might be a "superior citizen," i.e., when not "hitting the bottle," or "hitting a child/spouse." Regardless of the rationale, however, the abuser is responsible, not the victim.

The Victim: Victims tend to be socially isolated, ashamed to show their scars, not willing to expose their plight to others. Part of this social isolation is caused by the victim's internalization of the blame. The victim agrees with the abuser. "I deserve it." "I'm no good!" Invariably the victim believes strongly in family loyalty. One does not "rat" on a family member. Family secrets are guarded to the utmost. One maintains the family integrity at all costs.

Like the abuser, the victim is not a victim all the time. Sometimes, the victim has control, using the down-position to manipulate for new gains, but these manipulations do not last long, and the victim is a victim again. Still one does not choose to be a victim. A victim's behavior represents a means to survive; it also reflects a lack of access to failure of resources in our society.

The Rescuer: The well-meaning rescuing member of the family (or the counselor) starts out with good intentions. Most rescuers, however, enjoy controlling others and soon find themselves enmeshed in the problem they were trying to help. Suddenly, the rescuer is "triangulated." Each family member pulls and pushes the rescuer to take sides. When the rescuer does, he/she is immediately betrayed and blamed for everything. Then the rescuer becomes a victim.

What Can We Do? Some Tips, Some Pointers

Several steps may be taken to help families who are stuck with the "double trouble" of problem drinking (or alcoholism) and family violence. Helpers, whether professional counselors or Alcoholics Anonymous brethren, must avoid the rescuer position. Advice giver - yes. Trusted friend - yes. Reality tester and problem solver - yes. Rescuer - NO! Clarification of one's feelings about alcohol and family violence must emerge. Violent behavior, particularly in the home, must become unacceptable. The facts must come out from behind closed doors and out into the street. Provide shelters and "safety zones," where family members can negotiate, rest, and reconstitute their lives. Do not hesitate to ask, "How many times do you hit?" or "How often do you drink?"

Work with individual family members to set realistic goals to attain, then help re-establish that balance between the needs of the family and the needs of the individual. Battering stops and drinking stops having deleterious effects on the family as a whole when each individual family member becomes both an "I" and a "We."

Finally, to end on an encouraging note, alcoholics who are also physically abusive and still have intact families have a much greater chance of "making it" when problem drinking is a factor. This is partly due to (1) superior alcohol treatment options; (2) the family's option of saving face by blaming drinking (thus giving up alcohol), means giving up family violence); and, (3) the unmasking of denial as drinking decreases.

Alcohol and family violence are not new problems or new diseases. Nonetheless, today they re-emerge together because of the complexity of the present socio-political and economic climate. Perhaps this marks the beginning of an era when the multiple stress problems facing our burdened family structures will be faced. This beginning, toward exposure and ownership of these problems by our society, suggests we may be approaching a time of problem-solving and resolution.

Chapter Four
From 'Reconstruction' to 'Restoration'

Sharon Wegscheider-Cruse

Not long ago, I ran across a definition of experience as "history plus feelings." Perhaps the experience most common to every culture is that its children grow up in families—be they nuclear, extended or communal. Obviously, the family has a profound effect on the kind of adults we become. What, then, happens when children grow up in dysfunctional families such as those touched by alcoholism?

For myself, I know the answer. My family "history" is full of episodes associated with my parents' alcoholism. The "feelings" I had were a confused mixture of guilt, shame, and hurt when they were drinking and love, comfort, and security when they were sober. At either emotional pole, I had to wonder if I were not crazy to feel so pulled apart in my emotional life. I responded to all this by being super-responsible, so that I could be a rallying point for my parents, younger brother, and sister. I worked to be popular, became the star of the Debate Team and the apple of my father's eye. I succeeded in becoming the Family Princess, and yet my parents' drinking persisted. The message: Try harder! Small wonder, then, that the driving force of my adult life was to "try harder." And still, I could never be satisfied with anything I did. Life for me seemed an endless series of efforts that fell short; I was striving for an ideal that did not exist!

My own cycle of despair and confusion was broken several years ago by my "Reconstruction" with Virginia Satir. On that day, she guided me through a tableau of events from my family's past, lovingly re-enacted by her other students. With their support, I re-lived my childhood and felt, once again, the fear and confusion of seeing my parents

Reprinted with authors permission from FOCUS on Family and Chemical Dependency, Vol. 6, No. 5, Sept/Oct 1983.

fight at the dinner table, of seeing my father "asleep" on the floor, of feeling my mother's love and support for me drained under the pressures of the illness of alcoholism. I re-lived my teenaged and young adult years through recreation of other vignettes culled from my memory.

When the "Reconstruction" ended, I had re-lived a lifetime of pain. I had re-felt my feelings, discarded the ones which were no longer appropriate or useful, and paused a moment to cherish the ones that had given me pleasure. I made many choices the day of my "Reconstruction." And while I would not stop short of saying that I was reborn a healthy choicemaker in the space of that one day, I will say—unequivocally—that the experience turned my life around so that I could rebuild from a healthy base. I took control of my life, rather than to continue being controlled by feelings triggered by the illness of "co-dependency."

Today, one of the greatest joys of my life is guiding other people through "Family Reconstruction" so that they too many leave old issues behind and become healthy choicemakers. Virginia Satir's "Reconstruction" of me was of her very special style, and I am indebted to her. In the intervening years, I have evolved my own style of "Reconstruction" based upon additional families. This process has changed in many ways, and in order to separate and clarify the two processes, my "Reconstructions" in the future will be referred to as "Family Restoration."

The workshop always begins on a Sunday evening. At this point, most of the participants are strangers to each other. Each person introduces himself to the group and may talk about his personal goals over the next four days. The evening of introduction is always special to me, because I know that this group of strangers will know each other like family before the week is over.

Monday is a day of learning about alcoholism, drug abuse, family systems, and birth order. My professional life has been dedicated to changing our cultural and political views of alcoholism. It is not merely the disease of the Dependent Person (the afflicted); it is a family disease and a primary disease within every member of the affected family. When chemical addiction occurs in one family member, the other members adapt to that person's unstable behavior by developing behaviors of their own that cause the least amount of personal stress. This protects each person's feeling life, so the family survives—but only the most sick and deluded survival.

I talk about the family roles that I saw emerge in my own clinical experience: (1) The Enabler—(usually the spouse who does "everything under the sun" to make the drinking spouse stop—except what works: confronting the user or leaving the relationship. Enabling behavior is habitual; it will endure after separation from the Dependent unless treated.); (2) The Family Hero (who sees and hears what is happening and takes responsibility for the family pain by becoming successful and popular); (3) The Family Scapegoat (who rejects the family system by running away, withdrawing, or defiant behavior); (4) The Lost Child (who quietly and unobtrusively withdraws from the family system); and, (5) The Mascot (who hides his pain with humor and provides the system with "comic relief").

All these roles are symptoms of the disease of Co-Dependency, in which the primary compulsion is to act in a manner which accommodates the Dependent. It is a primary, progressive and chronic disease that stands between the afflicted person and his ability to act from free choice rather than to react, i.e., to behave the way he learned in order to survive a sick situation.

On Monday, many people who were previously unfamiliar with my work come to terms with their own knowledge and feelings about co-dependency. They see themselves for the first time as people who experienced a painful family system and never left it emotionally. With their family issues crystallized, they now have a hook into their own behavior patterns and feelings and something to work with over the next few days.

Tuesday morning, the psychodrama of "Reconstruction" (now "Restoration) begins. For the "Star," or person whose life we will be recreating all day and evening, the event began months before with his/her selection for that role. Once selected, the Star began amassing information about his family of origin, his grandparents' families, and the family in which he now lives. If he has done his job well, the Star will have a family tree, anecdotes and events of note securely in memory or on paper, snapshots, portraits, birth certificates, court records, adoption papers, and a clear idea of his goals for the day. For many of the Stars, this is a day of forgiveness, of letting go, of experiencing love they had forgotten they had, and sadness they thought they had buried. This day will bring up many issues they did not think they had brought with them, and from this re-experiencing and re-feeling will come new healing.

I prepare for my work with the Star by interviewing him/her extensively just prior to the workshop itself. The purpose of the interview is twofold: First, I must know the person's life thoroughly, in order to guide him/her through it. I need a sense of where they are stuck in terms of old issues, and what they are and are not willing to bring up before the group. Second, we need this time together in order to build the trust in each other that will make the journey a success.

Workshop participants are cast in specific roles in the Star's generational history. The casting process is mysterious, because many times, the person cast is trying to deal with his/her own family issues inherent in that role. For example, if the Star is a man who casts me in the role of his daughter, I become a daughter again. This is one of the many roles I have played in my life, but I have not been a daughter to my father in many years. As I feel myself in this role, memories come flooding back. I go with my feelings, paying attention to the situation the Star wishes to recreate, and our dialogue flows. Together, we re-live an event from his past, and both of us learn that in that situation, each person did the best he could. A healing takes place, not just for the Star, but for the person so fortuitously cast in the role of daughter, who healed in her heart a breach with her own father. I do not know why this happens; I only know that the Star's life is a vehicle through which others can work.

These vignettes are re-enacted all day, punctuated with pauses as the group gives feedback on the various scenes. Participants are not permitted to analyze events; rather, they must concentrate on the feelings that come up. If they are strongly identifying with the incident being staged, I encourage them to work through their feelings in demonstrative ways: scream, move the anger up through the stomach and out the mouth. Take a bataca bat and beat past hurts and rage onto a pillow. Cry. If we talk about how we feel, we may come up with valuable insights; but the only way to work through feelings is to feel.

The drama moves in reverse. The Star's current family is examined first, followed by his life in his family of origin, and then his grandparents' families. Where the Star is today is not the result of random circumstance; he comes to view his life as the only one he could have had, given the generational path cut long ago.

A successful "Restoration" ends not when the Star's work is done, but with the Star's awareness of where the work should begin. He now has choices, and he can make them freely and consciously.

Wednesday, the participants split into small groups for more individualized work. By this day, we have jelled into "family," and the small groups become very intimate. Those who surrender themselves to this feeling do the best work. In a loving, supportive atmosphere, the tears, rage, shame, pain, and ultimately the joy that people hide in order to live day-by-day come to the surface. It is, for many, the most exhausting and rewarding day of the workshop.

Thursday, we give a special party called The Parts Party. It is a Gestalt exercise in which one person lists his personal qualities, personifies them with well-known personalities, and casts one of the participants in each part. Then, as the "parts" sit down to a party with each other, the person walks the periphery of the "revelry," observing the interaction. Who dominates? Who brings the greatest joy? Who could best serve the party by leaving? As the person pauses next to each character, he may speak with them and negotiate terms under which they may stay. For example, the "comedian" at the party (often Rodney Dangerfield!) may stay if he does not dominate the loving, saintly Mother Therese! The Parts Party gives the "host" a chance to look at himself as the sum of his parts, to love parts of himself without loving all, and conversely to reject some parts of himself without despairing that he is "all bad."

On that note, we end the workshop with the Serenity Prayer and cling to each other for just a moment longer. The four days are over, just when they should be, as many of the participants are anxious to go home and put into practice what they have experienced here. For me, I leave each "Restoration" Workshop with a profound respect for the people who have surrendered themselves to the process and gratitude to the Higher Power for leading me to this work.

The change in name of this workshop from "Reconstruction" to "Restoration," fills me with new eagerness to continue the work. "Restoration" connotes a desire to return people to their "original personhood," i.e., to the person they were before they adapted their behavior to accommodate a sick system. We seek to "restore" rather than to change. It is my greatest hope and wish that everyone with unsettled family issues will someday surrender themselves to "Family Restoration." May it give each of you the same joy and hope it has given me.

Chapter Five
Hispanics and Alcoholism: A Treatment Perspective

Philip Oliver-Diaz and Ronald Figueroa

At the outset, we want to acknowledge the need to define what we mean by the term 'Hispanic' before discussing alcoholism in relation to this population. It has been our experience as substance abuse specialists who have developed culturally-appropriate treatment programs for Hispanic families, that all too often the general population has little knowledge of the cultural and socioeconomic realities of Hispanics. We can understand a treatment perspective for alcoholism for Hispanics only if we have a handle on the confusing demographics of this client group.

It is generally felt that a great need exists to develop new perspectives and methods for serving the Hispanic population, and most especially the alcoholic family. The alcoholism worker trying to work with a Hispanic patient often will be confronted with a close intermeshing of alcohol issues and sociocultural factors. As with most clients, the worker's desire to help the client understand the difference and deal with what appears as denial may seem justified and simple. This in fact may not be true. A better understanding of the multiplicity of problems and influences acting upon the family and of the different treatment possibilities within the client's realm of cultural experience is imperative. What continues to be painfully evident is that too large a number of Hispanics with alcohol-related problems are simply not being reached or drop out of treatment, while the rate of alcoholism among this population remains twice as high as for the general population.

In an overview of Hispanics in the United States, we most often refer to them as a single ethnic minority group, yet they consist of almost 20 million people of diverse origins and cultures. On one hand, Hispanics have been part of this country since its inception, yet on the other hand, Hispanics account for approximately one million new immigrants per year, emigrating from more than twenty different countries and territories in which Spanish is the native language. The racial composition of Hispanics as an ethnic grouping in the United States is virtually a microcosm of the world. Economically, Hispanics are represented in every level of society. As a result, Hispanics in the United States range tremendously in degree of cultural and linguistic adaptation. Therefore, to describe culture and its treatment implications in terms of the larger ethnic group of "Hispanic" would be too expansive and general a definition.

Socioeconomic Profile

One factor that does clearly impact on determining special needs and on the development of a cultural perspective for providing services to the majority of Hispanics in the United States is the fact that they live in depressed social conditions and constitute a good portion of this nation's lower economic class. Of those included in the most recent census, one out of four Hispanic families is at poverty level. This does not account for the uncounted illegal aliens of Hispanic background, which some estimates put between 3.5 and 6 million people; among this latter group, poverty level families would more likely number nine out of ten, if not higher. Unemployment figures for Hispanics consistently remain five to seven percent higher than for the general population. The median family income remains seven to eight thousand dollars less for Hispanics than for the general population. Fewer than half ever complete high school.

Services designed to reach the Hispanic population most effectively must first be sensitive to the economic realities of this population. From this standpoint alone, we find that those Hispanics most in need of health services, inclusive of alcoholism treatment, will consistently be the least able to avail themselves of existing services.

Historical Factors

Historical factors which impact on the definition of the Hispanic family need to be given careful consideration. For the purposes of this article, we will consider mainly the first and second generation of Hispanic immigrant families to the U.S. mainland.

This traditional family system has its roots in an agrarian society where economic survival is contingent upon a large, independent family unit with strong family bonding. The basic understanding is simple: the more members within the family system, the greater that family's chances of survival and improvement. Within this society, the family is often extended beyond the nuclear family to include grandparents, aunts and uncles, and "compadres," who serve as godparents to the children and participate in daily activity, decision-making, and distribution of responsibilities in order to further protect the family's survival. This may indeed be a crucial point for the service provider in seeking to determine who are "significant others" to a Hispanic person in treatment.

During the Spanish colonialist era, in which the traditional family reached its final stages of formation, two other factors came into play to further reinforce the "common sense of self" and the strong inner ties of the Hispanic family. One factor was the need for a family name which establishes status and prestige, signifies economic opportunities, and dictates marriage and property rights. As the distinct racial groups of three different continents (Native America, Europe, and Africa) met and merged within the colonial period, social mobility and status could no longer be measured as easily by racial criteria, and therefore a "good" family name of traceable lineage and strong family ties under that name became the vehicle. A second element of this period was the strong religious influence which continues to permeate every aspect of life. The Roman Catholic and fundamentalist Christian ideologies which serve to define individual and community roles, support those previously mentioned concepts of the Agrarian family: a large, patriarchal family system. Religious values are instilled in the family that preserve it through early marriages, the absence of birth control or abortion, and strongly defined sex roles. These become intrinsic parts of the Hispanic family's identity and measures of community standing.

Sex Roles

The sex roles within the traditional, non-assimilated Hispanic family have been very clearly delineated within traditional societies. The male role is that of father, protector, and hunter, and to him belongs the last word. The female role is that of mother, provider, and life-giver. Based on these primordial divisions of duties, there has developed an entire code of ethics and social expectations commonly referred to as "machismo," and its complement, "marianismo." These have become societal roles which act on the family from outside, with a great consistency of role modeling from within and without the family. The delegation of responsibilities must meet the established standards of what is socially deemed to be acceptably male or acceptably female.

It should be noted that much is said and written about the manifestations, nuances, and implications of sex roles and machismo. There are no simple formulas. What must be understood is that they are a powerful force which acts upon the family, and that those traditional roles do become altered to varying degrees according to the level of acculturation of the specific family and individual. It is essential to look for clues and not to assume that they have been altered, regardless of the worker's own feelings and biases in this area, letting the client define for the worker the former's perception of those sex roles.

Acculturation

Acculturation is a process of progressive adaptation to the dominant culture for the purposes of economic survival and mobility. In essence, it represents a continual assessment, compromising, and redefining of cultural values and perceptions in order to meet immediate needs.

The first stages of adaptation address: (1) environment or geography; (2) language; and, (3) employment and education. Adaptation at this point is marked by the need to survive, both as a family and as individuals. The non-assimilated family's identity, bonds, and roles are rigidly maintained, as well as the use of the native language and celebration of family rituals. Ties to "la patria" ("mother country") are also strongly maintained, and the adoption of new ways meets great resistance within the family.

Among Hispanic immigrant families, a pervasive sense of transience is characteristic of the first generation. Problem-solving and compromises are based on the premise of "returning home some day" in a better situation and to better economic or political conditions. This sense of transience serves as the proverbial "rose-colored glasses" through which life within the new dominant culture is perceived, interpreted, and survived on a day-to-day basis. The alcoholism worker, however, needs to understand that this is not just denial; it is an appropriate psychological coping mechanism.

Initially, housing and employment are sought where economic survival is attainable and where there is a cultural commonality, in "el barrio" or the Spanish-speaking ghetto. For the parents (first generation), the environment secured supports the family's identity, the language, the traditions, and the feeling of self-worth amidst the assault of mainstream culture, and the resulting culture shock. In this environment, the need to assimilate rapidly is diminished, and the process can be slowed. The parents' focus is primarily on the financial status of the family.

For the children (second generation), the transition is more immediate. Their daily school experience provides a disparate linguistic and cultural setting, alien to the home life shared with their parents. Survival for the child hinges upon the urgent acquisition of English language skills, understanding new rules which, in many cases, represent an almost constant conflict of value systems (traditional Hispanic versus new dominant culture), and accepting contrasting adult role models.

What arises is an intergenerational gap. Parent and child begin to exist respectively in separate milieus, a situation which produces separate perceptions of class, values, and language and two different rates of acculturation. The results can be subtle but devastating. The linguistic schism between parent and child creates two key, catalytic effects in the long-range disintegration of the family structure. The most predictable result is the slow deterioration of communication among family members, almost imperceptible at first. As the children continue to develop and to establish peer relationships, the new language (English) cognitively becomes the dominant one. Unfortunately, the new skills acquired initiate an emotional separation. Richard Rodriguez explains in his autobiographical *A Hunger of Memory* that a clear division is formed between the "public" language of success and the "private" language of intimacy. The nurturing and support that might otherwise be available in the traditional, monolingual family setting slowly becomes distanced. A second, compounding result of the child's rapid second language acquisition is the use of the child as family interpreter. What at first innocently addresses immediate needs, eventually begins to signal a significant role reversal between the parent and the child; the child is now taking care of the parent. In the traditional family, the child would be very aware of the rules and limits, even if necessity demanded that he/she speak on behalf of older family members. Within the acculturation process, however, the child is bombarded with new role models and new peer pressures, while simultaneously experiencing the loss of intimacy. Perception of appropriate roles become distorted and authority eroded.

During the initial phases of economic survival, a critical commodity that is sacrificed is the time the family spends together (dinner, vacation, holidays, etc.). While the parents try to hold down a couple of jobs, or to work whatever hours are available, the most basic family rituals are disrupted. Again, this is commonly viewed as a temporary solution to a temporary situation. In light of what else is simultaneously occurring to affect the individual family members, however, the isolating effects are greatly magnified. When those activities which constitute a symbolic form of communication are not given continuity, the family loses the collective sense of unity and the ability to mobilize during times of stress.

There are endless other factors affecting the family during acculturation. As the family is redefined, the members feel a sensation of belonging to a "shrinking family." Loneliness and feelings of "not being connected" are associated with the progressive loss and the geographical separation of the extended family. This becomes especially true of the single parent household, where the absent parent represents an emotional vacuum and remains "present" almost as a family ghost. Conflicts also can arise from the often greater employability of the female, or the children, over the male. This is interpreted as a role inversion, and a loss of purpose or usefulness is experienced by the male, which can lead to overcompensating with either exaggerated "macho" behavior or extreme withdrawal. Together, these factors help create fertile ground for even greater problems. All too often, alcohol abuse becomes a coping mechanism for those families in stress.

The Image of Alcohol Abuse To Hispanics

In order to understand alcoholism treatment for Hispanics, one must understand the traditional Hispanic views of substance abuse. One common perception is based on a fundamentalist Christian view of alcoholism as a sin. Alcoholism has traditionally been grouped together with a whole series of "sins" or transgressions that remove you from "following the will of God." All sin is viewed as spiritual disease. Yet, addictions are perceived as willfully contracted ones. "Giving in to temptation" or "succumbing to the flesh" are key phrases which emphasize the view of alcohol addiction as the result of a moral weakness, a hedonistic nature, or simply of "not loving God" (at least not enough to follow His will).

The cure, the only prescribed solution, is an immediate and total surrender to God's Will ("Giving your life to Jesus and putting yourself entirely in His hands"). This surrender is the remedy for all forms of sin.

One complication in addressing the issue of alcoholism and other addictions within this context is that it is difficult to perceive the person as a victim, because it is understood that we are all victims of a constant assault against our soul (or higher self) by invisible demonic forces, by the material world, by other sinners, and by our very own flesh (1 Peter 2:11, Eph. 6:11-12). Thus, our lives, all our lives, are a constant struggle against spiritual disease or the temptation to sin. Still another factor for the person accepting this view is the fact that sin is defined as compounding or multiplying itself and, in many interpretations, it is not measurable in qualifying degrees. In other words, if you get drunk knowing it is wrong, it is a denial of God, therefore, it is deceit, it is blasphemy, and is as bad as theft, adultery, or physically harming someone. Consequently, the amount of guilt associated with drinking, for breaking any one item within that doctrinal code, is also compounded. In effect, a person with an alcohol problem many times considers himself "the worst of sinners," no better than a thief or a prostitute. (We've seen it be a self-fulfilling prophecy of sorts, where the person actually transforms himself in dress, speech, attitude and actions into a veritable caricature of things perceived as evil or sinful: partying, wearing loud and revealing attire, excessive drinking, swearing, fighting, wearing make-up, being promiscuous, etc.). Thus, as one approaches this Hispanic family as a treater, one must keep in mind that for the family and the alcoholic, the battle for recovery is fought on the battlefield of Good and Evil. Usually, the only way to stop drinking is to become a "soldier of Christ." The treatment often needs to be presented in reference to its "spiritual results," not just its secular, therapeutic results.

For the Hispanic male, a second perspective of alcohol use and abuse is based on societal interpretations of the macho. In this context, alcohol abuse is simply another challenge in life, to be experienced and controlled the same way a true man, for example, faces sexual relationships, gambling, and all things that challenge his destiny. These are not to be avoided, but are, in fact, to be readily indulged in, maintained, and used as measures of one's manhood.

A.A., Al-Anon, and Hispanics

The primary recovery system for alcoholics in North America continues to be Alcoholics Anonymous. No other support system has been more effective helping non-Hispanic alcoholics maintain sobriety than A.A.

Alcoholics Anonymous, besides being a "spiritual route to recovery," is also a socio-political entity, a point all too often forgotten by the members of A.A. and the therapists who send clients there. Thus, A.A. mirrors the dominant culture and, of course, reflects the class and values of its members.

On the whole, A.A. in the United States is not an adequate alternative for the non-assimilated, Spanish-dominant alcoholic, and the same is true of Al-Anon and Alateen for the spouse and child. While there has been some attempt to have culturally specific groups and Spanish speaking A.A. and Al-Anon meetings, on the whole these groups do not exist in sufficient numbers to have an impact on the large number of Hispanics needing help.

Even where Hispanic Spanish-speaking groups exist, some of the aspects which are fundamental to A.A. and Al-Anon are diametrically opposed to the Hispanic value system. The independency and confrontative behavior that are encouraged in Al-Anon for spouses is antithetical to the image of the Hispanic female, and asks the Hispanic woman to break cultural barriers.

The same can be said of A.A. The idea of sharing one's personal problems in public, in front of other men, is antithetical to the Hispanic male's idea of himself and is therefore generally unacceptable. It is too powerless a position for the acculturating Hispanic male to put himself into. This is not to say that A.A. is not the key recovery system for Hispanics in the United States.

The Hispanic client often will be compliant, but not follow through on plans supposedly developed between therapist and client. It has been our experience that one primary recovery system for the chemically dependent Hispanic family is organized religious groups, in particular the charismatic or Pentecostal churches. Practitioners need to understand the significance of the churches to the Hispanic family as the primary helping system.

An important aspect of dealing with the church is the need to recognize that the church pastor is the source of all major decision-making for many acculturating Hispanics, one must have a concept of family which includes the Church. A true family session for an Hispanic family may include the pastor as well as a number of "hermanos y hermanas de la Iglesia." Without these participants, often no real change can occur for the family. In fact, for the chemically dependent Hispanic family, these other church members have become their extended family.

In particular, the pastor of the church plays a key role. The pastor decides what is secular and what is spiritual, and therefore decides what is to be taken seriously or to be ignored. It has been our experience that when the pastor is engaged in treatment, then client participation and cooperation are assured. This is because the pastor serves as gatekeeper of all activity in which members of the church may engage.

All Pentecostal churches have "obreros," workers for the church who serve as inhouse counselors and, in particular, deal with drug and alcohol abusing individuals. Through a planned system of intervention and spiritual nurturing, these "obreros" work with the family and the pastor to save the alcoholics.

One must keep in mind that to these people, alcoholism is a sin and is in reality a fight between good and evil which only the strong can win. It takes a real "Macho" to become temperant and receive the Lord. All this, of course, is culturally appropriate and looks into the Hispanic self-image as one of defeating alcoholism versus surrendering to it (which is the A.A. model). One explanation of the relatively high rate of success with alcohol abusing males who enter the fundamentalist Christian system of recovery is the language of that particular subculture, which utilizes Biblical terminology and militaristic symbols. This language reinforces the image of that strong, dominant male and arms him with a new definition of what a true macho is: one who can take up the sword of truth and the shield of faith in the battle against sin.

The record for how many alcoholics recover from alcoholism in the church cannot be estimated, but it is safe to say that the majority of non-assimilated Hispanics recover through this kind of intervention rather than through intervention practices at treatment centers. Thus, when working in an Hispanic community, one must identify the "obreros" and both validate their work and elicit their help in bringing the message of recovery to chemical dependent Hispanic families. When we worked in Hispanic communities and did community alcohol education, we would always include obreros as part of our panels of experts.

Almost equal in success and importance to Hispanic chemical alcoholics are curanderismo, santeria, espiritisno, and faith healing. While similar, these four types of spiritual healers are significantly different from one another and need to be understood. Each of these people represents indigenous healing systems which have a long cultural history of curing people and are often the source of recovery for Hispanic alcoholics. Without a clear understanding of who these people are and what they represent, one cannot truly understand the chemically dependent Hispanic family.

The roots of these traditions extend back to the native and African roots of the various Hispanic American groups in the United States. Simply speaking, a curandero is one who is practiced in the art of herbs and also can "heal by the faith." The curandero is part of the native thread of Hispanic tradition, similar to the idea of the medicine man.

The santeros and spiritualists are rooted in the African and some European traditions. They enlist the aid of spirits and potions in their healing. Faith healers are the same as those in the United States, so popular in the Southern white church tradition. All of these indigenous helpers need to be enlisted by the treatment system in order to truly exhaust all of the existing alternatives for recovery.

Spouses and Family Treatment

If the alcoholic is difficult to reach, the spouse and family are even harder to help. Intervention with the chemically active acculturating families is a confusing process at best, and can have disastrous results if the therapists have not sensitized themselves to the socio-cultural factors of their clients. No acculturating group has just one problem. Housing, employment, education, and immigration status are usually problems compounding the family system's stresses, in addition to the language problems. The old adage, "deal with the drinking and things will work out," does not fit poor, acculturating families.

If the drinking stops, the family situation often is not much better. The issues of poverty and racism are real and need to be addressed in the alcoholic family, in addition to the alcoholism.

It is also most important that the worker define with his clients what they mean by family. As we have often discussed, family too often means something very different to Hispanics than it does to non-Hispanics, and the therapist must gather data in a careful, thorough, and sensitive manner in order to know how large a unit is being treated and what the intergenerational issues are. Again, compounding the family treatment issues are also the various stages of acculturation in which the family system is engaged. A mixture of ethno-therapy, concrete casework, and chemical dependency counseling must take place.

This must all be done while keeping in mind not to disrupt the role of the wife in the family, yet teach her to separate from the alcoholic emotionally, and to stop enabling. If this work is done in the traditional, non-Hispanic way, and a feminist attitude is fostered in the female spouse, she may suffer severe rejection from the other female members in her family system who might view her confrontational style as a complete breakdown of expected dignity and respect. In this instance, the "politics of therapy" needs to be examined so that the spouse is clearly educated to help herself in the context of the cultural system within which she must live, rather than in the white middle class system of the therapist.

Children of Alcoholics/Children of Acculturation

In our work with acculturating children and children of alcoholics, we found that children of acculturation confront many of the same issues as children of alcoholics, even when drinking is not present in the system.

Children of acculturating families have all the problems of children of alcoholics. We have stated that they are often more competent in the dominant culture than their parents, thus they undergo a role reversal in which they take on a parenting role. They are forced to be interpreters for their families, especially where social agencies are concerned. Often insensitive caseworkers or alcoholism professionals will require children to ask questions of the most inappropriate and intimate nature of their parents, for the lack of an interpreter. It is the feeling of the authors that Hispanic children should *never* be asked to interpret for their parents, as it reinforces an inappropriate family position for the child.

Children of acculturation are often extremely ambivalent about their parents and feel guilty about their feelings. They love their parents, but are ashamed and embarrassed by their language, dress, and lifestyle. Children of acculturation also are forced to accept premature responsibility in having to take a leadership role in families far beyond their years. These children live in a world of mixed messages: become American, but don't lose your roots, learn fluent English, but don't speak English. Children who lose their capacity to speak Spanish often lose their ability to communicate in an intimate way with their family, for whom Spanish is the "language of the heart." This is a serious loss which makes the acculturating child struggle in his own house.

The feelings of mistrust, guilt, confusion, isolation and fear are as true for children of acculturation as for children of alcoholics. Accordingly, Hispanic children of alcoholics have a double burden to carry. Therapists need to understand that simply treating the Hispanic alcoholic does not necessarily eliminate the stress on the children; the acculturation issues also need to be addressed in treatment with the children.

In children of alcoholics groups, the therapist may need to help explain to other members some of the Hispanic family's methods for solving family problems. For example, the father of one of our young clients had gone to a "Bruja" (a witch) who put a curse on the child's mother. The child's mother got sick, and the child was very upset. The therapist had to interpret the incident to the group and to help the group understand that, while strange to many of them, this was just another case of the alcoholic acting against the spouse. The non-Hispanic children were very ready to help their friend, once they understood what had happened.

The other key concept in working with Hispanic children of alcoholics is the effect of the fundamentalist Christian belief that equates alcoholism with sin. We have worked with many children from Pentecostal churches. The children of alcoholics, especially those whose alcoholic parents had died of the illness, felt that their parents were in hell, being punished for their sins. Understanding the disease concept gave them real relief. Once they understood that their parents had a disease and were not at fault, they were able to let go of their belief that their parents were doomed "sinners," and to grasp the possibility that a loving God would not eternally damn the victim of an illness that preys upon the body, mind, and soul.

Summary

We cannot over-emphasize the need for chemical dependency workers to understand who the Hispanic client is before treating him. The worker needs to know what systems the client is using in the community and who needs to be included in treatment. The worker needs to include the full extended family system when doing family work, and needs to keep operative an understanding of cultural belief in non-assimilated Hispanics. Finally, the worker needs to remember that Hispanic children of alcoholics fall under all the same issues as children of acculturation, in addition to problems of alcoholism, and the therapist needs to help his clients with both realities.

Chapter Six

The Wisdom of Elders: Working With Native American and Native Alaskan Families

Jane Middelton-Moz

The metaphor which recently has been used to describe the alcoholic family system is that of a family with a huge elephant in its living room. The erratic and unpredictable behavior of the elephant is extremely frightening, and the family members learn to become cautious in their own behavior. In order to survive, they learn to minimize the effects of their often chaotic environment. They learn to adapt to and develop strategies to cope with the situation, and then finally they learn to deny the elephant's existence. No one talks about what it's like. No one even acknowledges that it exists. Painfully, the children in the family grow up doubting their own perceptions; they often feel tremendous guilt and shame — but they don't understand why. When the child is older, he might think he sees the elephant out of the corner of his eye — an elephant in his new living room perhaps — but the elephant is never discussed. Maybe it doesn't really exist; the child never knows for certain.

Over the past six years, through working with native American families on the reservations and working with many native Alaskan people, all of whom suffer the effects of substance abuse within their family system, it has become more apparent to me that within native culture, two elephants exist. The first is the effect of alcoholism on both the family and the community, and the second is found in the effects of the stigma and depression caused by forced acculturation. It should be noted that there are many differences between and among the tribes and villages which make up the native American and native

Alaskan cultures. There are also differences between Irish culture and Italian culture (although both cultures are European). Just as differences exist, so do similarities in values and in the effects of acculturation.

Often children from the majority culture, who have felt powerless in their alcoholic environment, find some sense of power, achievement and success in the broader world of school and community. Although a sense of poor self-esteem is still felt by these children, academic or leadership success does provide some positive feedback and a focus for energy outside the home. However, what does the Indian child do when he or she attempts to achieve in a white school and finds instead an unfriendly climate of racial prejudice? What does that child experience inside her/himself when he finds all teachers are white and so are all the powerful people in the broader community? What does he/she feel the first time he/she hears on a school bus that he/she is a "stupid Indian?" When I was a child, the Indian children (with few exceptions) sat in the back of the classroom and received very little attention from the instructors. It was as if, somehow, they didn't exist, as if they were not there. One boy I knew well wrote the most sensitive poetry I had ever read, but he was never called on to read it and he consistently got F's in English because he couldn't punctuate or spell correctly. He dropped out of school in the seventh grade. The prevalence of unemployment and alcoholism was virtually equal on his reservation, and the elder system was broken down by the impact of government service programs, yet there was constant talk by white members of the community about the "lazy Indians" who could get free college scholarships, but didn't have the "motivation" to take advantage of them. If they did apply, could they pass college boards with poor English and mathematics scores? Could they get good scores without the attention of teachers? Could they get the attention of teachers without learning to be more extroverted and to compete, when their cultural values were based on cooperation rather than competition and they were taught the power of silence rather than words.

In most of the families with whom I have worked, I have seen a pervasive sense of low self-esteem and powerlessness, depression, cultural disorientation, alienation from the power and strength of cultural values, and confusion about and distaste for the values of the new culture. The major resource of the native American and native Alaskan family has always been its community. To a native child, the family is more than a mother and father; it is a network of kinship and a network of relationships that extend far beyond the nuclear family unit. Yet the major effect of many federal policies has been to break up the extended family, the clan structure, and the village system of support.

The destruction of the native family has happened in three major ways. The first happened very early with the massive separation of Indian children from their families, both through foster home placement and through sending many hundreds of Indian children to boarding school. Many studies indicate that in the middle and late '70's, approximately 20 to 35% of all Indian children were separated from their families and placed in foster homes or adoptive homes. In many states, the number of Indian children in foster homes was 13 to 19 times greater than non-Indian children (Byler, 1977).

Many native children, taken from their families and placed in foster care, never reconnected with their families. Many of these foster placements were originally made because well-meaning social workers did not understand Indian cultural values, social norms, or the extended family system. I have worked with many urban natives who went through multitudes of different foster homes and never reconnected with their own families or their kinship networks. They felt alienated from the majority culture in which they lived, as well as the culture from which they came.

The Federal Boarding School placements had an even wider effect because of the numbers involved. Children sent to boarding schools often became strangers to their parents. The child's entrance into boarding school often meant a complete breaking of family ties. The children had to give up the values they learned at home and replace them with values of the majority culture. Adults with whom I have worked, and who spent many years in boarding schools as children, suffered cultural confusion and abandonment, not only through separation from parents, but through separation from the entire kinships network as well. Many did not return to their villages or to their reservations after finishing school. Those who did return found that they had difficulty using the skills they had learned. They wanted to stay in the culture, yet felt alienated from their own value system. They felt confused and depressed. This confusion was increased when these young adults, not raised by their own parents, parented their own children.

A child learns to be a parent through modeling after his/her own parents. He/she learns through his/her relationship with his/her parents as he/she grows through developmental stages. Children in overcrowded boarding schools from the ages of 10 to 17 or 18 did not have the benefit of that parent-child relationship. Many native adults have told me that they felt lost when their own children reached the age they had been when first sent to boarding schools.

Many native children, while allowed to stay at home, had to attend junior high and high schools off the reservation. For many, this was the first time they experienced conflict of values and prejudice. Indian children in their homes were taught by modeling the behavior of their elders and through the kinship network. The Indian child was allowed considerable responsibility in the home and often learned from the consequences of behavior rather than from external control. The child was taught that it was intolerable to tell another person what to do, was taught the value of silence and not to shout, was taught a universal flow of time rather than a linear one, and was taught to avoid conflict. When these children went into a majority culture school system, they were taught regimens of the mind and the body; they were forced to compete; they were taught time-oriented demands; they were told what to think, what to do and what to believe; they were taught to speak up and speak loudly; and for the first time, they faced racial discrimination.

Many adults with whom I work talk about their feelings as children, of being ashamed in front of the class or of being made to have their hair cut. On many reservations today, the school dropout rate increases dramatically in junior high and high school when the children on reservations are forced to attend majority culture schools. One native woman told me, "I didn't really want to leave home and go to boarding school, but it was a choice for me, where it had not been for my mother. The choice was to go to a boarding school far away from home where there were other Indian children or go to a school in a white town off the reservation and face prejudice every day on the bus and in school. I knew I wouldn't make it through the 7th grade in that town school. Boarding school was a far better choice."

Teachers in schools off the reservations often do not understand the values that Indian children are taught at home. Indian children are viewed as lacking motivation, interest and creativity. "The non-Indian has seldom appreciated Indian children's autonomous efforts. The Indian child may simply withdraw, wait, or use passive resistance to the onslaught of scolding by teachers and by other non-Indians" (Attneave, 1977). Many times I have been called to the home of an Indian family. The child has become ill two to three weeks after transition into the majority culture school. The family often becomes silent, while each family member quietly feels his own childhood pain and understands that the illness is often synonymous with shame. A native Alaskan woman told me, "Things that we were taught as natives were devalued in schools. We did not eat the right food; we did not talk the right way; we did not dress the right way; it was not the right way to be. I learned I was stupid."

The Tribal Association of a reservation with whom I've worked, recognized the problem with the increasing drop-out rate of their children when transferring to majority town schools. They fought for a secondary school on the reservation. The first year of its operation, the drop-out rate decreased 90%.

A second element that has served to break down the native family in community structure has been loss of power in self-determination. As one native said to me, "there is a difference in people telling us what to do, rather than asking us what would help. Government programs which foster dependence make us angry at ourselves and destroy self-esteem. People do everything rather than letting us depend on ourselves with help. That's how we grow dependent. We are hated for it and we hate ourselves."

The native culture had a strong community system. The main tribal resource was its people. Yet, because majority culture has assumed control over the native culture in finances and services, the tribal system has come to lack unity and cohesion. Wilkinson (1980) proposed that the intervention and the early absolute control by outsiders in the tribal communities has destroyed the classic interdependence necessary for community survival (Wilkinson). Members who were respected in the tribal community were displaced in their respective functions and fellow natives were seen to have less worth as a result of this role displacement. An Indian man told me of his sense of powerlessness. "A long time ago we were taught to respect our elders; to look downwards in respect; to only speak if we had something to say to our elders. So the white people came in and didn't listen. They asked us a question. Before we could formulate our feelings and thoughts, they'd answer it for us and then say we weren't motivated. We got intimidated. The dominant culture being white, dominates school systems and businesses. We'd get elected as tokens; try to communicate; get talked down; our opinions didn't seem valuable."

Wilkinson further states that the dominant society's method of dealing with community problems was to deal with a series of individual problems and this caused further community disintegration (Wilkinson). Increasing government regulations of hunting and fishing in native

American and Alaskan villages has caused an end to a subsistence lifestyle valued by the native culture, not only in physical survival but in its value of sharing with community. A native man stated, "We used to help out people who didn't get so much; now we need money, we learn to compete, and we don't respect each other's needs as much."

Rather than job training or providing consultation on developing industry, many tribal members receive intervention in the area of food stamps and welfare. As one native Alaskan woman stated, "Religion took over spiritual training of our people. Education was going to teach our people values and it rendered our elders useless. Welfare and food stamps rendered our people useless to each other. We became dependent on things, then had those things taken away abruptly. It made us feel even more powerless." A culture that has learned to feel powerless experiences depression and anxiety. Prolonged feelings of helplessness lead to a feeling of a helpless stance in life. Communities stop looking for resolutions and feel that they are unable to work through past problems. Their motivation is impaired and they begin to deny or miss information that suggests that control over their situation is possible.

The third factor that has caused family and tribal disintegration is stigma. When a culture is stigmatized, it is categorized and separated, making the people in it more stereotypical than individual. Native youth and families listen to statistics which state that their culture has greater incidence of alcoholism, drug abuse, suicide, health problems, and death at an earlier age than in other cultures. Although these statistics often result in more federal funds for services, they also result in native American people devaluing themselves. They rarely hear of the powerful strengths of native culture. Often there is a belief in the "drunken Indian," a belief in the hopelessness and powerlessness of the culture, and a further belief that somehow this reflects a genetic truth that influences the destiny of all native people.

Westermeyer in his article, "The Drunken Indian," talks about the invalidity of the genetic research on native American alcoholism. He argues that Indian people, as a group, have a good deal of similarity in numerous heredity characteristics to Asian people, and yet the same observations have been used to explain why Indians have a higher rate of alcoholism and Asians have less. He also states that it is a long step from merely demonstrating physiological differences, to explaining the role that etiology plays in alcoholism (Westmeyer, 1977). Many studies have supported the idea that perhaps such stressors as racial and ethnic prejudice, economic status, and outside control of education, religion, and health might play a larger role in the drinking patterns of natives that does genetics.

A native woman states, "We never used to need to use alcohol or drugs. We just got together and enjoyed each other in our own way. We supported each other in our own way, but we learned that that was different, strange. We learned we were wrong, and they laughed at us. Then we started getting together and drinking like they did. Then they told us we were good-for-nothing drunks." Westermeyer states that, the "stereotypical alcoholic drinking pattern" among Indian people is not that different from those observed in other men such as lumberjacks, fishermen, and military, who are separated from their culture in strange cities, and under the stress of culture shock (Westermeyer).

Dan Dodson has stated, "It would be impossible for a youth who is a member of a group which is powerless in the community to grow to maturity without some trauma to his perception of himself because of this compromised position of his group in communal life." He further states that as a result of this trauma, youth often develop apathy, low aspirational levels, and often, senses of low self-worth (Dodson). It was somehow projected in the American dream that if you worked hard enough, and were good enough, and studied hard enough, you would be successful. Yet, the majority of power figures to native American youth are not native, but white. Indian children learn, by this constant confrontation with white models, to devalue themselves and their own culture. Dodson believes that group self-hate and resulting devaluation of one's own people stems more from the unequal position of the groups with regard to power, than the fact that one is majority and the other is minority.

One of the saddest parts of the rapid development of low self-esteem among native populations has been an increasing tendency for natives to devalue natives. The feeling expressed by many native American and Alaskan people was that if they became educated and applied for open jobs on reservations or in villages, they would not be hired because they were native. One native woman stated, "Natives prefer non-natives over natives, at times with equal education, because we learn to believe that they do a better job than our people. We don't value our own people, and I oftentimes don't understand that."

The native American or Alaskan youth hears two opposing and equally stereotypical definitions of "Indianness." One is the "drunken Indian" with all the horrifying statistics which carry with them the message that to be Indian means to die at an early age, and two, the romanticized view of the solitary Indian — riding his horse on the plains, an ideal found in movies and museums but not on reservations of the 1980s. The power and value of his or her culture is not often heard in schools, nor is he or she often introduced to models of Indian doctors, teachers, lawyers, scientists or computer programmers.

One of the primary beliefs of the native American culture is the importance of community survival. Often peer pressure plays a fundamental role in the continuance of alcoholism and drug abuse. Many natives knew their group use of alcohol and drugs as a way to continue the community cohesion that is rapidly declining in reservations and villages. Alcoholism and drug abuse among many native poulations has served to ease their pain and has provided continued community networking and cohesion.

When working with native American families, I identify in each family member unresolved grief, often massive — grief from loss of culture, from loss of connection with the kinship network, from early losses of family due to children being sent away to schools, from loss of parents, from loss of self-esteem because of lack of family role or the effects of alcoholism. Most often, when communications in families are re-established and the family shares its grief together, there is a new sense of power in the family. A reconnection with the greater community develops, as well as a sense of responsibility to the kinship network. Almost without exception, in working with native men and women, there is a strong connection with the memories of their grandparents, their values and beliefs. In remembering, they find strength in those beliefs. They feel both joy and sadness in that remembered connection and also a sense of pride in being native American.

In much the same way that family members in an alcoholic family stay isolated from each other until they are brought together by a crisis caused by alcoholism, many native families most frequently feel a sense of kinship and community during weekend binge drinking. Many believe that the use of alcohol and drugs among native American people is an effort to retain "Indianness" in the culture.

It is important that native American and Alaskan people influence their own fate and their own destiny and that programs established with native populations be developed by native people. Alcoholism and drug abuse within native culture has been increasing at an alarming rate. As in majority culture, domestic violence and sexual abuse is widespread in families affected by alcoholism on reservations and in villages. Recent studies indicate that almost 90% of the reported cases of domestic violence, community violence, suicide, and sexual abuse within native populations are alcohol related.

The Adult Children of Alcoholics movement within the field has made professionals more aware that alcoholism is a family illness, not just an individual disease. With respect to native culture, it is a community disease as well. Often programs designed by professionals in majority culture have had little impact within native cultures, because they are designed to treat the individual rather than focusing on the interrelationship between the individual, family, and kinship network. Furthermore, outside interventions based on majority values are frequently not understood by Indian people. As stated by a a native elder, "It used to be that when one of our people became violent within his home, he would have to be responsible to the whole community for his actions. He would have to do a community service to benefit everyone. Our people would show him with their silences and eyes that his actions had affected all of us. He would learn by this." When individuals and families are sent outside their villages and reservations to treatment programs, they often experience the same confusion they did in school. Their silences and lack of understanding for works and interventions are frequently seen by treaters as unwillingness to cooperate or as lack of motivation.

It is important to re-involve the elders in the education of children, to help them understand their contribution and value to their family and to their community. Native children are raised with positive values within their extended family system and then expected to function in a system that rejects the values of their own culture [Pedigo, 1983]. It is important for the elders of the tribe to demonstrate that the native American culture is a thriving one. Youth need to see that native people have learned to feel a sense of strength in native values while also successfully bridging with the majority culture.

It is important to recognize the need for family counseling and network strengthening on reservations and family and native peer counseling in urban areas. It should be recognized that, in the process of working with the family where alcoholism is an issue, it is not enough only to treat the alcoholism and its effects, but the underlying grief also must be treated. "There is no moving beyond loss without the experience of mourning; to be unable to mourn is to be unable to enter into this great human cycle of death and rebirth; to be unable, that is, to live again" [Lipton, 1975]. The major skill of the family therapist is to aid the family in reconnecting with each other, re-establishing that network of self-support, and re-establishing connections to the major resource of the family, the community. This can be accomplished only after the grieving process. It is important to aid the family in understanding that the major solutions to the problems they face are in the values of their own culture. The therapist also needs to assist the family in understanding the process of building a bridge to majority culture, in understanding majority values while keeping native values as primary. Families need to be helped to realize that positive solutions exist within their own communities (Westermeyer).

There has been a continual increase in domestic violence on reservations, most of it alcohol-related. The domestic violence literature includes studies which theorize about methods for reducing violence, of which one study by Strauss, in, *Behind Closed Doors*, is representative. He proposes the following solutions: "1] to eliminate the norms which legitimize and glorify violence in society and in the family; 2] to integrate families once again into a network of kinship; 3] to reduce violence-provoking stress created by society in the areas of joblessness, stigma and poor health; 4] to change the sexist character of society and replace it with values placed on being men and on being women; 5] to break the cycles of violence in the family and replace punishments which are physical with alternate practices of child-rearing (Strauss, 1981)."

It is interesting to note that with the exception of the stresses of unemployment, that many of the solutions arrived at in regard to domestic violence are the values that have been inherent in native American and native Alaskan culture prior to the effects of acculturation. Native values include: 1] the value of the community above all else —generosity, sharing of goods and services; 2] the belief that the individual is expected to take full responsibility for his or her own actions; 3] the belief in non-interference and the respect for other's values and beliefs; 4] respect for the environment—adapting to the environment in order to co-exist and survive within it and respecting all life: man, animal and the earth; 5] to rear children by the example of modeling —that children are to be prized above all else (the child is taught to look out towards the environment from the earliest years in the cradle board and learn its lessons and to follow well-established traditions set by the life cycles, the environment and their elders); 6] the belief in non-materialism, non-ownership and sharing.

Many values that majority culture are now looking to recreate in the home and in the community in order to stop domestic violence are many of the same values held and prized in the past by native American and Alaskan people. Yet majority culture is having difficulty attaining these values in a culture based on power and fierce individualism, and native American and Alaskan people are losing their own strong community values, suffering the effects of alcoholism, and experiencing increased domestic violence following acculturation with the dominant culture. It should be noted that new understandings by medical science related to combating disease and illness are akin to the healing practices that native American people have used for hundreds of years. These practices include ceremonies focused on the body, the spirit, and the mind and the power of focused self-healing.

The Task Force 11 report (1976) emphasized the need for preventive education strategies that stressed the needs of native American cultural beliefs. Three recommendations were made in this regard:

"[1]. Giving the building of comprehensive preventions and preventative education strategy a high priority, stressing community leadership and involvement in changing behavior patterns and development of alternatives to drinking and drug usage;

[2]. Building prevention strategies emphasizing the strength of the Indian culture; and

[3]. Building upon familial and community ties (P. 26, Task Force 11)."

I have found in my work with native American and Alaskan people that the statistics on the "number one" cause of health hazard to natives, alcoholism, can be reversed if those individuals and programs responsible for alcoholism treatment are sensitive to the strengths and power of the culture and the values of the people. All too often alcoholism programs for Indian people have been designed by those from majority culture and incorporate majority values, not native ones. These programs have often failed to achieve success in the sobriety of Indian people, not because of the "lack of motivation" or "resistance" of the natives involved, but because the programs designed have failed to take into account both the power and strengths within the culture, and the uniqueness of cultural values in evaluation and treatment.

One native woman I worked with in urban Seattle had previously been through five inpatient and three outpatient alcoholism programs. Evaluations I received indicated that she was "resistant to treatment." As well as being diagnosed as "alcoholic", she also carried the diagnosis of "antisocial personality disorder," "hystrionic personality disorder," and "battered woman syndrome." Her use of alcohol and drugs began when she entered a white school system off her reservation in the seventh grade. She stated that this was the first time she realized that she was "stupid." She talked about being teased constantly in school and felt bad about herself, which she had never felt before. Both of her parents were alcoholic, but she said that she had always been cared for by her aunts and grandparents when her parents were drinking. She felt her childhood had been happy. Her grandmother had taught her the strengths and values of native culture, but she had often felt confused because her parents had never reinforced those values and seemed to feel "shame" at being Indian. She left the reservation when she was eighteen to get a job in the city. She said she liked being with people and always let people who didn't have a place to stay or the money for housing stay with her. She was often confused when they would steal from her or beat her up, but said that she couldn't say "no" when someone was homeless. She had tried to kill herself once when she was drunk and consequently entered treatment. The only Indian in the treatment program, she felt alone and didn't understand what was being taught. She said she felt stupid, as she had felt in school.

Another woman with a similar experience told me, "My grand-mother taught me that the heart tells you what to do and you should always listen to your heart for its lessons. Then you learn in school that your head should tell you what to do. The mind tells you something different — that the heart is not the way white people tell you to be. It's really confusing."

Throughout treatment, neither of these women had been asked about the values they had learned in their culture, the strengths they felt concerning those values, or their confusion; neither had been asked about their grief concerning early education experiences or of the grief they felt in their parents; neither had been asked about their kinships network, the experiences of reservation life; and neither, even though one woman lived with her family on the reservation, had been asked to take part in family treatment.

It is important to understand that where native people are concerned, alcoholism is often a "community disease," and programs designed to treat the individual separate the person from the most powerful source of healing, the kinship network. Treatment programs designed in sepa-ration from the culture often ignore the grief and depression resulting from acculturation, the effects of stigma on the culture, as well as ignoring one of the most powerful tools in the healing process, the strength of the values of native American and Alaskan people. Often not considered as well, is the powerful impact of peer pressure on the native person. Programs which remove the individual from his/her kinship network are destined to make statistics a self-fulfilling prophecy.

There is a world of difference between "help" and "empowerment," and many times, services that have been designed for alcoholism treatment on reservation and in villages inadvertently become one more statement by majority culture of a refusal to share power. As stated by Dodson, "power has to be taken. It cannot be given"(Dodson). One native woman told me, "It is important for people to realize that recovery from alcoholism is possible on reservations and in villages. Recovery happens when natives have native models for recovery, not white ones. More and more people on my reservation are sober and helping others to become sober. We are learning from each other the strength of the family and the community and the pride of being Native American. I believe that my sobriety has happened because I have returned to the values my grandmother taught me to live by, while understanding majority values as well. I learned as my family counselor put it, 'to bridge the river.' "

As an Alaskan native said so well, "One of the solutions to the problems that we are experiencing today is to learn from our elders. It is true our elders didn't go to school. It is true some of them don't know how to speak English. But, they somehow are a lot smarter than those individuals who have gone to college. Their wisdom can be used as tools to alleviate some of the problems we are experiencing today. Traditionally, professionals have not recognized those elders as having solutions to the problems" (Bill, 1983).

REFERENCES

Attneave, Carolyn, "The Wasted Strengths of Indian Families" in *The Destruction of American Indian Families*. Association of American Indian Affairs, 1977.

Bill, Daniel. *Village to Village: A Discussion Guide by Rural Alaskans About Family Violence*. Juneau, AK; Pouch N. Alaska State Department of Public Safety, 1983, p.33.

Byler, William. "The Destruction of American Indian Families" in *The Destruction of American Indian Families*. Association of American Indian Affairs, 1977, p.1.

Dodson, Dan W., "Power as Dimension of Education", *The Journal of Educational Sociology*. New York, N.Y.

Lipton, J. in *The Inability to Mourn*. Alexander and Margarete Mitscherlich [editors], New York, NY., Grove Press, 1975.

Predigo, Jill. "Finding the Meaning of Native American Substance Abuse: Implications for Community Prevention", *The Personnel and Guidance Journal*. January 1983, p. 273.

Strauss, Murray A., Gelles, Richard J. and Susan K. Steinmetz. *Behind Closed Doors: Violence in the American Family*. Garden City, NY., Anchor Press, 1981.

"Alcohol and Drug Abuse" in *Report on Alcohol and Drug Abuse*. Washington, D.C., Task Force Eleven, American Indian Policy Review Commission, 1976.

Westermeyer, J. "The Drunken Indian: Myths and Realities" in *The Destruction of American Indian Families*. Association on American Indian Affairs, 1977, p. 22.

Wilkinson, F.T. "On Assisting Indian People", *Social Casework*. 1980, 61:451-454.

Chapter Seven
Alcoholism and the Black Family

Gael Lanier Caution

The impact of alcoholism has touched every family in America either directly (i.e., through having an alcoholic member, friend, or associate, etc.) or indirectly (through increased costs of insurance policies, increased taxes, or absenteeism, etc.). This impact is significantly multiplied when one examines the black American family, given its pre-existing vulnerabilities. Alcoholism has been called the number one health and the number one social problem in Black America (Harper, 1978; 1976a; 1976b). This "symptom of oppression" and other indicators of stress have remained consistently high in the black community (Akbar, 1980; Bowman, 1980; Caution, 1979; Dennis, 1980; Martines, 1978; Rice, 1980; Skolnick, 1954; Stern & Pittman, 1972; Winbush, 1980).

Although there is a little information on the overall health status of black Americans, the limited information available shows them to be a high risk group for major illnesses, which correlate highly with stress. For example, hypertensive heart disease, malnutrition, cancer of the cervix/-prostrate, and diabetes are much higher in the black community than in the general population (Harper, 1976a; U.S. Public Health Service, 1981). Surprisingly, research has shown that even middle-class blacks suffer from deficiencies in vitamins A,C,D, iron and calcium (U.S. Public Health Service, 1981).

There are also indications that blacks surpass their counterparts in rates of the occurrence of alcoholism (Cahalan, 1970; Caution, 1979; Davis, 1973; Haberman, 1970; King, et. al., 1969; Larkins, 1965; Malzberg, 1955; Rimmer, Pitts, Reich & Winkur, 1971; Warheit, Grey & Swanson, 1976). Physiological illness resulting from alcohol abuse is also greater among blacks, according to some reports (Harper, 1978). These factors, along with the indication that the progression of alcohol-related illnesses is further along before blacks seek treatment, makes the black community extremely vulnerable. For example, Harper (1978; 1976a; 1976b) found blacks to have a higher rate of admissions to hospitals due to alcoholism (52%) than whites (11%), and those blacks admitted tended to be younger than whites. Black adolescents who drink report a greater number of health problems, with a correlation between pregnancy and drinking for young black females, which has significant implications for fetal alcohol syndrome (Harper, 1976b). The inference from this limited data is that even with the historical strengths of the black family (Nobles, 1980a; 1980b; 1978; 1974), the likelihood of full self actualization and marital and/or family stability for these teenage mothers is significantly reduced given the already present conditions of oppression (Baldwin, 1985).

Although alcoholism is widespread in the black community and has such devastating effects on the black family, it has been largely neglected by researchers (Bourne, 1973; Dawking & Harper, 1983; Harper, 1976). This research and theoretical void exists, despite the fact that counselors, therapists and social scientists working in the treatment of alcoholism in the black family have observed values, practices and behaviors unique to black clients and therefore, have called for modalities that fit the "black experience." For it is clear to those in direct care, that the alcoholism treatment modalities built on Western European values, principles, worldview, or cosmology are not always applicable to African-American families and actually can create greater conflicts and dysfunctions (Akbar, 1981; Jackson, 1980, Nobles; 1974).

Given the seriousness of alcoholism among black families and the need for appropriate treatment interventions, this paper attempts to present a progressive approach to conceptualizing the black American family from a cultural/historical perspective (worldview and oppression). It is hoped that these concepts will explain some of the phenomena observed by other therapist and researchers in the area of black American alcoholism (Harper, 1978; 1986a; 1976b; King et.al., 1969; Larkins, 1965). The ultimate goal, of course, is to develop appropriate, affirming, and applicable treatment modalities that are in harmony with the African-American worldview and that work (Association of Black Psychologists, 1985; Baldwin, 1985; Brown, 1978; Carruthers, 1972; Headley-Knox, 1981; Jackson, 1980; Nobels, 1980a; 1980b; 1978).

Regardless of their race, the vast majority of counselors working with alcoholic black families have been trained from a European-American worldview and operate from assumptions which may not be therapeutic for their clients. Our formal education (or miseducation) has actually trained us away from working with various ethnic groups in general and with black Americans in particular. We have been taught to use the same traditional psychotherapeutic models (or other European-based models, including behavioral approaches) for all segments of the population. Counselors rarely recognize that the Euro-American values of competition, rugged individualism, and objectivity shape the way we conduct therapy, design treatment programs and conceptualize healthy family functioning. This continues, despite the recognition that these paradigms were designed for white, middle-class Americans and really do not fit the black community. For example, black alcoholic clients rarely return for a second visit to an outpatient mental health center, no matter how great their need (Harper, 1981). One of the most pervasive mistakes taught to counselors is to ignore our client's ethnicity. We are taught that "people are just people ... we are all the same." Although our humanness connects us all, and the techniques recommended for black clients may apply to the general population, our ethnic/cultural identity shapes who we are. When serving any group of people through working with their families, we must examine, appreciate, understand, and respect their culture. To do otherwise would lead to a greater disruption in an already stressed family system and would assist in their oppression. To ignore a people's culture is to dismiss their values, beliefs, and assumptions about the universe (i.e., worldview). This dismissal of the client's culture, of course, renders the counselor powerless to promote self-affirmation and change within the therapeutic relationship. Thus, the counselor working with black American alcoholic families must have knowledge of the African-American worldview and its impact on black American drinking patterns.

The African-American Worldview

Counselors working with black clients should understand that the nature of the African-American family is neither the "deprived" version of the European-American family, nor just the remnants of the experience of slavery in America, as most traditional concepts perport (Nobles, 1974). The fundamental African-American definition of "family" has its basis in West African culture with its unique values, customs, attitudes and norms (Nobles, 1980a; 1978; 1974).

The following represent some of the basic value themes that pervade the African-American worldview:

1. **Oneness with Nature/Spirituality** - This is the foundation of

the value themes that pervade the African-Cosmological system (world-view).

This system asserts that all things in the universe (including God, man, and nature) are interconnected and mutually dependent upon each other for existence. Therefore, the universe is interdependent much like a spider web; anything that touches one part vibrates or affects the whole. It is through religion, however, that this philosophical system is expressed. In this sense religion and philosophy are the same pheno-menon. Therefore, people are their religion, and there is no distinction between the act and belief.

2. *Collectiveness/Survival of the Group* - Emanating from these first themes are the values of collectiveness and the survival of the group. These are based on the West African value of the priority of the "tribe" which defines one's self (collective self), thus the West African saying of "I am because we are." In other words, one's definition of "self" cannot be separated from one's group and its culture, history, and traditions, etc.

3. **Family/Elders/Children** - The clan is the basic unit of the family. In West African culture the concept of "family" is much more complex than in Western-European societies. African cultures include the horizontal as well as the vertical spheres when referring to "family." The horizontal consists of the living (relatives, friends, and other black people or members of the tribe) as well as the vertical (those ancestors who are dead and those yet to be born). Therefore, the "family" is based on the continuity and unity of one's people (the collective). The most obvious aspect of the West African values of collectiveness can be seen by the counselor in the black American emphasis on the extended family. In African societies, one's role within the community (family) is clearly delineated. Older people (elders) are respected for their spirituality, age, and wisdom. This tradition carried over into Black America. One of the most obvious forms is for blacks to address each other using their titles when someone older is present in social situations. If one is close to the older person being addressed, the title (Mr., Mrs., Miss) is placed in front of the first name to show familiarity with deference. Children in African cultures are viewed as the link between the past and the future. They are of "God" and thus are innately good. In addition, children are born complete beings, with natural, God-given wisdom. At birth children are believed to possess a distinct nature and personality because they reflect or possess the wisdom of their ancestors.

4. Spiral Concept of Time - In African cultures time is denoted by events, with the focus being on the people. Events do not begin until the people arrive. Time is perceived as being very elastic. Time is viewed as something to be experienced rather than a commodity to be invested. This is carried over into the black American concept of time (often called C.P. time) where the designated starting time for an event is just a reference point. The event really doesn't begin until enough of the "group" arrives. This often translates into average events beginning anywhere from 15 minutes to 45 minutes after the stated time. This is very different from the Western European concept of time which influences most of the systems serving black clients.

These cultural differences in viewing the world and in perceiving families have significant implications for therapists and counselors working with African-American families. Often the differences between the African-American and European-American worldview creates great stress when black families come into contact with social institutions (values, norms, customs, etc.) and with service providers and counselors (i.e., family therapists) who operate according to the European—American worldview. Although the surface structure of the Black family has been modified, due to the external forces of oppression and existing in an alien (Western-European) culture, the fundamental Africanisms are still present, influencing the values, beliefs and behaviors of African-Americans at a subconscious level.

Culturally Specific Drinking Patterns of Black Americans

The worldview of a group of people shapes every aspect of their functioning, from child rearing practices to alcohol consumption patterns and to perceptions of "deviant" behavior. In the black community this shaping of perceptions through one's culture is clearly seen in drinking patterns. For example, the following has been noted by Fred Harper (1978; 1976a; 1976b), one of the leading experts on alcoholism in Black America:

1. Blacks tend to be group drinkers, drinking with friends and relatives rather than solitary drinkers.

2. Lower income blacks often drink in public on street corners, outside liquor stores, in automobiles, in front of homes, store-front businesses, and in public taverns and "joints."

3. Black men and women often drink heavily in the party and group context especially on the weekends.

These patterns correlate very highly with the aforementioned African-American value of survival of the group or collectiveness. This translates into the sharing of one's resources with the "group," including sharing alcohol. Therefore, social activities or activities which involve the collective are viewed as an opportunity to "share a taste." In middle class gatherings, this sharing takes the form of "only sharing the best" with their friends; a high value is placed on drinking expensive brands of liquor, especially scotch for the men and gin or wine for the women (Dawkins & Harper, 1983; Harper, 1976a). The rich, functional African-American values can become distorted, dysfunctional and eventually destructive in oppressive environments (Amurelu-Marshall, 1985; Baldwin, 1985; Bowman, 1980). One only has to look at the incidence of alcohol-related crime and violence in the black community to recognize that the reactions to surviving in an oppressive society have become very misorienting for black American families (Akbar, 1980; Amurelu-Marshall, 1985; Bowman, 1980).

Treatment and Intervention Strategies

Given that alcoholism in black American families is a complex phenomena shaped by West African culture, the experience of oppression in American culture, and the resulting misorientation, the counselors working with black families should be willing to grow and change deeply ingrained values in themselves and in the systems in which they work. It should be recognized that racism and oppression are contributing factors that lead to escape drinking in blacks. It should also be recognized that the black community distrusts mental health centers and alcoholism treatment programs located outside of the community. Therefore, increasing the number of outreach programs in the black community, staffed by black professionals and paraprofessionals, will increase the quality and utilization of services.

Where these services have not been made available to the black community, counselors in predominately white mental health centers and drug treatment centers may become conscious that due to the closeness which develops in therapeutic relationships that the issue of the therapist's or counselor's race cannot be ignored. There are many subtleties of existing racism in institutions of which most non-black counselors are unaware. Therefore, if the counselor is not black, it is important that they make arrangements to work with the assistance of a black therapist or co-therapist. If arrangements cannot be made for before the first session, it is important that the therapist make his/her intentions known to the family in the first session. If done properly, this will increase trust and retention.

The following are some general considerations, adapted from the work of Dr. Daudi Azibo (a leading researcher in the area of black personality development) that may serve as guidelines for institutions to follow for cost effective means to support black professionals or para-professionals to effectively work with black clients:

1. Acquire knowledge of black (i.e., African) culture and its positive impact on current and past civilizations (James, 1972; Jones, 1980; Setima, 1985; Williams, 1976).

2. Affiliate with black professional organizations which have expertise in alcoholism and mental health problems facing the black community (i.e., Association of Black Psychologists, Association of Black Social Workers, and the Natinal Council on Black Alcoholism).

3. Acquire knowledge and understanding of black personality models (e.g. Baldwin, 1981a, 1981b; Semaj, 1981; Williams, 1981; Wright & Isenstein, 1978) and models of psychological Africanity-development (e.g. Cross, 1973, 1978; Thomas, 1971; Tolson & Pasteur, 1975) and the theoretical underpinnings of black personality (Akbar, 1979, Azibo, 1984; Baldwin, in press).

4. Understand conceptualizations of disordered black psychological functioning from Afrocentric frameworks (Akbar, 1981; Azibo, 1984; Baldwin, in press).

5. Familiarize himself or herself with culturally specific assessments of black personality (e.g. Cross, 1979; Wright & Isenstein, 1978).

6. Become proficient with psychotherapeutic models developed for African-Americans (e.g. Tolson & Pasteur, 1973, 1981; Tounsel & Jones, 1980).

7. Be motivated to see black families grow and become proud of their African heritage and thereby increase their positive self-concepts.

Within the context of the African-American worldview of oneness with nature, a holistic approach toward the black American family is very important. Therefore, counselors working with black families should recognize that the family may expect the counselor to address a variety of its needs, including housing issues and health concerns, as well as the traditional family dynamics within the therapeutic situation. The counselor can act as a link between the family and other service providers by assisting them in making contacts and by helping to empower the family. It is important that the counselor not become an additional enabler but a source of information.

Specifically, the practitioner working with the black alcoholic family should understand the following:

A. Black families often do not view alcoholism as a primary issue (correctly), but rather as secondary and symptomatic of poverty and racism (Taylor & Bell, 1984). Therefore, counselors must acknowledge the complexities of social problems plaguing the black family, while simultaneously making the family feel empowered enough to begin changing theur own situation along with larger social inequities. Alcohol ism must be viewed as a lifestyle, therefore it takes a change in lifestyle to overcome it.

B. Within the African-American value system of survival of the group, the use of supportive organizations within the black community such as church groups and black educational and cultural institutions can provide leadership, support, and healthy care for the black alcoholic family. The starting of black alcoholics support groups so that black alcoholics can get assistance without leaving their community, has proved to be beneficial. Therefore, counselors working with black families have to be willing to be change agents while also being able to assist the family in constructing the types of supports that they perceive are needed for a healthy recovery and continued sobriety.

C. One of the most difficult issues to address when working with black families is the creation of leisure time activities which are festive while remaining alcohol-free.

Dancing card-playing and just getting together in a healthy way without succumbing to the pressure to include alcohol will be a major challenge for the family as a whole. Thus, preplanning activities and clearly stating to friends and relatives that it will be a "teetotaler" affair, will be an important parameter for the family to establish. For the identified black alcoholic, this calls for a change in lifestyle. For example, the "brother" that gets off from work and "shares a taste" with his friends, or the "sister" who goes to "happy hour" with a girlfriend so they can relax and "eye" the opposite sex, will need the aforementioned support groups or activities to fill this void.

D. The two African-American concepts of the **spiral concept of time** and **respect for elders** affect the interactions between the mental health system and the black family directly or most obviously. Counselors in mental health settings often complain that black families are often late for appointments without recognizing the cultural differences in conceptualizing time. For the sake of the counselors' mental health functioning within the boundaries of the mental health system, it is important to discuss these cultural differences regarding time and to reach an agreement (perhaps by consciously and overtly setting the time of the appointment 15 minutes earlier than the actual time).

E. Western-European culture (white society) has a culturally different standard of interacting with the elderly than with blacks. Therefore, they often unknowingly insult blacks who are older than themselves by addressing them by their first name. No greater insult can be heaped on members of an extended black family than for a young white mental health worker to address their grandmother by her first name.

F. Alcoholism counselors often use the Western-European definition of the nuclear family when working with black families. Black alcoholic families often don't have any model for what a "normal" family functions like. Therefore, it is extremely important for the counselor and the members of the family to jointly and realistically determine the ideal functioning for that particular family. This determination must be made within the appropriate cultural framework (Browing, 1985).

G. Some of the historical strengths of the black family also present some unique difficulties. For example, multiple enablers (including friends) may be more common in extended families. In addition, the resolution of family disputes may be quite difficult with so many parents in control. Privacy for the couple is also often an issue. The recovering alcoholic father, in this context, may find it extremely difficult to exert his authority. Increased physical violence is often a symptom of this power struggle and needs to be addressed in therapy. Black women significantly outnumber black men (Wheeler, 1978). Black males have twice the infant mortality rate of whites. Black males are sixteen times more likely to be shot as white males, and have a much shorter life expectancy (Wheeler, 1978). In some cities, the eligible black females outnumber the eligible black males 12 to 1. These effects of racism result in significant modifications in male-female relationships. Frequently, polygamy is acceptable in black males, while the female is expected to be monogamous. Many women have chosen to accept lower standards of behavior in their men rather than face the possibility of living "without a man."

H. One by-product of racism is a tremendous sense of frustration, anger, and helplessness, exacerbated by a system that perpetuates wrongs and unresponsiveness. The result is what has been termed by Louis Ramey (in Akbar, 1980) as "free-floating anger." The real frustration arises from institutional factors that encourage economic, social, and psychological victimization of blacks. Unable to identify the cause of the frustration, the person directs the anger toward a specific person. Displaced aggression may, therefore, enter into the family counseling session. The counselor must, as a result, be able to set clear rules (i.e., no physical violence); however, the venting of frustration should be acceptable. Racial pain, like other forms of pain, needs to be examined in counseling.

Therapists therefore, cannot afford to be culturally naive, given that alcoholism in Black America is a complex phenomenon shaped by African culture, the experience of oppression in American culture and the resulting misorientation. The counselor working with black families must be willing to grow and change his or her own deeply ingrained values. A culturally-specific approach to working with alcoholism in African-American families based on the Africentric values of oneness with nature, survival of the group, kinship, spirituality, and the African-American cultural-historical configuration is recommended. For, as we have seen, the drinking patterns of American blacks are grounded in their unique and complex culture and require a holistic Africentric intervention.

REFERENCES

Akbar, N. (1981). Mental disorders among African-Americans, *Black Books Bulletin*, 7(2), 18-25.

Akbar, N. (1980, November-December). Causal factors (of homocide among black males). *Public Health Reports*, 95(6), 554-555.

Amurelu-Marshall, O. (1985, April). The role of psychologists in preventing and reducing the incidence of black violence. Paper presented at the *Southern Regional Conference on Violence in the Black Family and Community*: Sponsored by the Atlanta Chapter of the Association of the Association of Black Psychologists. Atlanta, Georgia.

Association of Black Psychologist National Convention (1985). *Black Psychology: A Tool for Black Liberation*. Chicago, Illinois.

Azibo, D. A. (August, 1984) *The Black Personality: Selected Papers of Dr. Ajani Ya Azibo*, (private publishing), Washington, D.C.

Bacon, S. D. (1951). Studies in Jewish culture: General Introduction. *Quarterly Journal on Studies of Alcoholism*, 444-450.

Bailey, M.B., haberman, P. W., & Sheinbery, J. (1965, August). Distinctive characteristics of the alcoholic family. *National Council on Alcoholism Report*, New York, N.Y., 31.

Baldwin, J. A. (1981). Notes on an Africentric theory of Black personality. *Western Journal of Black Studies*, 1981, 5, 172-179.

Baldwin, J. A. (1985). African self-consciousness and the mental health of African-Americans, (In press).

cross-cultural study of drinking. *Quarterly Journal of Studies on Alcohol*, Suppl. No. 3.

Bales, R. F. (1946). Cultural differences in rates of alcoholism. *Quarterly Journal of Studies on Alcohol*, 6, 480-499.

Bourne, P. G. (1973). Alcoholism in the urban Negro population. In (P.B. Bourne & F. Fox eds.), *Alcoholism: Progress in Research and Treatment*, New York: Academic Press.

Bowman, P. J. (1980, November-December). Toward a dual labor - market approach to Black-on-Black homocide. *Public Health Reports*, 95(6), 555-556.

Brown, R. E. (1978). *The Relationship of Moral Conscience, Discipline and Culture Among Black Children*, Unpublished doctoral dissertation, The University of Michigan.

Browning, T. (Spring Quarter, 1985). Culture in the Black family: the key to good mental health. *Black Family*.

Cahalan, D. (1976). Observations on methodological considerations for cross-cultural alcohol studies, in *Cross-Cultural Approaches to the Study of Alcohol*. (Everett, J.O., Waddell, D.B., & Heath, eds.) Srcid, Paris: Mouston, 403-406.

Cahalan, D. (1970). *Problem Drinkers*, Jossey-Bass, San Francisco.

Cahalan, D., & Cisin, I. H. (1976). Drinking behavior and drinking problems in the United States. *The Biology of Alcoholism*, 4, 77-116.

Campbell and Stanly, J. C. (1966). *Experimental and quasi-experimental designs for research*. Chicago: Rand-McNally and Company.

Campbell, D. T. (1964). Distinguishing differences in perception from failures of communication in cross-cultural studies. In (P.S.C. Northrop and H.H. Livingston eds.) *Cross-Cultural Understanding: Epistomology in Anthropology*, N.Y.: Harper.

Carruthers, J. H. (1972). *Science and Oppression*. Chicago: CICCS, NIU.

Caution, G. L. (1979). *Ethnic Drinking Patterns of Jewish Americans, Black Americans and Native Americans: A Critical Review of the Literature*. Unpublished comprehensive paper, University of South Carolina.

Child, I. L., Bacon, M. K., & Barry, H. III. (1965). A cross-cultural study of drinking. Descriptrive measurement of drinking customs. *Quarterly Journal of Studies on Alcoholism*. Supply No. 3, 1-28.

Cross, W. E. Jr. (1973). The Negro to Black conversion experience: An empirical analysis. In J. Lander (Eds.), *The Death of White Sociology*. New York: Random House.

Dawkins, M. P., & Harper, F. D. (1983). Alcoholism among women: A copmparison of Black and White problem drinkers. *The International Journal of the Addictions*, 18(3), 333-349.

Davis, F. T. (19730. *Alcoholism Among American Blacks*, National Council on Alcoholism, Inc., New York, New York.

Dennis, R. E. (1980, November-December). Social costs to families and communities. *Public Health Reports*, 95(6), 556-557.

Field, P. B. (1962). A new cross-cultural study of drunkenness, in (D.J. Pittman & C.R. Snyder eds.) *Society, Culture, and Drinking Patterns*. Wiley, New York.

Glad, D. D. (1947). Attitudes and experiences of American-Jewish and American-Irish male youth as related to differences in adult rates of inebriety. *Quarterly Journal of Studies on Alcoholism*, 8, 406-472.

Haberman, P. W. (1970). Denial of drinking in a household survey. *Quarterly Journal of Studies on Alcohol*, 31, 710-717.

Harper, F. (1978). *Background Review, Analysis and Guidelines Toward Three Workshops on Alcoholism Treatment and Blacks*, Initial Report prepared for NIAAA.

Harper, F. (1976a). *Alcohol and Blacks: An Overview*. Douglass Publishers, Alexandria, Virginia.

Harper, F. (Editor), (1976b). *Alcohol Abuse and Black America*, Douglass Publishers, Inc., Alexandria, Virginia.

Headley-Knox, D. (1984, February). Culture and mystical beliefs: Issues in the Black family. *National News and View: The National Black Alcoholism Council Newsletter*, No. 5, 7-8.

Jackson, G., (1980). The African genesis of the Black perspective in helping, in (eds, R. Jones) *Black Psychology: Second Edition*. Harper & Row, New York, 314-331.

Jacobs, R. (1975). *A Study of Drinking Behavior and Personality Characteristics of Three Ethnic Groups*, unpublished Ph.D. dissertation, California School of Professional Psychology, Los Angeles, University of Microfilms (No. 76-10421).

James, George G. M. (1972). *Stolen Legacy*. The African Publication Society, London, England.

Jellinek, E. (1959). *The Disease Concept of Alcoholism*. New Haven College and University Press.

Jessor, R., & Brunum, K. (1970). The triethnic study and the problem of culture. *Quarterly Journal of Studies on Alcohol, 31*, 272-277.

Jones, R. Editor, (1980). *Black Psychology: Second Edition*, Harper and Row, New York.

King, L. et. al, (1969). Alcohol abuse: A crucial factor in the social problems of Negro men. *American Journal Psychiatry*, 125, 1682-1690.

Kunjufer, J. (1984). Developing positive self-images and discipline in Black children. *African-American Images*, Pub., Chicago, Illinois.

Larkins, J. (1965). *Alcohol and the Negro: Explosive Issues*. Zebulon, North Carolina: Record Publishing.

Malpass, R. S. (1977, December). Theory and methods in cross-cultural psychology. *American Psychologist*, 1069-1079.

Malzberg, B. (1955). Use of alcohol among White and Negro mental patients: Comparative statistics of first admissions to New York State Hospitals for mental disease, 1939-1941. *Quarterly Journal of Studies on Alcohol, 8*, 668-680.

Martinez, F. (1978, May 22-24). Close encounter of the worst kind: The mental health care of minorities. Unpublished paper prepared for the *National Conference on Minority Group Alcohol Drug Abuse and Mental Health Issues*, Denver, Colorado.

Nobles, W. (1974, June). Africanity: Its role in Black families. *The Black Scholar*, 5(9), 10-17.

Nobles, W. (1978). The Black family and its children: The survival of humanness. *Black Books Bulletin*, 6(2), 7-14.

Nobles, W. (1980). African Philosophy: Foundations for Black psychology in (Eds. R. Jones). *Black Psychology: Second Edition*, Harper & Row, New York, 23-26.

Nobles, W. (1980). Extended self: Rethinking the so-called Negro self-concept in (Eds, R. Jones). *Black Psychology: Second Edition*, Harper & Row, New York, 99-105.

Rice, D. (1980, November-December). Homicide from the perspective of NCHS statistics on Blacks. *Public Health Reports*, 95(6), 550-552.

Rimmer, J., Pitts, F. N., Reich, T., & Winkur, G. (1971). Alcoholism II: Sex, socio-economic status and race in two hospitalized samples. *Quarterly Journal of Studies on Alcohol, 32*, 942-952.

Robins, L. N., Murphy, G. E., & Breckinridge, M. B. (1968). Drinking behavior of young urban Negro men. *Quarterly Journal of Studies on Alcohol, 29*, 657-684.

Room, R. (1968). Cultural contingencies of alcoholism: Variation between and within nineteenth century urban ethnic groups in alcohol-related death rates. *Journal of Health and Social Behavior, 9*, 99-113.

Semaj, L. T. (1981). The Black self, identity, and models for a psychology of Black liberation. *Western Journal of Black Studies, 5*, 158-171.

Sertima, I. V., Editor, (1985). *Nile Valley Civilizations*, Journal of African Civilizations Ltd., Inc., New Jersey.

Skolnick, J. (1954). A study of the relations of ethnic background to arrests for inebriety. *Quarterly Journal of Studies on Alcohol, 15*, 622-630.

Sterne, M., & Pittman, D. (1972). Drinking patterns in the ghetto (2 volume unpublished research report). St. Louis: Social Science Institute, Washington University.

Taylor, P., & Bell, P. (1984, April). Alcoholism and Black families. *Focus on Family and Chemical Dependency*, U.S. Journal, 7(2):34, April.

Thomas, C. W. (1971). *Boys No More: A Black Psychologist's View of Community*. Beverly Hills, California: Glencoe Press.

Toldson, I., & Pasteur, A. (1975). Developmental stages of Black self-discovery: Implications for using Black art forms in group interaction. *Journal of Negro Education, 44*, 130-138.

Toldson, I., & Pasteur, A. (1981). Black oral art forms: Guided group interaction techniques. *Journal of Non-White Concern in Personnel and Guidance, 9,2*, 50-59.

Tounsel, P. & Jones, A. (1980). Theoretical considerations for psychotherapy with Black clients. In R. Jones (Ed.) *Black Psychology: Second Edition.* New York: Harper & Row.

Warheit, G. J., Grey, S. A., and Swanson, E. (1976). Patterns of drug use: An epidemiologic overview. *Journal of Drug Issues, 6,* 223-237.

Wheeler, W. H. (1978). Socio-sexual communications between Black men and Black women, in *Issues in Black Mental Health,* Southern Region Education Board, Atlanta, Georgia. NIMH Grant 12679-04.

Williams, R. The death of White research in the Black community in (Eds. R. Jones). *Black Psychology: Second Edition,* Harper & Row, New York, 314-331.

Winbush, R. A. (1980, November-December). Toward a microcosmic view of crime in African-American communities. *Public Health Reports,* 95(6), 557.

Woititz, J. G. (1983). *Adult Children of Alcoholics,* Health Communications, Inc., Pompano Beach, Florida.

Part Two
Children of Alcoholics:
Childhood Without Youth

There are an estimated 6.6 million children of alcoholics under the age of eighteen in the United States. In part two the impact of parental alcoholism on these children and their response to this impact are presented. Being in a position of powerlessness is one of the major problems for the young child of the alcoholic parent, and it is a problem that extends over a minimum of three issues. First, the child is powerless over the drinking by the alcoholic parent. Children cannot get sober for their parents. Second, children are powerless over the relationship between their parents. In research on children of alcoholics, it was found that children consider the troubled relationship between their parents as more detrimental than the drinking by the alcoholic parent. Where there is parental alcoholism in the family, it is doubtful that an ideal spouse marital relationship exists. Third, the young child cannot leave the situation, thus the ability of the child to survive the alcoholic family becomes dependent on the child's ability to adjust and adapt to the situation. The question then becomes, what price does the child pay for this adaptation to a dysfunctional family?

The authors in part two explore many of the difficulties and outcomes of parental alcoholism on young children. In chapter eight, Barbara Naiditch makes the argument for working with children of alcoholics. Chapter nine, by Ellen Morehouse and Tarpley Richards, discusses the need for and the problems associated with working with young children of alcoholics. Claudia Black, in chapter ten, offers various models and roles of adaptation that children of alcoholics often knowingly or unknowingly fulfill. Finally, in chapter eleven, Rokelle

Lerner describes the impact of family confusion and inconsistency on the young child and the possibility of these experiences affecting the child in later life.

Chapter Eight
Why Work With Children of Alcoholics?

Barbara Naiditch

There are approximately 28 million children (of all ages) who have at least one alcoholic parent. These children are at highest risk of developing alcoholism themselves or of marrying people who became alcoholic. Children of alcoholics often adapt to the chaos and inconsistency of an alcoholic home by developing an inability to form close relationships, an inability to trust or express feelings, and an inability to develop a sense of their own worth. Children who grow up in alcoholic homes are at risk of developing physical, developmental, and psychological problems. These problems surface in school as attention deficit disorders, in law enforcement agencies as child abuse, incest, or neglect cases, or in doctors' offices as fetal alcohol syndrome or other alcohol-related birth defects. In the past, these children have received little attention from society. The problems of most children of alcoholics remain hidden because their coping behaviors tend to be approval-seeking and socially acceptable. However, a disproportionate number of those entering the juvenile justice systems, courts, prisons, and mental health facilities are children who have grown up in alcoholic homes.

Children of alcoholics continue to be the most underserved population today in the continuum of care in the alcoholism recovery field. There are AA programs for the alcoholic, Al-Anon for the co-dependent, Alateen for the adolescent, but virtually nothing to provide support for the elementary age child. Most treatment centers do not include these children in family programs, most therapists are not qualified to counsel the total family, and schools do not have community approaches to prevention. The problems that exist for these children of alcoholics need to be the concern of the entire community.

Parents and other adults who interact with children can help young people develop into capable people. According to Stephen Glenn in *Developing Capable People*, children need to feel capable, to feel powerful, to feel significant, and to be a contributor to life. In order to perceive meaning, purpose, and significance, they must believe they are understood, accepted, and significant. Children of alcoholics usually do not feel capable. When there is active alcoholism taking place during the first ten years of their life, they usually do not receive the reinforcement from their parents—thus, they do not feel understood, accepted, or significant. As an adult then, these issues need resolutions in order to affirm feeling capable, powerful, and significant, and making a contribution to life. More adults need to be motivated to intervene with children of alcoholics. Children who understand alcoholism can be potent catalysts to family recovery. Young children growing up in alcoholic homes desperately need information.

What is the family environment like to a child affected by parental alcoholism? Chaotic and unpredictable behavior by the adults who parent usually present extreme inconsistencies to the child. There is usually inconsistent emotional care and inconsistent responsiveness to the children. Childhood in many cases is shortened or non-existent. These children become "divided spirits." They are not children, but little adults who also learn to manipulate the action of others.

Parents do the best they can with the information they have. The difference between treating adults and treating children is that adults choose spouses and are free to leave home. Even though that decision is difficult, it is still a choice. Children have neither the choice, nor the mobility to leave home. Adults *feel* trapped. Children *are* trapped.

Children need intervention. Those who live in high-stress, alcoholic environments learn to manipulate and to live with inconsistency, insecurity, and fear. What these children do not learn is to establish relationships, to develop a strong sense of self-esteem and trust, to overcome shame, and to accomplish healthy coping skills. Programs are needed for teaching children ways in which to establish lasting relationships, methods for developing their self-esteem and trust of others, means for overcoming shame, and systems for learning sound coping skills. Children Are People's support group model has proved highly successful with elementary school-age children of alcoholics. This agency continues to prove over and over again, that children need to be involved in recovery.

The major issues for children to deal with in recovery programs are those dealing with control, mistrust, avoidance of emotions, inability to define boundaries and, over-responsibility. Where there are no intervention programs for assisting children in working out these problems, they grow in magnitude and become very large therapeutic issues for adults to tackle in their own recovery programs. Thus, early intervention programs for children are a must. As a child receives help, the key ingredient is integrating a belief system which legitimatizes self-acceptance. We need to teach children how to view the world more positively. In order to do this, therapy programs for children must be aimed at the following:

—Building self-esteem;
—Building a personal identity apart from the alcoholic;
—Assisting the family and the child to set limits for behavior;
—Establishing consistency;
—Encouraging healthy interaction between the child and other children and adults;
—Allowing the child to be open and honest in relationships;
—Expressing feelings openly;
—Learning to trust others;
—Being able to ask an adult for help;
—Learning about "healthy touching and abusive touching"; and,
—Teaching that it's "OK to be a child."

Too often children from alcoholic homes have been untreated, misdiagnosed, and ignored. We can provide these children with the tools they need to become healthy adults. Adults who come in contact with these children can help them to understand what is taking place in their families. Traditionally, society has ignored the needs of this forgotten age group.

To break the cycle of chemical dependency in our generation of young people, help must be available. Family recovery would be ideal, but in many cases, this is not a reality. Nonetheless, children deserve to get help even if their families do not enter recovery. More prevention programming needs to be available in school districts. Treatment programs need to establish after care and family programs which include children. Community Mental Health Agencies need to do grass roots work and educate clients on the effects of chemical dependency on children. Those of us who work in this field have an obligation to break the pattern of dependency by involving children creatively in the continuum of care cycle. There is hope for the children, but there must be help for the children. Communities should take action against the epidemic of alcoholism by beginning early intervention programs for people of all ages.

Chapter Nine

An Examination of Dysfunctional Latency Age Children of Alcoholic Parents and Problems in Intervention

Ellen R. Morehouse and Tarpley Richards

INTRODUCTION

The characteristics that are common to most children of alcoholic parents [Cork, 1969; Morehouse, 1979], roles that they can assume [Wegscheider, 1979], and the negative impact of parental alcoholism on children [Booz & Allen, 1974; Keane & Roche, 1974; Fine, 1976; Haberman, 1966; Bosma, 1972; Kern, 1981; Richards, 1980; Black, 1979; Chafetz, 1971] have been well documented. A number of factors influence how a child is affected, and because of these factors some children are more adversely affected than others [Wilson & Orford, 1978]. In examining the negative consequences of parental alcoholism, there is general agreement that parental alcoholism has the capacity to adversely influence the emotional, cognitive and social functions of children who are exposed over a long period of time to this parental illness. The inability to establish satisfactory relationships is a specific difficulty which has been mentioned repeatedly in the literature, by both other investigators and adults who grew up in an alcoholic home. It is the intent of this study to examine this observation/complaint and to point out how faulty parenting patterns in alcoholic caretakers affect a developing child's ability to relate with others in mutually enhancing ways.

In the first section, the authors will present a description of parental

Permission has been granted to reprint this article which appeared in the Journal of Children in Contemporary Society, Vol. 15, #1, Fall 1982. It also appeared in a monograph, *Children of Exceptional Parents*, Haworth Press, 1983.

functions which are believed to be essential to a child's healthy growth and development and then will describe how alcoholism damages or destroys these functions. The next section will focus on interpersonal problems of latency age children of alcoholic parents who are seen in psychotherapy or alcohol educative counseling groups by the authors. The article concludes with a description of problems encountered by the therapist in working with these children and offers specific recommendations to mental health practitioners in confronting and working through the faulty relationship styles many of these children bring to the treatment setting.

IMPORTANT PARENT FUNCTIONS SUBJECT TO IMPAIRMENT IN THE ALCOHOLIC PARENT

Parenting styles are extremely varied. Nonetheless, there are particular parental functions that are present to a greater or lesser extent in all nuclear families. [The four parental functions discussed here are selected because a parent's having varying degrees of these attributes appears to be of particular importance in understanding the child in therapy who has an alcoholic parent.]

Role Stability

A child in a family needs to feel a consistent ongoing emotional relationship with the parents. This is an unconscious process. For there to be role stability, there must be a consistent ongoing emotional relationship between the child and the parents, as well as a consistent emotional reaction among family members. The role specificity, i.e., who goes to the office, who cooks, who reads bedtime stories or whatever, is not as important. What does seem to be important to the child is that whatever the family roles are, they remain constant. No family can boast uninterrupted role stability. Mothers may start to work outside the home. Parents may choose to live apart and divorce. However, following these sorts of role changes, there is usually a restabilization of parental roles and the child adjusts.

In the alcoholic home, role stability is frequently replaced by role confusion, leaving the child little chance to adjust to any clear role assignment on the part of the parent. The following examples illustrate this point:

1. In a home where a mother is alcoholic, a daughter may from time to

time take the place of the alcoholic wife and be cast as the confidant and love-object of the father.

2. A wife with an alcoholic husband sets the stage for the rest of the family to relate to father as an authority figure when sober, and as one of the children when drunk.

Environmental Consistency

Parents create an environmental home for their children that is conducive to caring for their young. Types of homes vary but by definition all homes should offer a place to sleep, clothing, food, and safe shelter from the weather and outside danger. Homes are usually equipped with house rules regarding these factors. For example a child's home should offer rules as to where the child sleeps, with whom he sleeps, and when he sleeps. Clothing is provided suitable to the season and the circumstances. Not only does the home offer shelter from the outside world, it also offers a safe and secure place within.

Environmental consistency in alcoholic homes has a tendency to be replaced by environmental chaos. The following clinical case illustration is presented to show the difficulties many children of alcoholic parents encounter in getting their most basic and routine needs met.

An eight-year-old boy who was presented for treatment with hyperactivity and sleep disturbance, was never sure where or with whom he would sleep when bedtime did arrive. His father was alcoholic. If father was "too drunk," mother came into the child's room and ousted him from his bed, and the boy was sent to another of his sibling's rooms to sleep in either a top bunk bed alone, a double bed with his sister, or a single bed with another brother.

Dependability

A child needs to be able to count on a parent doing what the parent says he or she will do. It is unlikely that any child will survive childhood without some parental disappointment. It does happen that a parent sometimes promises, for example, a trip to the zoo, only to be called away at the last minute because of an emergency at work. The average parent feels the need to follow through and does so most of the time. In alcoholic homes, disappointment in parental dependability can be alarmingly routine:

— A father stands up his son's little league championship game

because he was drinking in a bar and lost track of time.
— A mother promises to take her daughter to buy a prom dress but is
passed out at the time the trip was to have occurred.

Not following through on commitments and promises is especially
baffling to a child when the alcoholic parent experiences a "black-out"
[memory lapse while drinking]. How can a parent forget something he
or she definitely said or did?

Emotional Availability

Being available or being present to the child in an emotional sense is
difficult to define, yet children know when this quality is absent.
Alcohol interferes with a person's ability to be truly empathetic, truly
giving, or truly self-denying, which are crucial ingredients to emotional
availability. Chronic, heavy drinking produces an increasing self-cen-
teredness in the user and a diminishing capacity to interact effectively
with others.

As a result, when the alcoholic parent is drinking, the children's
needs are often ignored. When the alcoholic parent is sober, the lack of
emotional availability may continue or the parent's irritability may
alternate with periods of overindulgence in an attempt to alleviate guilt
over prior emotional neglect. See Figure 1.

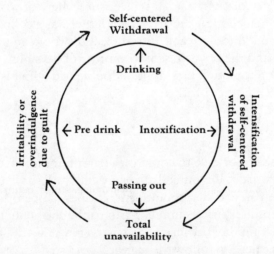

Figure 1

INTERPERSONAL PROBLEMS OF THE LATENCY
AGE CHILD OF AN ALCOHOLIC

Prior to age five or six, the family is the center of the child's world. Even though children younger than this have friends, visit neighbors, stay with babysitters, and go places, the pre-school child remains primarily connected to home; the very young child does not venture far. When a child begins school, she/he is exposed on a regular basis to different adults, different values, and different expectations. The majority of children adjust to school, their first step in negotiating with the world at large. Temporary setbacks such as displeased tone from a teacher, a fight with a new friend, can be repaired at home where the child can retreat, nurse wounds, get special attention, and prepare to return the following day. Many young children of alcoholic parents feel thrown unprepared into the world of school, or worse, they often have no place to which to retreat.

In addition to learning reading, writing, and arithmetic, the elementary child begins to practice getting along in a social structure with others. [It is in the arena of social structure and social interaction that many children of alcoholic parents have difficulty.] The chart below indicates various types of interpersonal responses of children of alcoholic parents which from the author's experience seem to be related to impaired parenting patterns. The descriptions that follow indicate how the social/interpersonal response of the child results from the impaired parenting patterns of the alcoholic parents.

Parenting Pattern	Social/Interpersonal Response of the child
1. Role instability	pseudoadult, overdependence
2. Environmental chaos	patsy, clinging, oppositional
3. Undependable	exaggeration, lying, stealing, manipulation
4. Emotional Unavailability	demanding, selfish, obnoxious, withdrawing, fantasizing

Response to Parental Role Instability

The child who has experienced great fluctuation in parental role stability may feel it is unwise to be a child [dependent and needy] and the resultant behavior pattern may be pseudoadult behavior. The child may set herself/himself apart from other children and relate to them as a superior sophisticate. She/he may look down on peers for their "childishness" and have no friends as a result.

The opposite of pseudoadulthood is an overdependence in which the child may be school phobic or when at school will avoid interaction with peers and find ways to cling to adults, spending a lot of time in the nurse's office with a stomach ache, or sitting next to the teacher at every available opportunity.

Response to Environmental Chaos

When the child's physical environment is insecure and unstable, the youngster may try to securely attach him/herself to a friend or a group of friends in such a way as to become an unwelcome permanent fixture. The child is usually viewed by these friends as a nuisance and is frequently the butt of practical jokes. The child appears willing to accept any mistreatment or will do anything to have a friend even if the child's personal safety is at risk. Another response to environmental chaos can be attempts to perpetuate this chaos in interaction with peers by being unconsciously but purposely oppositional in play. The child may intentionally ruin a game or unravel a team play only to keep friends as off center and unsettled as she/he feels.

Response to Undependability

The child who has been repeatedly and severely disappointed by parents tends to respond by being devious in interactions with friends because a child feels the only way to get something from someone is to grab or take before the offer changes. The following example illustrates this.

> A sixth grade girl who admired a girlfriend's bicycle was told by the friend that she could ride the bicycle after school. The girl took the bicycle during morning recess and told the teacher she had permission to ride it.

Technically, the girl stole the bicycle and lied about the permission. Behind this manipulation or "conning" is an interpersonal style which is evident in many children of alcoholics, who feel that in order to insure getting everything they have to set up situations in advance or take early advantage of others. Often their experience has been that to trust in others means disappointment and deprivation.

Another response to undependability can be exaggeration. Parents' frequent disappointment of children can lead to feelings of worthlessness. When children feel worthless, they believe no one will like them for what they are so they exaggerate to make themselves feel they will be "worth" other children's attention and interest.

> A fifth grade boy who was promised by his father that he would be taken to a major league baseball game was disappointed because his father was severely "hung-over" and told the boy he was too sick. The boy then told all his friends that he went to the game and had dinner with his father who is best friends with the star players.

Response to Parental Emotional Unavailability

Empathy, giving, and self-denial are qualities which generally are passed on from parents to child. If the child does not receive these gifts, he or she will be hard pressed to pass them on. In addition, children who are disregarded, not listened to, and not understood by their parents, will go to great lengths to obtain these attentions from other people or they will withdraw into fantasy. Children whose alcoholic parent[s] has been emotionally unavailable may be unreasonably demanding in their relationships with peers. They may be obnoxious with teachers, worrying that if they do not go to extraordinary lengths to be noticed they will go unnoticed. Some of these children are totally unknowing of what is reasonable to expect from another person in terms of time and attention. In any interaction with peers the primary focus is self-centered and the goal is to constantly get for themselves. They have difficulty sharing themselves and their possessions for fear that they will have to give everything and be left with nothing.

Sometimes, to avoid this hurt, they choose not to risk or assert themselves and instead prefer the safety of withdrawing into a fantasy world. For example, a nine-year-old girl often talked about, and to, her best friends who are all imaginary.

Interventions with Children of Alcoholics

Services for children of alcoholics usually tend to be short-term supportive educative sessions that increase the child's understanding of the alcoholic and the family's reaction [NIAAA, 1981]. With increased understanding many of these children experience a lessening of painful feelings [such as feelings of responsibility], feel less burdened by the alcoholism, feel less anxiety ridden and less depressed. As a result, the child's functioning usually improves.

Regardless of the modality, working with children of alcoholics usually includes the following ingredients [Richards, 1982]:
— demonstrating an understanding of how children of alcoholics are affected by parental drinking
— establishing trust
— working with a child's ambivalence about discussing the parents
— giving the child an opportunity to express feelings either verbally or through play materials
— educating about alcohol and alcoholism
— helping the child develop concrete solutions for coping with the alcoholic's behavior and the child's own upset feelings
— examining the child's own behavior for the purpose of modifying dysfunctional behavior patterns that may have developed as a reaction to the parental alcoholism.

PSYCHOTHERAPEUTIC INTERVENTION

If the child has developed dysfunctional behavior or interpersonal relationships that cause problems, such as some of the examples described earlier, then the child may need more intensive treatment that focuses on helping the child to change. Treating a dysfunctional child of an alcoholic presents a number of problems and issues for the therapist that makes working with this child different from working with other dysfunctional latency age children.

Parental Issues

The most noticeable differences in treating latency age children of alcoholic parents as compared with children from non-alcoholic homes is the role of the parents. In working with children, it is important to have parental involvement. The younger the child, the more crucial the involvement of the parent. The parent is needed to give a developmental history, to give an ongoing report of the child's functioning at home, and to assist in implementing the treatment plan. When a parent is drinking actively, the parent is unable to be effective in carrying out these tasks.

Inaccurate Reporting

Most parents of children who are having problems feel some degree of guilt for causing or contributing to the child's problems. This is always true with the alcoholic parent who is able to identify the drinking as causing the problem. However, the actively drinking alcoholic parent utilizes denial — denial that the drinking could cause the child's problems and denial that abstinence will alleviate them. The alcoholic parent alternates between feeling guilty and being in a state of denial. As a result, she/he tends to minimize the child's problems, thereby making it difficult for the therapist to make an accurate assessment of the child in the family situation. For example, an alcoholic mother of a seven-year-old boy reported that her son did fair in first grade and got mostly Cs when he really did very poorly and got mostly Ds.

The actively drinking parent also tends to be an inaccurate reporter of ongoing events. In addition to guilt and denial, blackouts also interfere with the parent's recall.

> A nine-year-old girl told her therapist she was very upset that her father did not come to visit on a weekend when he had visitation and promised to visit. The father told the therapist that he told his daughter he would be on a business trip and might not be back for the weekend.

In this situation it was hard to know if [1] the child distorted what the father had said because she wanted to see him, [2] the father promised but forgot because of a blackout and therefore really believed he never made the promise to his daughter, [3] the father distorted what was said so he would not "lose face" with the therapist, or [4] the father consciously decided not to see his daughter because he was too drunk and too embarrassed to call.

The parent's inaccurate reporting not only makes it difficult to make an assessment, but it also makes it more difficult to judge the child's reality testing. The more dysfunctional the child, the more difficult yet important this aspect of treatment becomes.

Overdependence on the Therapist

The alcoholic parent often feels she/he is unable to parent adequately. When the child develops symptoms/problems, the parent sees this as confirmation of inadequate parenting skills and in effect tells the therapist, "you take care of my child — I can't!" The parent with this attitude will inappropriately want to speak with the therapist about every decision concerning the child because there is no confidence in the parent's own judgment.

Another way this is manifested is by the non-alcoholic spouse, who often feels she/he has no one to consult with because the other parent is unavailable to discuss decisions concerning the child or to provide emotional support. In this situation, the non-alcoholic spouse uses the therapist as a co-parent in place of the alcoholic. The result of these situations is more frequent phone calls and requests for appointments.

Parental overdependence on the therapist can benefit the child but it can also evoke negative counter transference because the therapist has to give more of her/himself.

Inability to Assist in Treatment

In working with young children, the parents often meet with the therapist to discuss ways the parent can assist in the child's treatment, such as waking an enuretic child to go to the bathroom, monitoring the child's intake of food, enrolling the child in activities, etc. The alcoholic parent's drinking often makes it impossible to carry out these tasks. The non-alcoholic spouse may not have dealt with his/her own angry feelings and therefore may be too emotionally needy to help the child.

> An eight-year-old boy with no friends was living with his depressed mother. The alcoholic father was living with another woman. The mother was depressed because of the husband's alcoholism and desertion. The therapist recommended that the boy be involved in after school structured activities with other boys his age. The mother didn't want him to be because she wanted him home right after school to keep her company so she wouldn't be so lonely.

Inconsistent Involvement

The episodes of heavy parental drinking often cause or contribute to cancelled appointments, broken appointments, lateness, the child not being picked up on time, and non-payment of fees; all of which interfere with the child's involvement in treatment. The parent's drinking also affects the parent's involvement. As Figure 1 indicates, the parent can alternate between total non-participation and disinterest in the child's treatment while drinking, to wanting to be the ideal parent, and be actively involved when not drinking.

The issue of inconsistent involvement is the most difficult, because it directly affects the child's access to the therapist. As a result, the therapist is often more reluctant to confront an alcoholic parent than a non-alcoholic parent because of the fear of an unpredictable response from the alcoholic that can result in the parent's removal of the child from treatment.

ISSUES FOR THE CHILD

All the issues around the parent's involvement and treatment are issues for the child. However, there are also a number of issues that the therapist must deal with directly with the child in session. These include: [1] the child's feelings about missed appointments and lateness; [2] the child's guilt for expressing angry feelings about the alcoholic and non-alcoholic spouse; [3] the need to discuss "slips" [returns to drinking after a period of non-drinking] which come without warning and interfere with the treatment work on the child's behavior; and [4] the intensified transference where the child sees the therapist as a parent.

The child of an alcoholic parent will typically put the therapist in the role of the idealized parent. When this happens, the child can make impossible infantile demands on the therapist to be taken care of, the child can become overly dependent on the therapist, the child can start an emotional moving away from the parent, and the child can act out the conflicts she/he has with the parents through the therapist.

These issues need to be handled carefully because they serve as the basis for the corrective emotional experience that will help repair the faulty relationship style described earlier. When a child acts out a faulty relationship style, the therapist should identify it and interpret it to the child. This should also be done when the child describes interactions with other children. The following example taken from clinical experience illustrates how this can be done.

A ten-year-old girl constantly made unbelievable exaggerations to her friends, because she felt so worthless. As a result, her friends labeled her a liar. When describing her first quarter marks to the therapist, she reported a big improvement from last year, from Ds to As. The mother later expressed her concern for her daughter's poor grades of Cs. In the next session, the therapist was able to interpret to the girl her fear that the therapist would be disappointed by the low grades and not "like" her because she did not improve more. The girl's wild exaggeration to her friends and their dislike also provided a punishment for her angry feelings and wishes toward her alcoholic father. She felt she was a "bad girl" and therefore, deserved bad treatment from her friends.

Careful listening to the child's report of interactions, either verbally or through play, and attention to the child's interaction with the therapist provide the basis for assessment and interpretation of relationship style. Through interpretations, the child can gain greater understanding of his/her feelings and behavior and be in a stronger position to make behavioral changes.

REFERENCES

Black, C. Children of alcoholics. *Alcohol, Health and Research World*, 1979, 4[1], 23.

Booz, Allen, & Hamilton. An assessment of the needs of and resources for children of alcoholic parents. National Institute on Alcohol Abuse and Alcoholism, 1974.

Bosma, W. Children of alcoholics—a hidden tragedy. *Maryland State Medical Journal*, 1972, 21[1], 34-36.

Chafetz, B., & Hill. Observations in a child guidance clinic. *Quarterly Journal of Studies on Alcoholism*, 1971, 32, 687-698.

Cork, M. *The Forgotten Children*. Alcoholism and Drug Addiction Research Foundation of Ontario, Toronto, Ontario, 1969.

Fine, E.W., Yudin, L. W., Homes, J., & Heineman. S. Behavioral disorders in children with parental alcoholism. *Annals of the New York Academy of Science*, 1976. 273, 507-517.

Haberman, P. Childhood symptoms in children of alcoholics and comparison group parents. *Journal of Marriage and the Family*, 1966, 28, 152-154.

Keane, A., & Roche, D. *Developmental disorders in the children of male alcoholics*. Paper presented at the Twentieth International Institute on the Prevention and Treatment of Alcoholism, Manchester, England, 1974.

Kern, J. D., Hassett, C. A. Collipp, P. J. Bridge, C., Solomon, M., & Condren, J. Children of Alcoholics: Locus of control, mental age, and zinc level. *Journal of Psychiatric Treatment and Evaluation*, 1981, 3, 169-173.

Morehouse, E. Working in the schools with children of alcoholic parents. *Health and Social Work*, 1979, 4 [4], 144-162.

National Institute on Alcohol Abuse and Alcoholism. Services for children of alcoholics. Research Monograph 4, 1981 [DHHS Publication No. [ADM] 81-1007].

Richards, T. Splitting as a defensive in children of alcoholic parents. In M. Galanter [ed.], *Currents in alcoholism*. New York: Grune and Stratton, 1980.

Richards, T., Morehouse, E., & Seixas, Kern, J. Psychosocial assessment and intervention with children of alcoholic parents. In *Social work treatment of alcohol problems*, 5, from the Treatment Series, New Brunswick: Publication Division, Rutgers' Center of Alcohol Studies, 1981.

Wegscheider, S. The family trap . . . No one escapes from a chemically dependent family. Minneapolis, The Johnson Institute, 1976.

Wilson, C., & Orford, J. Children of alcoholics. *Journal of Studies on Alcohol*, 1978, 39, 121-142.

Chapter Ten
Children of Alcoholics

Claudia Black

The method being developed in our program, which stresses prevention as well as intervention, could be implemented in most alcoholism treatment facilities. Before looking at our program, we need to explore the dynamics of the child exposed to alcoholism. Typically parents and professionals do not acknowledge the need for bringing children into the treatment program, except to treat a behavioral or disciplinary problem or to assist in a confrontation among family members. The tendency is to focus on a problem child who is often stereotyped as a potential future alcoholic: one who exhibits the defined high-risk characteristics of: 1] having a low self-concept; 2] being more likely to perform poorly in school; 3] being more easily frustrated; and 4] having adjustment problems in adolescence and early adulthood [Bosma, 1974]. I believe, however, that the child with behavioral problems in the alcoholic home is in the minority. Although he or she may receive attention by drawing notice to him or herself, I believe that all children in alcoholic homes have a high risk of becoming alcoholic and that the majority of the children, those who appear to have adjusted and so are not focused on in the research, are easily overlooked.

We find in our groups that children of alcoholics, like most alcoholics themselves, according to research, are bright and of above average intelligence. People often admire the roles these children have adopted in reaction to their chaotic and inconsistent family setting.

Three role patterns which seem to allow children to survive in alcoholic homes appear regularly. The dynamics discussed here are not revolutionary psychology, but rather are similar to Adler's birth order and the more recent family systems approaches. However, I do not believe these concepts have been generally related in practice to the children of the alcoholic. We have labeled these role patterns as 1] The Responsible One: 2] The Adjuster; and 3] The Placater. A child may adopt one role or any combination of the three. As will be illustrated, these roles create strengths which in turn hide the scars that develop from living in an alcoholic family system. It is important to recognize the deficits in such roles in order to believe in and to support the need to address all children of alcoholics. Family system theorists view the family as an operational system and believe that "change in the functioning of one family member is automatically followed by a compensatory change in another family member" [Bowen, 1973.] To each action there is an equal and opposite positive reaction in the family. The roles these children play are compensatory changes or reactions to parental alcoholism, allowing the children to maintain a sense of balance or homeostasis to survive.

THE RESPONSIBLE ONE

The role most typical for an only child, or the eldest child in a family, is one of being responsible not only for him or herself but for other siblings and/or parent[s]. This child typically provides structure and stability for him or herself and others in an often inconsistent home setting. An example is the 10-year-old daughter who took it upon herself without telling anyone to complete the household chores daily and to oversee the other two children. Aware of the plans of every member, she attempted to organize the family. She felt this role was necessary because the mother was working seven days a week, 10-14-hour days, and the alcoholic father was not working and was not responsible to anyone in the home for his whereabouts. In this situation where the child assumed the responsible role, one that provided order for her, she carried this sense of responsibility to other areas of her life. She excelled in school, for she learned to structure good study habits. She learned to manipulate others about her to get done what was necessary, thereby developing leadership qualities. She became goal-oriented on a daily basis. She learned not to project ahead, knowing her alcoholic father could interfere, so her goals became realistic. A sense of self-worth developed as she accomplished these goals.

THE ADJUSTER

Another role that may be combined with the previous responsible role, or adopted separately, is that of the adjuster. This child easily follows directions, not feeling the great responsibility the elder child feels or to whatever is called for on a particular day. For example, a 28-year-old man, the son of a male alcoholic, describes his childhood as "bouncing from one extreme to the other." He said he fluctuated physically and emotionally—never knowing what to expect from either parent. One day his mother was leaving his father and the next day she was behaving as if the thought of separation could never enter her head. For weeks at a time, the child would sit outside a bar in the car, waiting while his father drank for hours. Other weeks, his dad would not drink at all. Another young woman said she too learned to be flexible in her alcoholic family—she felt she had little choice but to adjust. In the most extreme situation, she could not follow through with her plans because her parents would move without notice. And these were major moves—from the Northeastern States to Florida, to California. Adults who were "adjuster" children say that, as a result, they see themselves as flexible and able to adapt to a variety of social situations.

THE PLACATER

The placating child greatly needs to smooth over conflicts. This child, often very sociable, develops the admired quality of helping others to adjust and feel comfortable. This child often adopts his role to alleviate a sense of guilt that he caused the alcohol problem. An example is the 22-year-old daughter of a male alcoholic who talked of being aware since age six of tension in her family, especially great sadness in both parents. So she spent years trying to help both parents feel good. Every time her dad said, "Hey, let's go for a ride," she'd go, later reflecting that the ride always resulted in a series of stops at local taverns. She combined the placating and responsible role, additionally doing a great amount of housework to please the mother who worked because the father did not work. For hours at a time she would wait on and listen to her father's buddies as they drank and talked. She said she did not understand what was happening in the home, but she knew people hurt, and she would do whatever she could to please them, thinking it would take away the pain. Strengths developed out of this role. She felt she was popular and got many strokes for helping others, being sensitive to their feelings and listening well.

SURVIVAL IS KEY

I have found that children in alcoholic homes are busy surviving. We admire the way they assume the roles that make[s] the most sense to them—roles that will help bring peace to the chaotic, denying family in which they live. Displaying behavioral problems is not a role that helps attain peace. We do see some—but not most—children from alcoholic homes in the acting out role. Unfortunately, it is easy to overlook the children who are responsible, adapting, sociable, and bright but they are possibly being set up to be 50 to 60% of society's future alcoholics. Whatever role these children adopted in the family, there still will be some negative consequences for them.

As these children reach their late teens and early twenties, they often are busy leaving the primary family. They make decisions on education, employment, marriage, and childbirth. Focusing on their futures, these children usually are unaware of the negative effects of their alcoholic upbringing. They often recognize their strengths because they have been rewarded for being so healthy. As adults, they say they often heard from others and/or told themselves, "You've really done well in spite of your home life." Again the scars are unseen, even by those who are close.

These children whose roles have allowed them to survive do not change roles just because they leave the alcoholic environment, however; these roles become patterns carried into adulthood. It is after the children have begun to lead settled lives as adults that they begin to realize that old methods of coping are no longer working to provide a sense of meaningfulness to their life. It is at this time the effect of living in the alcoholic home begin to show. These adults often find themselves depressed without understanding why; life seems to lack meaning. They feel a loneliness, though many are not alone. Many find great difficulty in maintaining intimate relationships. And many become alcoholic and/or marry alcoholics.

In addition to the strengths developed through adopting these roles, there are some equally powerful deficits. Many of these children learned it was not all right to experience certain feelings like anger or sadness. It did not help to feel. When they showed their sadness, their fear, no one was there to comfort them. When they became angry, they found themselves punished. Or when they wanted to talk about anything important, they simply found themselves ignored. It did not take long for these children to learn first, not to express their feelings, and second, not to feel. The 25-year-old daughter of a male alcoholic gave a good example of how her fear of anger has had a major effect on her adult life already. She talked of learning to please others, always avoiding conflict because she feared anger. She said her alcoholic father was extremely violent when he drank. She generalized her fear of his anger to anyone's potential anger. Thus, she negated her own anger, and possible satisfaction of her wants, by continuing to placate. She was unaware of this dynamic until she walked out of a marriage of five years, a marriage in which she had never argued and only felt depressed. Several months in therapy helped her acknowledge her fear of anger and her own anger and to begin working on acceptance of that feeling in herself and others, but all of this was too late to save this first marriage.

Children who ascribed to the responsible role often found their leadership and self reliance led them to being "too alone," unable to depend on another person, to trust that another person would be there for them when they needed someone. This can carry over to adulthood. Many of these "responsible" children have talked about their "need to be in control" which has led to difficulty in relationships at work and socially. These children, too, end up often working alone and not having meaningful relationships. A classic example was the 31-year-old daughter of a male alcoholic. She was bright and a successful lawyer, but she worked alone and had no close friends. Her third marriage was failing. I definitely believe her fear of trusting others, as well as her fear of her own feelings, which she learned in her alcoholic family, were responsible for her confusing, lonely life.

"Adjuster" children become "adjuster" adults, unless there has been some direct intervention as a result of their own insight for a need to change. They continue to allow themselves to be manipulated by others, thereby losing self-esteem and power over their own lives. Their option is to invite someone into their lives, often an alcoholic, who has problems or creates problems. This allows them to continue their reacting role.

Adult placaters will try to continue the childhood habit of taking care of and trying to please others. Both adjusters and placaters often will not respond to or even be aware of their own feelings and desires. As one woman said, "After I raised my kids and only had my husband to please, it seemed life had little meaning, and before long, I was here in the hospital for alcoholism."

The examples given have been those of adults who were raised in alcoholic families. I have used adult examples because most of the children still at home appear to be doing well; not until adulthood do negative consequences become apparent, but the pattern begins at a very young age. I see denial systems starting to develop in 5, 6, and 7-year-olds. Nine-year-old Melody was in group for more than two months before she responded to a question with anything other than "I don't know." A breakthrough came when she was able to say, "Sometimes I pretend that my Mom is not drinking... when she really is. I never even talk about it." The denial usually is not apparent to outsiders. I see these young children learning to find the role that helps them feel better, either taking care of others and the environment [being "responsible"], adjusting, not questioning, or busy trying to please others and trying to take away others' hurt. Melody summed up the roles in her family clearly when she said, "My younger brother worries—I don't know—my Dad takes care—my Mom drinks." As Melody says, she "doesn't know," she simply asks no questions, makes no statement, does what she has to to get through the day. As her dad said, she "adjusts" very well.

PREVENTING THE "ALCOHOLIC PERSONALITY"

These children may be physiologically predisposed to be alcoholic, but we, the professionals in the alcoholism field, can help them to not have the emotional and psychological "alcoholic personality" that may feed the physiological predisposition. Recognizing this, I began to see the young children of our patients individually. I found the children were attentive, listened, asked a few questions, but seldom mentioned their feelings. Finding the interaction was more meaningful when I saw three to four siblings versus an only child or two siblings, I decided to start a group. The group began in April 1978 with a brother and sister; it took three to four months before a core group developed. Since then the group has grown from the core of four or five to 15 to 20 children each week.

The group is open to any child being affected by alcoholism. This includes biologically natural children who live with the alcoholic, those who no longer live with the alcoholic, stepchildren of the alcoholic, and "common law" children related to the alcoholic. We have two sets of grandchildren. One set lived with their alcoholic grandmother and alcoholic grandfather. The other set seldom saw their alcoholic grandmother, but were being affected by their mother's reactions to the alcoholism. During the early sessions of the group, the leaders and the children discuss alcoholism and read stories about it. Sometimes the children who have been in the group longer explain alcoholism to new members. When children first join the group, we try to give them a basic understanding of alcoholism and to build their trust in us. When we later focus on the children's feelings, they are acclimated to the group and have heard other children with whom they can identify talk about their feelings. Typically, the children prefer to talk about what the alcoholic and non-alcoholic parents do and say to each other, rather than to share their own feelings. Films, games, and puppets help elicit feelings. The children continue to express these feelings of their perception of the illness when they draw pictures or write stories.

Art therapy has been the group's most valuable tool. When the children are not able to verbalize their feelings, they are often willing to illustrate them on paper. After thoughts and feelings are on paper, they then find it easier to verbalize. The pictures the children draw are not shown to their parents. The children let the group leaders know from the inception of the group that they would be more honest with their pictures if their parents were not going to see them. In their drawings, the youngsters deal with such parental behavior as the hiding of bottles, arguments, and violence. Approximately 50% of the children we see witness or experience violence related to drinking in the home. They usually do not openly talk about it or about how they feel, but being scared is the feeling the kids identify with most. Another theme we see in drawings is guilt; many children feel they have caused the drinking.

These children, if they have already begun denying feelings, will continue to do so when the alcoholic person recovers. I believe, as Margaret Cork found in her study of children of alcoholics, that family life does not become significantly better when the drinking stops (Cork, 1969.) For the alcoholic, recovery is a process that only begins with abstinence. There is a period of years before the parents may be healthy role models. We cannot rely on parents to undo the emotional damage to their children. They are not apt to recognize any problems when the children outwardly appear fine. Yet the children have developed and are using a very sophisticated denial system and certainly need an ongoing recovery program—as much as the parent—to get well. The group is a safe place for them to learn to trust and to express thoughts and feelings. It is a place in which they do not have to be Responsible, to Adjust, or to Placate others. It is a place where they can rely on others and better understand what is happening in their own home. Treatment professionals need to evaluate their concept of the family illness and, I hope, to incorporate children's groups. As treatment professionals we can do prevention work; this is our responsibility.

REFERENCES

Bosma, W. Alcoholism and Teenagers. Maryland State Medical Journal, 24[6]: 62-68, 1975.
Bowen, M. Alcohol and the family system. The Family, 1[1]: 20-25, 1973.
Cork, M. The Forgotten Children. Toronto: Addiction Research Foundation, 1969.

Chapter Eleven

Co-Dependency: The Swirl of Energy Surrounded By Confusion

Rokelle Lerner

What are the special needs of children of alcoholics? You won't find out by asking one, because they don't know what their own needs are. CoAs are so focused on others that they haven't a clue as to their own needs. They have no sense of identity; they don't know who they are or how they feel. It's like the joke about the drowning co-dependent. With his last breath, he saw someone else's life flash before his eyes.

Emotionally, the untreated co-dependent does drown, and I will attempt to explain how that happens. I will define co-dependency, discuss how an alcoholic family breeds co-dependency, and examine aspects of recovery for young and adult children of alcoholics. I work with each, and both confront the same issues. The term "Adult Children of Alcoholics" does not come to us accidentally. Across the country are millions of people who call themselves "grown-ups" but who are still children inside, struggling to get their unfulfilled needs met. Perhaps it would be useful at this point to acknowledge several assumptions I make before addressing co-dependency per se.

First, alcoholism is a family illness. If we really believe this as professionals, then we should be providing treatment to all members of an alcoholic's family. As it is, the alcoholic receives the thrust of treatment services—which he deserves—but the rest of the family too often is left to get well, somehow, by osmosis. That recovery just doesn't happen.

A family out for a Sunday afternoon drive provides a good analogy. It's a lovely day, and father is driving. There's a terrible accident, and the whole family is hurt. The ambulance comes, and the paramedics

Reprinted with author's permission from *Focus on Family and Chemical Dependency*, Vol. 8, No. 1, Jan/Feb 1985.

pick up the father and rush him to the hospital . . . leaving the rest of the family, injured, lying in the street. Like the crash victims, the people affected by the alcoholic's disease have a right to receive treatment, too. Now, it is hard to talk about children of alcoholics without inferring a lot about parents. I believe that parents do the best they can. I've yet to meet in therapy the mother who wakes up in the morning and decides, "Gee, I think I'm going to screw up my kid today." The parents in an alcoholic household do the best with what they have; many simply don't have any tools to work with.

My third assumption is that laughter and joy are very serious elements of the healing process. Connecting the head and the heart through humor and play can be just as healing as the work we do with anger, misery, and anxiety.

Defining Co-Dependence

In our field these days you are in danger of being labeled a co-dependent if you bring me a cup of coffee, turn on the lights for me, or help me out of a car. I hope to heaven that our approach to recovery doesn't develop a therapeutic group of thoughtless people. To define the co-dependent, we use words like controller, fixer, intensity junkie, relationship junkie, and all the "overs"—over-protective, over-achiever, over-controlling. All of these are true, but the central feature of co-dependency is the high art of never giving up control:

"I know how things are supposed to be, and I know how things are supposed to go, and I will not deal with you as you are . . . I will deal with you as you should be, could be, might be, ought to be, as your mother promised me you would be . . . Because I wrote to God, and I have the blueprints, and with just a little adjustment here and there, I know I can help you." That's a difficult way to live. I assume that alcoholic families would prefer to live differently, but they just don't know how.

A definition I like is that co-dependency is a learned behavior, unlike alcoholism, which is not learned. This definition describes co-dependency as an unhealthy pattern of learned behavior, attitudes, and feelings that make life painful. It is a dependency on people and things outside the self to the point of self-neglect and diminished self-identity. The important words here are "learned" and "pattern." If co-dependency is a learned behavior, it can be un-learned by changing patterns.

If we fail to apply this definition to the treatment of children of alcoholics, we risk self-deluding cures, like geographic solutions.

Members of alcoholic families look for the "Big Fix" in life, "magical cures" for being human. Co-dependents are always explaining, "If only I get out of this relationship," or, "If I could only stop controlling, then I'll be fine." But there is no easy way out. Children of alcoholics share others' co-dependent characteristics. They are very much other-directed. They are very verbal, and appear to be very capable, achievement-oriented—super moms, super cooks, super business people. But inside there's a vacuum—no clarified ego, no sense of self. They are full of guilt. A CoA is a swirl of energy surrounding confusion. Once in a while, when they are fed up, angry, tired of giving and doing, they experience "tolerance breaks" and spin away from the swirl of co-dependent energies, but guilt, like an anchor, drags them back into the system.

The Family Dynamics

How do alcoholic families breed co-dependent people? How are these behavior patterns learned?

If you come from an alcoholic family, you may believe that yours is the sickest—it's terrible, awful. But no family is bad all the time. In alcoholic families, there are occasions of intense joy and loving and caring, but it's intermittent. And intermittent reinforcement has a powerfully addictive effect on children. It keeps them hooked, waiting and waiting and waiting for more of the good times.

Roots and Wings

Minuchin teaches us that a family should provide a sense of belonging and separateness, giving children "roots and wings," a balance. In alcoholic families, there is no balance, no stable core. Instead, there are extremes, family members are either over-involved or under-involved with one another. In the under-involved family, Johnny doesn't show up for dinner, no one knows why, and no one really seems to care.

It's the over-involved family that I see most often in treatment, however, and they are just like a junior high class [I'm a recovering junior high school teacher]. In school, someone burps in the back of the room, and everybody responds. In an alcoholic home, the same thing happens. Everyone is involved in your feelings; you are not entitled to your own reactions. You cannot be an individual in an over-involved alcoholic family. You are part of the "Big Us." You are absorbed in an undifferentiated ego mass; when you were born, it absorbed you.

Minuchin uses "enmeshment" to describe this family. If the alcoholic is up, everybody's up. If the alcoholic is down, everybody's down. And if the alcoholic is angry—watch out! Family members are so wrapped up with each other that boundaries are confused: "I don't know where you begin and I end . . . if the alcoholic gets a headache, I take the aspirin . . . If the alcoholic is depressed, I'm the one who is sad." Messages are so distorted that children learn very early that what is said and what is done do not match. The alcoholic promises to quit drinking, but doesn't. The spouse vows to leave, but stays. Double binds are puzzling: "I'm your parent: take care of me . . . Everybody knows Mom is drinking, but no one can talk about it." The children learn to live with this inconsistency, confusion, and fear. They try to control situations that are uncontrollable, and they become afraid to live in the present, because it is too intimidating. These children come out of their families with great guilt and anxiety, and, what is guilt but a state of living in the past? Anxiety then is a state of living in the future, and there is no energy left for the present.

Need Attainment

A family should also provide "need attainment"—if children find their needs are met, the chances are good that they will become healthy adults. Children of alcoholics do get their needs met, but not in the conventional fashion. I asked a 13-year-old girl to explain when she feels closest to her parents. She told me: "I'm closest to my mom when she's complaining about the marriage. I'm closest to my dad when he's complaining about my mother's drinking."

CoAs commonly assume emotional roles to get their needs met—caretaking, by being desperately needed, by being rebellious, by being sick or debilitated, by being smothered. As the children grow, the means to need fulfillment continue to be confused. I agree with J. Greenleaf who says that CoAs learn to rely on twisted emotion equations:

Being loved = being desperately needed.

Being loving = caretaking.

Spontaneity = rebellious behavior.

Needing = being sick.

Intimacy = smothering.

There is no balance in an alcoholic home; it is either fusion or isolation.

Child Development Issues

In alcoholic homes the children of alcoholics grow up too fast, too soon. By examining the developmental issues shared by the children of alcoholics, we can see how this happens.

1. The "dance of development" that takes place between parent and child during the early stages in life is crucial, but for children of alcoholics, there is no partner. They dance alone. They turn to the outer world for their "goodies," because they get so little from their parents.

2. Trust is undermined in an alcoholic family. If the alcoholic is drinking, the child lives in an alcohol-centered, not a child-centered, home. Attention is diverted from the child, who doesn't understand.

   Neither parent may respond when the baby, left wet for hours, cries. The child may be offered scalding bottles, or held in an uncomfortable way for long periods. The infant learns that people cannot be trusted to furnish physical and sometimes emotional care. To overcome mistrust between birth and age five is critical. This is when we learn to trust our environment, and the people in it. This does not occur in an alcoholic family when the child is secondary to the family's involvement with the alcoholic.

3. Alcoholic families are shame-based. Shame is rampant, with name-calling, negative compliments, blaming.

   As a result, the child develops an eagerness to please. But what is pleasing during drinking time is not always pleasing during sober time. The inconsistency generates a sense of shame, which children learn to disguise:

   With courage: "If I am not courageous, you'll see how shameful I am."

   With ambition: "Don't see me as I am; see me as I want to become."

   With judgments: The child who feels powerless will become dominating, shaming others.

4. Boundaries block identities. Part of a child's developmental task is to separate from the parents. This starts at two years, when kids drive parents nuts by saying "no!"—an important word to learn.

   You need to become angry to see yourself as a distinct person, to be able to separate, but for CoAs, saying "no," being angry at parents is not okay. Every time they feel that natural urge to separate, they are ashamed for it. It starts when they are very young; the incantations are familiar;

"How can you do this to me?"

"You make me so mad!"

"You drive me crazy."

Gradually, this conditions them to surrender themselves and to assume responsibility for the feelings of others. In an alcoholic family, it is almost a duty to feel intruded upon. Children learn "space invasion"—the seductive forms of intrusion which come in the guise of over-loving and over-protecting. It becomes a struggle to mature and a difficult process ever to leave home emotionally. As adults, they remain terrified of losing themselves if they become too close to people; they fear becoming enmeshed, with good reason. The family boundaries have interfered with their ability to be intimate, and the degree to which we can be intimate depends on how separate they are emotionally from their families.

5. Parents sometimes withdraw from parenting very early. You will hear adult children admit that they felt more competent at age eight than they are today. The CoA often is pushed into early ego development, giving up childhood quite early.

Because many of them did not get their dependency needs met as children, they learn to hurry up and grow up, covering their inferiority by appearing to be super competent and fearing the world will see their anxiety . . . or they stay "little," soaking up dependency fulfillment they never got at home. As a result, some children of alcoholics become victims as adults:

The martyr—CoAs who play the game of "ain't it awful," making lists of how bad things are, and comparing miseries with other CoA victims.

The saint—the professional caretakers, giving to the extreme, hoping that by over-giving, they might get something back.

The perfectionist—hard on themselves and everyone around them. They are high achievers, self-starters, and very effective, but if you ask why they do this, they answer, "I don't know." If you ask them to stop, they reply, "I can't."

Recovery for Children

I could tell you sad stories about children, but that is not what this is all about. Dealing with the past, with young children, is only as important as it relates to the present. From children of alcoholics, I have learned that they desperately need information: they need to know what is going on in their alcoholic homes. Any caring adult can give these children the information they need. Some therapists specialize in grief, anger, or anxiety, but how many work on joy and laughter? Children have shown me a magical connection between the head and heart. When the two come together, healing ensues.

The children I work with show me a remarkable flexibility to pass through pain and to see the paradoxical, sometimes humorous truths of an alcoholic family. Sometimes, children can acknowledge the hurt through the paradoxical intervention of humor. A primary problem I have with children of alcoholics is denial. It takes these children a long time to grasp why they are in therapy, but we can find ways to break through the defenses. Utilizing laughter and play is one powerful tool.

Recovery for Adults

I agree with Sondra Smalley; recovery for adult children of alcoholics takes place in three phases:

Phase 1— "I" —Learn to observe yourself by journaling, by finding the right therapist, by joining adult children's support groups, and Al-Anon. Find out who you are; form your own identity.

Phase 2—"Me"—Observe yourself in interaction with others. Co-dependents do not have a clue how they relate to people. They must learn by doing.

Phase 3—"We"—Discover intimacy, which can come only after you find yourself. CoA's collect friends and lovers in "pseudo intimacies," but have never experienced the real thing.

Therapists working with CoA's sometimes just attack the focus of the person's addiction, the relationship of the moment. This doesn't work, in the same way that attacking an alcoholic's drinking habits doesn't work. These same therapists will chase a co-dependent around a circle with exchanges like this:

Co-dependent: I've got to get out of this relationship. It's driving me crazy. It's making me sick. I can't stand it any more.

Therapist: By all means, then. Get out of the relationship.

Co-dependent: Oh, but I can't, he loves me. He needs me. He does so much for me. When things are good, they are so very, very good.

Therapist: Well, then stay in the relationship.
Co-dependent: But can't you see what it's doing to me?
In other words, it doesn't matter what you say when you attack the focus of the addiction. Adult children of alcoholics sometimes are mis-diagnosed in this way. Now, the art of Al-Anon teaches you how to be okay when others around you are not. Al-Anon doesn't tell you to get out of a relationship; Al-Anon tells you to mind your own business. Those of us who treat CoAs need to remember that.

Many adult children of alcoholics begin to get better almost inadvertently, as they come to realize what their own business is. According to J. Bowden and H. Gravitz, adult children of alcoholics seem to follow a continuum in recovery which starts with survival. They know something is wrong with their lives, they're not satisfied with their work, they drift from one relationship into the next. They are limping through adulthood, just surviving. Then they attend a conference, or read an article in the paper, or open a magazine and, suddenly, they find out what alcoholism is all about, how it affects the family. There is a wonderful realization: "Ah ha, that's why I felt crazy all these years!" Emerging awareness draws them along the recovery continuum, leading them to breaking the alcoholic family's rule of silence. In the next stage, they address the core issues of the learned patterns of behavior which have molded them. Therapy and Al-Anon lead them further.

Finally, they achieve integration, as they begin taking care of themselves for the first time. They stop ignoring their own needs. They begin to play and to have fun—sure signs of recovery. Working on recovery is life-long, because they can never run away from their alcoholic family for good. The only way into the family is through birth, adoption, or marriage, and the only way out emotionally is death. They can't resign; they can't get fired, or let their membership expire. That invisible string which binds them to their family of origin is tied to them wherever they go; it determines who they are and what they do.

For CoAs, that string will become a rope that can strangle them, unless they deal with the Three C's of CoA's: I didn't cause it, I can't cure it, but I can cope with it.

What it is all about is in a poem a friend in recovery gave me:

> *After a while, you learn the subtle difference between*
> *holding a hand and chaining a soul;*
> *And you learn that love doesn't mean leaning, and company doesn't mean security;*

*And you begin to learn that kisses aren't contracts, and
    presents aren't promises.*

*And you begin to accept your defeats with your head up and
    your eyes ahead, with the grace a man or a woman,
    not the grief of a child.*

*And you learn to build all your roads on today, because
    tomorrow's ground is too uncertain for plans.*

And futures have a way of falling down in mid-flight.

*After a while, you learn that even sunshine burns if you ask
    too much.*

*So you plant your own garden, and decorate your own soul,
    instead of waiting for someone to bring you flowers.*

*And you learn that you really can endure, that you really are
    strong, that you really do have worth.*

*And you learn, and you learn, with every letting go, and
    with every good-bye, you learn.*

This, to me, is the meaning of recovery for the children of alcoholics—
to learn how to decorate their own souls.

Part Three
Adolescent Children of Alcoholics: Family Confusion and Identity Diffusion

Part three presents essays on adolescent children of alcoholics in various settings. Rather than being a descriptive narrative on adolescent children of alcoholics, this section is concerned with intervention, associated problems, and alcohol and drug abuse among adolescent children of alcoholics. In chapter twelve, Ellen Morehouse offers concrete guidelines for working with adolescent children of alcoholics in groups. Beginning with a discussion of the benefits of a group experience for adolescent children of alcoholics, this chapter also includes a section on the common feelings of these adolescents and procedures for implementing these groups. Patricia O'Gorman and Robert Ross, in chapter thirteen, discuss the high probability of some adolescent children of alcoholics being in the juvenile justice system and the need for the system to understand the dynamics of the alcoholic family and its impact on adolescents. In the last chapter of this section, Tim Allen addresses adolescent substance abuse and the role of families, schools and communities in prevention and intervention of substance abuse by adolescents and particularly by adolescent children of alcoholics.

Chapter Twelve
Counseling Adolescent Children of Alcoholics in Groups

Ellen R. Morehouse

INTRODUCTION

Adolescents are extremely peer oriented. They care what their peers think and do, and use their peers to measure their own actions against and to help form an identity. Adolescent children of alcoholics are no exception. Given the inconsistent responses they receive from an alcoholic parent, however, the role of their peers in shaping an identity becomes even more important. Although not all adolescents are suited for participation in small groups, groups offer a number of advantages for adolescents. Typical behavioral patterns are shared leading to a decrease in feelings of isolation and of being peculiar, with a rise in self-esteem. Groups foster new ways of dealing with situations along with an evaluation of techniques already in use. They provide the adolescent with a feeling of protection in interacting with an adult who may be initially distrusted by the adolescent. Participating in groups seems less associated with being ill than does receiving individual counseling from an adult. Finally, group participation provides an adolescent the opportunity to appreciate and reduce the blocks to warm, honest, non-exploitative relationships with others [Berkovitz, 1975].

BENEFITS OF GROUPS FOR CHILDREN OF ALCOHOLICS

A number of people have documented the positive results experienced by children of alcoholics when they participate in groups that focus on being the child of an alcoholic [Miller, 1983; Hawley, 1981; Deckman, 1982; Peitler, 1980; Hughes, 1977; Fairchild, 1974; Weir, 1970]. DiCicco et. al. also documented the positive results for adolescent children of alcoholics when they participated in integrated groups that provided general alcohol education [DiCicco, 1984].

Groups can be a particularly strong modality for working with adolescent children of alcoholics. By participating in a group with other children of alcoholics, the adolescent child of an alcoholic will experience the following benefits:

1. **Reduced Isolation**

   Adolescent children of alcoholics grow up learning never to talk about the parent's alcoholism. As a result they often think they are the only one experiencing the kind of anger, pain, confusion, frustration, and guilt that occurs when one is a child of an alcoholic. Learning that others also feel this way will result in the adolescent child of an alcoholic feeling less different and more self-esteem.

2. **New Ways of Coping**

   By participating in a group the adolescent child of an alcoholic will learn new ways of coping with the behaviors and situations that can occur when an adolescent has an active alcoholic parent. Learning what to do when one cannot do homework because of noisy arguing at home and learning how to increase the chance that parental promises are not broken are just two examples of information that is needed by most adolescent children of alcoholics. Learning new ways of coping will occur as members share ideas and experiences of what does and does not work for them and as the group leader also offers ideas

3. **Positive Peer Support**

   The positive peer support in making healthy changes is one of the factors that helps adolescents translate new knowledge into new action. Trying out a new behavior can be scary for an adolescent; especially when the old behavior has become ingrained and the outcome of the new behavior is unknown. The encouragement and empathy provided by peers lessens the adolescent's resistance to making healthy changes. Frequently the positive peer support extends outside the group. It is common for members to exchange phone numbers, become friends, and call each other when problems occur.

4. **Practice Sharing Feelings**

   The group provides a laboratory to test new behaviors and is a "stage" to act them out and get feedback. Children of alcoholics need help to learn to break the "don't talk," "don't feel," and "don't trust" rules that they have learned to help them survive living with an alcoholic parent [Black, 1982]. The group becomes a safe place to break these rules and provides an opportunity to get reactions from others.

5. Confrontation When Needed

Adolescent children of alcoholics, like all others who are learning new behaviors, often will slip back to the old ways of responding. Empathetic confrontation from peers can help motivate the adolescent child of an alcoholic to make positive changes. Hearing one group member telling another group member, "You can't keep blaming your poor grades on your mom's drinking. We discussed several weeks ago how you could stay after school to study," forces the adolescent to examine why she/he is not taking responsibility for his/her behavior and eliminating less productive behaviors.

6. Increased Readiness for Alateen

Most adolescents participating in Alateen have parents participating in Alcoholics Anonymous, Al-Anon, or in treatment. It is extremely difficult for an adolescent to leave the house to go to an Alateen meeting without a parent knowing or to tell a parent that she/he wants to participate. Group involvement prepares the adolescent for dealing with parental resistance to Alateen participation and educates the adolescent about the importance of participation.

FORMING THE GROUP

Each potential member should be seen individually for screening and orientation before he/she joins the group. The adolescent children of an alcoholic bring the ambivalent feelings they have towards their parents to the adult counselor. It is difficult for those adolescents to trust adults, to feel that adults are consistent, and to anticipate an adult's behavior when the parents have provided an inconsistent atmosphere at home (Morehouse, 1979). The individual meeting provides an opportunity for the adolescent to begin to know the adult counselor. During this meeting the adolescents should be screened to make sure they are developmentally, intellectually, and emotionally appropriate for the group. During this individual session the counselor also needs to learn about the adolescent's family situation to determine what specific topics the group should address.

In situations where the adolescent has never discussed what occurs in the home, it is important for the counselor to demonstrate an understanding of what it is like and how it feels to live in a home with an alcoholic parent. This is necessary because the adolescent has learned never to talk about this and, therefore, believes that she/he is the only one experiencing what has happened. The adolescent also may believe his/her feelings are not valid because parental reactions to past expressions of feelings were inappropriate. As a result, the child of an alcoholic is skeptical that the counselor will understand. When the counselor demonstrates an understanding, the adolescent becomes less skeptical and has an easier time expressing his/her feelings about what is going on at home. The discussion should acknowledge the following feelings that are characteristics of most children of alcoholics [Morehouse, 1979; Cork, 1969].

1. Children feel responsible, directly or indirectly, for their parent's drinking. They may be told, for example, "If you wouldn't bother me all the time, I wouldn't drink." Even if they are not accused directly, they may feel responsible for causing the parent to get angry, which then brings on drinking. Or they are told by the nonalcoholic parent when the alcoholic is abstinent, "Don't upset your father." This makes the child feel that the nonalcoholic parent believes that the child's behavior may be responsible for the drinking.

2. Children equate their parent's drinking with not being loved. They feel, for example, "If dad really loved me, he wouldn't drink." They feel hurt by the actions of the alcoholic parent, which are often characterized by broken promises or inadequate attention, affection, or material goods. They feel that if the parent loved them, he or she wouldn't hurt them.

3. Children feel angry with the nonalcoholic parent for not making things better and for not providing protection from the alcoholic parent's violence, for not getting a divorce, and for not lessening their responsibilities for assuming parental roles. Frequently, the anger is a result of the child's sense that the nonalcoholic parent is responsible for the alcoholic parent's drinking. For example, they may think, "If Mom wouldn't nag Dad so much, he wouldn't drink."

4. Children fear that the alcoholic will get hurt, sick, or die as a result of being intoxicated. Worrying that "Mom will fall asleep with a lit cigarette and cause a fire" or that "Dad will have a car accident on the way home from work" sometimes makes it impossible for the child to concentrate in school. In extreme cases, the adolescent will want to

stay home from school to take care of the parent.

5. In situations in which the alcoholic parent is more permissive or affectionate while intoxicated, the adolescent may want the parent to drink but then feels guilty.

6. Children always feel confused by the difference between "dry" behavior and "drunk" behavior. Not understanding blackouts, for example, proves to be very frightening. Initially, blackouts make children think the parent is "going crazy." Often things are unfairly blamed on the adolescent as a result of the parent's blackout. They are confused about how the alcoholic parent really feels. Many adolescents believe that alcohol acts as a truth serum. For example, one teenage girl was punished for coming in late when in fact she had come in on time and had spoken with her alcoholic parent. Another girl was verbally insulted and accused of being promiscuous by her father when he was intoxicated. When sober, he would frequently say how proud he was of her. The unjustified criticism almost always left this adolescent so angry, frustrated, or sad that it was impossible for her to do homework. Feelings are similar if the verbal or physical abuse is directed at the non-alcoholic parent. If the child feels responsible for causing an argument between the parents, these feelings are intensified.

7. Parents' inconsistent behavior makes adolescents reluctant to bring friends home because they never know what to expect. This inhibits close peer relationships. Adolescents are sensitive to social reciprocity and after visiting a friend's house many times, an adolescent feels obligated to reciprocate. Many adolescents avoid close friendships because of this problem. Usually the adolescent will have one close friend who knows of the parent's alcoholism. Many adolescents also become tense just before returning home or just before the alcoholic is to arrive home because they do not know what to expect.

8. Once children are old enough to realize that alcoholic drinking is frowned upon by others or is "different," they always feel shame and embarrassment. Many adolescents are willing to take criticism from friends or teachers rather then "expose" their parent's problem. The child's sense of shame increases when the nonalcoholic parent tells the child not to discuss the drinking with anyone outside the home. The nonalcoholic's attempt to "cover up" the drinking also lets the child know that it is to be kept secret. When this is done with friends and family members, the child gets a clear message that "Mom's drinking is so terrible, we can't even tell Grandma." The drinking then becomes a

crime in the child's mind. By the time the child reaches adolescence, his or her feelings of embarrassment and stigma have intensified. Several high school students believed that the parents of some of their peers did not want their children to go out with them because of their parents' drinking.

Once the counselor has demonstrated an understanding of what it is like to live with a parent who drinks too much, the adolescent usually has one of three reactions. The first reaction is a surprised and tearful, "How did you know?" The "floodgates" open and the adolescent spills what has been kept inside and unspoken for so many years. With this reaction the counselor should let the adolescent ventilate and provide support and comfort by letting the adolescent know his/her reaction is not at all unusual and that his/her perceptions and feelings are valid.

The second reaction is a minimizing, "Things aren't that bad in my house. Dad has never hit mom or done any of the other things but he yells a lot, mom cries, and I feel scared." When this reaction occurs, the counselor should acknowledge the adolescent's concern and add that it might be helpful also to discuss the other things and feelings that are not occurring so if they ever do, the adolescent will be prepared.

The third reaction, is a somewhat hostile, "Those things may occur in other homes where a parent drinks too much but none of that is occurring in my home." When the adolescent reacts with denial, the denial should be respected and the counselor can say she/he is glad these things and feelings are not occurring. As with the minimized reaction, the counselor should point out that discussing some of the issues and feelings mentioned can be helpful, so if they arise the adolescent will be prepared. With this procedure the adolescent can receive some help without having to acknowledge to the counselor what is occurring at home.

Providing the adolescent with an opportunity to express concerns about family members or self is the next step. These concerns and how they can be addressed will serve as the basis for discussion in the first few group meetings. The adolescent should be told that his/her concerns are shared by most other adolescents with parents who drink too much. Therefore, discussion will benefit all group members.

ORIENTATION TO GROUP PARTICIPATION

Unfamiliarity with counseling, some degree of mistrust of adults, and fear of not being in control all make the adolescent child of an alcoholic uneasy about participation in a group. This uneasiness can be minimized by providing prospective group members in the individual screening with a detailed orientation of how the group will work and what will occur at the first meeting. Points to be covered include the time that the group will start and end, number of group sessions, what will take place, the policy for new members entering, the number of adolescents that will be participating, the age range of group members, confidentiality issues, and parental consent issues. In addition, it is important to acknowledge the adolescent's reluctance about participating and ask him/her to describe his/her worst fantasy. When one can actually verbalize one's worst fears and then discuss the likelihood of them occurring and steps that can be taken to prevent them from occurring, the fears are minimized. It is also important to acknowledge that: the adolescent will be nervous, as will all other group members; she/he does not have to say anything if she/he wishes; it is okay to come and listen; and finally that she/he should try the first meeting and she/he does not have to return if she/he does not want to. Acknowledgement of fears should be balanced with the discussion of how the adolescent will benefit from group participation. The group should be presented as being helpful to the adolescent by providing concrete solutions for coping with the parents' drinking and resultant behavior. It is the author's experience that with these guidelines, most adolescents are willing to attend the first group meeting.

Sometimes it is necessary to see the adolescent two to three times individually before she/he is ready for participation in a group. If the adolescent is seen too many times individually, the adolescent may become more resistant to group participation because she/he has already been able to obtain the information and help needed, may not want to share the counselor, and may not want to change what has been a helpful counseling routine. Therefore it is a delicate balance between seeing the adolescent individually for enough time so there is a willingness to participate in group and seeing the adolescent too many times so there is resistance to group participation. It has been the author's experience that two to three times is ideal.

GROUP COMPOSITION

Group composition issues that are usually considered in forming an adolescent group are not as important in the group for adolescent children of alcoholics. The fact that all group participants have a parent who drinks "too much" overrides most other composition issues and makes the group homogeneous enough to develop cohesiveness quickly. If there are large enough numbers of adolescents who want to participate and it is possible to form several groups, then traditional group composition issues should be considered. Assuming this is not the case, the following guidelines are recommended:

1. A minimum of four adolescents and a maximum of ten, with an ideal size of six to eight.
2. Adolescents grouped by grade range of the school they attend, i.e., one group for adolescents in junior high school and one group for adolescents in high school.
3. Either no siblings or siblings from more than one family. When there are siblings from one family, they have assumed different roles and perceive the drinking and non-drinking parent differently. As a result they will disagree on issues in the group. If there is more then one sibling set, this phenomenon can be interpreted and discussed. If there is only one sibling set, it has been the author's experience that one or both will drop out of the group.
4. All members should be in the normal range for intelligence. Adolescents who are intellectually limited or are not able to read will have difficulty with informational booklets that are not geared to their level and, therefore, should be grouped together or seen individually.
5. Severely acting out, psychotic, or adolescents with severe impulse disorders should not be included in a group with adolescents in the normal range of personality function because they will disrupt the group.
6. If possible, there should not be "one of any kind" of adolescent, i.e. try to avoid putting one male in a group with all females, one freshman in a group with all juniors and seniors, one black adolescent in a group with all white adolescents, one "preppy" in a group with all tough adolescents, etc.

STYLE OF LEADERSHIP

The model presented in this chapter uses a more educational style as opposed to a psychotherapeutic style. The reader who is used to conducting adolescent psychotherapy groups or "rap" groups should think of this more as a mini course or workshop for adolescents in which the adult leader acts more like a teacher than a therapist. Just as education is an essential ingredient in the treatment and recovery of the alcoholic, it is also essential in helping the adolescent child of an alcoholic. This educational approach suggests a directive leader, giving out reading assignments, providing factual information, and "calling" on the adolescent group members as a classroom teacher would "call" on students. Printed material written for and about adolescent children of alcoholics is important, because it demonstrates to the group that they are not alone. It also is important because individual adolescent group members will not all be able to absorb the material at the same time. Some adolescents will need more time before they are emotionally able to absorb some of the facts and concepts related to alcoholism and how it affects the family [Gravitz & Bowden, 1985]. The adolescent will find it helpful to be able to re-read the printed material when the group is over. Printed material and films also are good catalysts for discussion in the group.

Other ways the leadership style differs from the adolescent psychotherapy or rap group are: in the children of alcoholics group the leader creates commonality and stimulates cohesiveness instead of waiting for it to emerge, the leader provides a safe structure instead of relying on the healthy process of the group, and the leader switches from a teacher student model in the early stages of the group to a self-help model that encourages the members' own resourcefulness.

GROUP STAGES

It has been the author's experience that the group will go through four stages. In the first stage the group members want information about alcoholism, its effects on the family, and how to manage their reaction. They also will be testing the group experience to determine how the leader will respond and how the other members will respond. Most of the communication will be leader directed and interaction among group members will be minimal.

In the second stage the group members begin to share feelings about what is going on at home and have built up enough trust to share with each other. Communication is less leader directed and more spontaneous.

In the third stage there is less of a need to discuss parental drinking. Friends' use of alcohol and drugs is usually discussed in this stage. Adolescent children of alcoholics who do not use alcohol or drugs are frequently upset by a friend's experimentation and perceive the friend's use as a betrayal to them. One adolescent described how she was so angry at her best friend for using alcohol and stated, "For all these years we've talked about how bad mom's drinking is, and now she [the best friend] is doing it, too!" It is not uncommon for adolescent children of alcoholics to be "against" alcohol use and therefore feel betrayed when a friend drinks. Often, the adolescent assumes the group leader is also opposed to alcohol use and the discussion of a "friend" is sometimes a "test" to see how the leader will respond to a group member's own use of alcohol. The subject of alcohol use with adolescent children of alcoholics requires much discussion. While it is clear that adolescents should not use alcohol, and it is clear that children of alcoholics must be made aware of the special risks in using alcohol, it is also clear that they have difficulty in forming attitudes about alcohol use [Weir, 1970.] Reconciling "upbeat" advertisements for alcoholic beverages with the devastating consequences of a parent's abuse is a difficult task. Therefore it is helpful to discuss this in the group.

In the fourth stage of the group, the focus is more on the here and now, their current relationships and problems. Group members are less burdened by the parental alcoholism and now able to focus more on themselves.

THE FIRST MEETING

At the beginning of the first group meeting there is shyness, nervousness, and embarrassment. Often group members are surprised to see others they know but didn't know had an alcoholic parent. The group leader should begin by speaking for the members and acknowledging these feelings. The leader should then restate the rules of the group so each member knows that all members have heard the same rules. They should also repeat the common feelings of adolescents who live with a chemically dependent parent, so each member knows that these are permissible topics to be discussed. Repeating for the entire group what has been stated to each member individually is necessary, because the "don't talk" and "don't trust" rules mentioned earlier make each member wonder, "Is it really okay to discuss these feelings?" Restatement of the rules to the entire group helps free the adolescents to discuss these issues.

The next step is for the leader to read a list of topics that were compiled from the individual meetings. The leader can say these are some of the topics that the group will be discussing. Examples include blackouts, enabling, addiction, fighting, being embarrassed, not being able to do school work, etc. The leader should add that these topics reflect the concerns of the group members and that it is anticipated that other topics will be added. Before discussion begins, the leader should prepare the group for joking and help members understand that laughing about situations does not necessarily mean that a group member thinks that a particular situation is funny and not serious. This lessens the likelihood of one group member's being offended by another group member's response.

The group then can begin by members introducing themselves and the leader selecting the first topic for discussion. The first topic should be one that is applicable to everyone, such as parents' arguing. Asking each group member to describe the arguing that can result when a parent drinks too much allows each member to talk generally on the subject or to personalize the discussion and share his/her experience.

The leader should make participation as comfortable as possible. Turning to his/her right, the leader can ask the adolescent immediately on the right, "Can you describe how arguing can result when a parent drinks too much?" The phrasing of this question and the process of "calling on" an adolescent can reduce an adolescent's uneasiness about participating. Using a "go around" where each group member is asked the same question in the order in which they sit is similar to classes where a teacher asks for responses in the order of how chairs are arranged in the classroom. The "go around" technique results in reactive participation by all members and does not require a conscious decision to volunteer by an individual member. In the first "go around", each group member should give only a brief response. This can be controlled by the leader's verbal and non-verbal cues. The brief response demonstrates that participation can be easy and prevents a group member from sharing too much and then feeling guilty. This procedure helps group members learn to break the "no talk" rule and keeps guilt to a minimum. When the "go around" is completed, the leader should summarize the group's response and create commonality by focusing on the common points in everyone's response, as opposed to the differences. This should be followed by the leader beginning to educate group members in terms and concepts they can understand about their concerns. For example, the "go around" on arguing can be followed by a discussion of how intoxication changes the nature of an argument if the intoxicated parents' perceptions are distorted by the alcohol, etc.

It is important for the alcohol education to be focused directly at the adolescent's concerns rather than what the leader thinks is most important. However, it is important to discuss the information about alcohol, alcoholism, and alcoholism and the family that will help the adolescent feel less burdened by the parent's drinking and the family's reaction. It is also helpful toward the end of the first meeting to prepare group members for the possibility of feeling guilty after the meeting for violating the "no talk" rule. Ending the group simply by stating, "We've run out of time. We will continue discussing topics next week," and assuming everyone will attend, reduces the anxiety that occurs when members must think about their participation. Therefore, it is suggested that the leader does not end by asking what group members thought of the group.

THE SECOND AND THIRD MEETING

In the second and third meeting, the communication continues to be primarily leader directed, the members are still testing, and the leader is modeling structure and creating a safe, trusting, and consistent atmosphere. Topics continue to be discussed, commonality is created, and education takes place. The leader can begin to ask "How is it for you?" and can begin to ask members for solutions for coping with the situations of other group members. Discussing solutions for coping demonstrates members' resourcefulness and willingness to help each other. The leader also should play an active role in helping members evaluate the appropriateness of the solutions. The format of starting each meeting with a topic should be continued. More verbal adolescents may suggest which topics are discussed first. Members should also be encouraged to use role play in a limited way. By the end of the third meeting, most groups will be entering stage two.

THE FOURTH AND FIFTH MEETING

In the fourth and fifth meeting, the communication among group members is more spontaneous and less leader directed. Group members are volunteering what is going on at home and reacting to each other. The guilt about sharing has been reduced or eliminated and ventilating becomes a positive experience that leads to closeness among group members. In this stage of the group, the leader should allow ventilation but again provide safety by ensuring closure about what has been said. For example, if a group member shares her anger about all the broken promises made by the alcoholic parent and other group members share their similar experiences, the leader should acknowledge the universality of this and the accompanying feelings but also ask for suggestions on how to deal with broken promises and check that members feel they have usable techniques.

THE SIXTH AND SEVENTH MEETING

If discussion of friends' use of alcohol and drugs has not been initiated by group members, the leader should bring up the topic. The leader should also start discussion of their attitudes regarding alcohol use. Discussion of the vulnerability of children of alcoholics for developing alcoholism and the special risks associated with their use of alcohol should be included. If group members are not familiar with Alateen, Alateen should be discussed, and Alateen literature should be distributed. After advance notice to the group, it is helpful to have an Alateen member come to the group to give a brief presentation on Alateen. This meeting should be followed by the entire group attending an Alateen meeting together and then discussing their reaction to the Alateen meeting at their next group meeting.

Many resistances or barriers to participation can be worked through by introducing Alateen participation while the adolescents are still participating in a professionally led group. This procedure increases the likelihood that the adolescent will make the transition from the professionally led group to Alateen.

When the group is halfway through the planned number of meetings, the leader should remind the group that they are at the halfway point and there are "x" number of meetings left. The short-term groups for adolescents and children of alcoholics are difficult to end for both the leader and the participants. Being aware of the number of group meetings left stimulates involvement in Alateen because group members want to continue to be involved in a supportive group experience and accept that their group will be ending.

THE EIGHTH AND NINTH MEETING

By the eighth meeting a high level of trust and cohesiveness has developed. Group members may have exchanged phone numbers and started to have contact outside the group. As new friendships develop, the group leader has to be alert to alliances and the phenomenon of "sub-grouping" in the group. While it is beneficial for group members to provide support for each other outside the group, the support in the group can inhibit constructive confrontation. As group members increase their understanding of alcoholism and its effects on the family, they can be more objective in examining their own behavior. They can begin to identify the adaptations they have made to their family situation and decide, with the group's help, if those adaptations can and should be modified. Destructive and dysfunctional behaviors need to be changed and constructive and healthy behaviors should be substituted. The following example illustrates how the group can assist with this process:

> In the third meeting, 16-year-old Jane talked about how all the fighting and tension at home made it difficult for her to study and do homework. As a result she was not doing well in school. When this was discussed, group members suggested staying after school or going to the library before going home as a way to ensure that homework and studying would get done. Jane agreed she could do this. Two weeks later, Jane complained about an argument with her parents about her poor grades and blamed her parents for her poor grades. Several group members confronted Jane by reminding her of their earlier suggestions and asking why she was not acting on what she had agreed was a workable solution.

ENDING

As mentioned earlier, ending is difficult for both the group leader and the group members. The group provides a nurturing experience that most adolescents want to continue. The leader is able to receive a high degree of satisfaction from seeing the positive effect of the group experience and wants to continue feeling helpful. In addition, the experience of not getting enough nurturing at home, having a relationship with a caring adult [group leader] who is consistent, and having a place to talk about what was never discussed before result in the members' not wanting the group to end. Some adolescents slip back into the "if you loved me you wouldn't end the group" feeling that was a reaction to disappointment by their parents. This reaction has to be identified and discussed. As with other groups for adolescents, "acting out" to show that the group is needed, not attending, and direct expressions of anger are other common reactions to ending and must be worked through.

The leader has to identify his/her own resistance to ending, which includes enjoying being needed, enjoying helping, believing no one else can be as effective, and viewing ending as an abandonment.

Sometimes it is appropriate to decide to recontract for an additional set number of meetings. Not having Alateen and identifying appropriate new tasks or issues that group members want to discuss are two reasons why a group may extend the number of meetings. When this occurs, however, it is important for each group member to have a clear understanding of the contract, i.e., the purpose of the additional meetings. In ending, the leader should identify what the members have accomplished by participating in the group and help members to identify additional goals and how they plan to work on those goals. The leader should reinforce the gains made by members and stimulate confidence in their ability to sustain those gains. Resources for additional help should also be discussed. The leader also may want to schedule individual meetings with each group member to evaluate more fully a member's unmet needs, additional goals, and need for counseling or treatment. This individual session is particularly useful when a group member needs ongoing counseling or treatment but is resistant to a referral. In this instance it may not be appropriate for the leader to confront the group member in the presence of other members who may not need treatment.

Additional Issues

Wegscheider [1981] and Black [1982] have described survival roles that are adopted by children of alcoholics to help maintain the alcoholic family's homeostasis. Although these roles are useful for the family, they can cause problems for the child as an individual. It is common for children of alcoholics who have adopted these survival roles to stay in these roles in the group. For example, a group member who is the "super coper" or "family hero" at home will act as the assistant group leader. The mascot who provides comic relief for the tension filled family will crack jokes in the group when a tense or serious situation arises. It is important for the group leader to point out when this occurs and to remind members when they are acting out their roles. A discussion of these roles should occur around the half-way point of the group.

No Alateen

If there is no Alateen meeting in the area, the group leader should contact Al-Anon about identifying someone who could lead the Alateen groups. Having a core of members increases the chance that the Alateen will be successful in terms of attendance. Ideally the Alateen leader should have worked through his/her own issues about being the child of an alcoholic and/or the parent of a child of an alcoholic, so as not to "shut off" expressions of feelings by Alateen members.

PARENTAL ABSTINENCE

A parent's sudden abstinence as the result of involvement in treatment, Alcoholics Anonymous, or some other means will warrent significant attention and discussion. In addition to providing information on recovery, slips, relapse, treatment, and Alcoholics Anonymous, group members also will need to know how the family is affected. "Survivors guilt" in the group members whose parent becomes abstinent and scapegoating by other members are possible, therefore a thorough discussion and monitoring is recommended. The shock that abstinence does not necessarily result in things improving for the adolescent, must also be discussed [Oliver-Diaz, 1985].

INDIVIDUAL APPOINTMENTS

It is common for group members to ask for an individual appointment with the leader to discuss something they do not feel comfortable discussing in group. Incest, sexual abuse, child abuse, and pregnancy are areas that most adolescents do not feel comfortable sharing in group. While it is appropriate for individual appointments to take place, the leader should be careful in conducting individual appointments because they can interfere with the group process. It takes skill in deciding how to balance group members' needs for an individual appointment with maintaining meaningful group discussion and sharing.

PARENTAL CONSENT

The setting and the state where group is held will determine the need for parental consent. If parental consent is required, the following issues must be considered. Is consent from one parent enough? Does it matter if consent is given by the drinking or non-drinking parent? Does the adolescent have to tell the parent she/he is participating in a group for children of alcoholics, or can she/he say it is an alcohol education group or an adolescent pressures group of a group to build self-esteem, etc?

A second issue is: should the adolescent tell the alcoholic parent she/he is in group for children of alcoholics? This should be an individual decision for each member. The most important factor in this discussion is what the outcome will be. Feeling guilty about discussing what is occurring at home, hoping that telling the parent about group participation will result in the parent's getting help, and wanting to "get back at the parent" are three of the more common reasons that adolescents have for telling their parents about group participation. Assisting the adolescent in identifying the reason for wanting to tell the parent and then projecting possible and likely outcomes is an important function for the leader. This issue should be discussed in the second and third meeting before the adolescent tells the parent and then again in the second half of the group meetings as group participation becomes more meaningful for the adolescent. Using role playing, in which the adolescent plays his/her parent and another adolescent plays the adolescent, is particularly helpful with this issue.

FOSTERING DEPENDENCE

The leader will feel that this group is a "needy" group and may unintentionally foster a dependence. It is helpful for the leader to view himself/herself as a guide who teaches information, communication, and coping techniques and who introduces resources that will help the adolescent survive in the healthiest way possible as part of an alcoholic family. If the leader allows the adolescent to become dependent and to view him/her as a substitute parent, the adolescent will be harmed by unfulfilled expectations and have one more disappointing relationship. To avoid this situation, the leader should frequently clarify his/her role and check that members have a clear understanding of it.

CONCLUSION

Leading a group for adolescent children of alcoholics is helpful for the adolescent and satisfying for the leader. Using a directive leadership style and educational approach will increase the adolescent's understanding of their parents' actions and the resulting behavior. This increased understanding leads to a reduction in painful feelings, worries, and dysfunctional actions that ultimately leads to healthier functioning for the adolescent. Although group participation is not recommended for all adolescent children of alcoholics, it is the approach of choice for most of them.

REFERENCES

Berkovitz, I. and Sugar, M., "Indications and Contraindications for Adolescent Group Psychotherapy" in *The Adolescent in Group and Family Therapy*. Max Sugar, ed. pp. 1-22, New York: Brunner/Mazel 1975.

Black, C., *It Will Never Happen to Me!* Denver, MAC Printing and Publications Division, 1982.

Cork, M., *The Forgotten Children*, Alcoholism and Drug Addiction Research Foundation of Ontario, Toronto, Canada 1969.

Deckman, J. and Downs, B. A group treatment approach for adolescent children of alcoholic parents. *Social Work with Groups* 5: 7377, 1982.

Oliver-Diaz, P. "Self-Help Groups: Through the Child's Eyes - Tempering Commitment with Compassion" *Focus on Family and Chemical Dependency* Vol. 8, No. 2, 1985.

DiCicco et al, "Group Experiences for Children of Alcoholics," *Alcohol Health and Research World*, Vol, 8, No. 4, 1984 pp. 20-24, 37.

Fairchild, D.M., "Teen Groups 1: A Pilot Project in Group Therapy with Adolescent Children of Alcoholic Patients," *Journal of the Ft. Logan Mental Health Center* 2, 1974, pp. 946-947.

Gravitz, H. and Bowden, J. *Guide to Recovery* Learning Publications, Holmes Beach, Florida 1985.

Hawley, N.P. and Brown, E.L. The use of group treatment with children of alcoholics. *Social Casework: The Journal of Contemporary Social Work*: 40-46, January, 1981.

Hughes, J.M. Adolescent children of alcoholic parents and the relationship of Alateen to these children. *Journal of Consulting and Clinical Psychology* 45: 946-947, 1977.

Miller, N. "Group Psychotherapy in a School Setting for Adolescent Children of Alcoholics" *Group* Vol. 7, pp. 34-40, 1983.

Morehouse, E. "Working in the Schools with Children of Alcoholic Parents," *Health and Social Work*, Vol. 4, No. 4, pp. 144-162.

Peitler, E.J. A comparison of the effectiveness of group counseling and Alateen on the psychological adjustment of two groups of adolescent sons of alcoholic fathers. *Dissertations Abstracts International* 41: 1520-B [Order No. 8021807], 1980.

Richards et al, "Psychological assessment and intervention with children of alcoholic parents," *Social Work Treatment of Alcohol Problems*, Vol. 5 of the Treatment Series, Rutgers Center of Alcohol Studies, New Brunswick, NJ, Lexington Press, 1983, pp. 131-162.

Wegscheider, S. *Another Chance: Hope and Health for the Alcoholic Family*. Science and Behavior Books, Inc. Palo Alto, Cal. 1981.

Weir, W.R. "Counseling Youth Whose Parents Are Alcoholic: A Means to an End as well as an End in Itself," *Journal of Alcohol Education* 16, 1970, pp. 13-19.

Chapter Thirteen
Children of Alcoholics
in the Juvenile Justice Systems

Patricia O'Gorman and Robert A. Ross

A significant proportion of youngsters in the juvenile justice system are children of alcoholics. Although no national statistics have been compiled, a local survey conducted by the authors indicates a potentially high correlation between juvenile justice system involvement and alcoholism in the families of those involved in that system.]

A review of intake material at Berkshire Farm and Center for Youth in Canaan, New York (a 232-bed, non-secure, residential treatment facility for adjudicated male minors), indicated that alcoholism was by far the most frequently reported problem affecting the families of these boys. More than 55% of those in placement came from homes where there was an alcoholic parent or other adult. The data also showed that 18% of families had been investigated by Protective Services for child abuse or neglect.

Further, 60% of the incarcerated youngsters whose records were reviewed indicated alcohol and drug usage problems of their own. Thirty-seven percent of these came from homes whose alcoholism in a family member was indicated. Since this survey relied only on intake material, these estimates must be considered conservative. The authors believe that a complete assessment would reveal an even higher incidence of family and personal alcohol problems among juvenile offenders.

The phenomenon of the alcoholic family producing children who frequently commit crimes was chronicled long ago in such works as *Ten Nights in a Bar-Room* (published in 1899). However, no serious attention has been paid to the connection between parental alcoholism and

Reprinted with authors' permission from *Alcohol Health and Research World*, Vol. 8, No. 4, Summer 1984.

juvenile justice problems until recently. The intent of this essay is to bring attention to the fact that alcoholism may be present in the homes of a significant number of those served by the juvenile justice system, and that a response to the family member's alcoholism problem may be essential to successfully addressing the problems of these youth. More widespread understanding of, and commitment to, this issue is also a prerequisite to developing the research and prevention efforts needed to establish meaningful intervention efforts for those children of alcoholics currently receiving juvenile justice services.

Interventions for the Family in Trouble

Often what is found when a parent or someone in the community lodges a complaint against a child, bringing him or her into the juvenile justice system, is that not only is the child before the judge in crisis, but that the whole family also is troubled. The child's crisis—usually acting-out behavior—is frequently only one visible manifestation of the family's problems.

States and counties differ in the degree of assessment done on the family and the child. Alcoholism, however, is usually identified only if an enlightened probation officer or social worker knows the right questions to ask. Such questions are not a part of the routine information gathered.

After some assessment, the child is brought into family or juvenile court to appear before a judge. The court can make a number of dispositions concerning the child, but it is important to note that the court does not mandate any intervention or treatment for the parents, since they have not been brought before the court. The only exception to this (at least in New York State), is if Child Protective Services investigates a family and mandates treatment because child abuse or neglect is occurring. Through adjudication, the child can be placed in a detention center, in foster care, or in a group home, usually consisting of 6 to 12 youngsters who reside in a community home with staff. If a child is in need of greater structure, the child can be placed in a residential treatment facility.

Treatment Programs

Often, when a youngster comes into treatment, he or she provides a fuller picture of the family. If a family member's alcoholism is identified as a contributor to the child's problems, a range of interventions is available to the child and the family, depending upon resources available in the placement setting. For example, if the child is placed away from the home, the child's return to the home can be made conditional on the parents' acceptance of help for the alcoholism problem. The threat of having the child placed away from the home, or of not being returned permanently to the home, may be a strong motivation for a parent to address his or her alcoholism initially. In other cases, residential treatment facilities may bring family members in for regular contact with the adolescent during placement. Through this method, all members of the family can receive counseling, following the standard intervention models.

While it is highly desirable to involve the family, quite a bit of work can still be done with the youngsters in cases where families are either not available, or are resistant to any involvement. As our intake survey indicated, many children of alcoholics who enter a juvenile facility have their own alcohol or drug abuse problems. In these cases, our experience has been that it is most effective to have the adolescent address parental alcohol abuse first as a way of "de-dramatizing" their own usage. Adolescents at a juvenile facility frequently exhibit much bravado concerning their own alcohol and drug abuse. Focusing on the parental drinking problems allows the youngster to admit that alcohol abuse does cause people serious problems without directly admitting their own loss of control, at least initially. Children of alcoholics are best treated initially as part of Alateen, and in short-term groups that focus first on parental drinking, and then on their own alcohol and drug abuse.

Self-Identification and Motivation

Sometimes, youngsters not identified during intake as coming from an alcoholic home later identify this as a problem. This is most likely to take place if a climate of acceptance has been established by counselors. At Berkshire Farm Center, one short-term group was established for boys identified at intake as children of alcoholics. Boys being treated in this group then began to identify peers as being in need of this service. Staff members began to ask more questions about alcohol problems among the boys and their families, and began to find that many more youths identified such problems when asked about them.

Information about alcoholism and children of alcoholics was provided in staff training sessions, and a traditional alcohol awareness week was held at the facility. The boys also received information on alcohol via affective education techniques in the classroom, as well as in individual and group counseling sessions. The response was significant. What motivated these boys to seek help with their own and family alcohol problems? Children in the juvenile justice system have been identified as being "the problem" in their families. On some level, most are aware that all is not their fault. No matter how "hardened" they may appear, they all are concerned about family members and are trying to help their families.

Sensitizing the Juvenile Justice System

The experience at Berkshire Farm and Center for Youth is rare. More juvenile justice facilities need to become aware of the familial alcoholism crises experienced by the youth in their charge. If we are to freely address this problem, however, we must not only train staff at juvenile facilities, but also train family court judges, probation officers, and community mental health personnel—all of whom are involved with problem youngsters prior to their admission to the juvenile justice system.

Will addressing family and personal alcohol problems early prevent the type of deterioration of the family and the child that results in juvenile offenses? On the basis of our experience, we would say "yes," but this needs to be documented through research, as do a number of other issues. What interventions work best with which clientele? What sequence of interventions portends the best results? The investigation of such questions raise additional concerns. For example, should alcoholism evaluation or treatment also be mandated whenever child abuse occurs? Such policy might require training for child protective workers, as well as a change in the confidentiality regulations covering alcoholism treatment. Preventing involvement with the juvenile justice system and facilitating intervention with troubled families are important objectives for the juvenile justice system. There is great potential for success, but only if this area receives attention from researchers, treatment professionals, juvenile justice workers, and policymakers.

Chapter Fourteen

Adolescent Substance Abuse and the Role of Families, Schools, and Communities

By Tim Allen

No Man Is An Island

No man is an island, entire of itself;
Every man is a piece of the continent,
A part of the main;
If a clod be washed away by the sea,
Europe is the lesser;
As well as if a promontory were,
As well as if a manor of thy friends,
Or of thine own were;
Any man's death diminishes me,
Because I am involved in mankind;
And therefore never send to know
    for whom the bell tolls
It tolls for thee.

John Donne

Many centuries ago in English seacoast towns, the local town crier would ring a bell if residents of the village were lost or killed at sea. When the bell sounded, a member of seagoing families would be sent to find out "for whom the bell tolled." If the bell signaled the loss of a member of another village resident, a sense of relief and happiness was experienced by all but the grieving families. The point of Donne's poem is that each man's death is a loss to all mankind.

It is this timeless realization which establishes the necessary focus on adolescents and their use of, abuse of, and dependency on chemicals. Each year, studies indicate the mortality rate of adolescents and young adults increases. Most of these deaths can be attributed directly to drug and alcohol related accidents or situations. These findings are tragic, as our nation's most valuable resource, young human life, is diminished by a force which can be dealt with effectively.

The realization that the existing problem can be handled, has moved several communities and school districts to address this issue. Certain barriers must be overcome and new information must be provided, however, in order for old ideas and attitudes to be changed and replaced. Where adolescent chemical abuse is concerned, attitudes still are marked by much confusion and ambiguity. There is no concensus or consistent public attitude toward adolescent chemical abuse. For some, adolescent chemical use has become "normal" and "typical kid behavior."

The primary barrier to overcome, then, is the pervasive denial that a problem does exist. This attitude is evident in almost every community, every school system, and every family throughout the country. Most systems will admit that if a problem does exist, it is probably worse in other cities, schools, or families. The fact remains: The slightest indication of the existence of a chemical problem must be addressed quickly and correctly, rather than overlooked or minimized. Even when it is not clearly evident, the chances are great that there actually is a need for concern and for the creation of some type of program to address the problems and concerns related to chemical use and abuse. Among adolescents, the use and abuse of chemicals has reached almost epidemic proportions, with far-reaching and even devastating results. Each year, various studies provide statistics which indicate all age levels continue to increase consumption of chemicals, with the concurrent increase of social and family problems. Aggressive and disruptive behavior and deterioration of academic performance, as well as other problems related to adolescent chemical use, continue to increase. Whatever else the statistics may reveal about increased chemical use, they confirm the existence of the problem, deny it as we may, and demand that it be addressed.

In the past, communities and school districts have expressed a sense of hopelessness and helplessness. As people became more aware and more angry at the senseless loss of human life and potential, active substance abuse programs began to emerge. Groups of parents, educators, and community members coordinated efforts, gained insights necessary to create a change, gathered information, assessed needs, and created effective programs. Control was returned to families and to school campuses and classrooms as mutually acceptable standards were developed and enforced (See Figure 1).

Throughout the late '60s and early '70s, children were allowed to "do their own thing." They were "Spocked," not spanked. They grew up in what came to be labeled as the "me-oriented society." Many children grew up lacking clear-cut standards, guidelines, and controls. By 1978 and 1979, the NIDA household survey on drug abuse reported over 10% of the high school seniors were smoking marijuana daily. Many others were drinking on a regular basis and experimenting with other illegal drugs. This increased chemical abuse resulted in increased problems for schools and families. Violence on campus, discipline problems and disruptive behavior, and student walkouts and demonstrations all increased.

Programs were developed to ease the tension and to focus on the "drug culture." "Innovative" programs were funded by federal and state agencies. Quite often, the funds ran out after a couple of years, and programs were discontinued. These programs failed primarily because of the lack of consistent understanding of how to develop, create, and sustain changes in the system, and because the focus of education was primarily on the pharmacology of drugs alone, rather than on all other pertinent and relevant factors as well. Topics which were not addressed included: the concept of alcoholism as a disease; the stages of dependency; how substance abuse affects the family; "how to say no;" the true facts about drugs and alcohol, and much more.

The '80s, however, have become the time for real change. Grassroots efforts are resulting in communities, schools, and parent groups working together closely to solve a common problem. These groups are learning that, in order to make an impact and to be successful, programs designed to address drug and alcohol abuse must be comprehensive and include many of the following components:

1. Educational programs, techniques, and strategies;
2. All-inclusive prevention programs, K-12;
3. Awareness programs covering a variety of topics from substance abuse to sexual abuse;
4. Discipline procedures and policies, well defined and articulated;

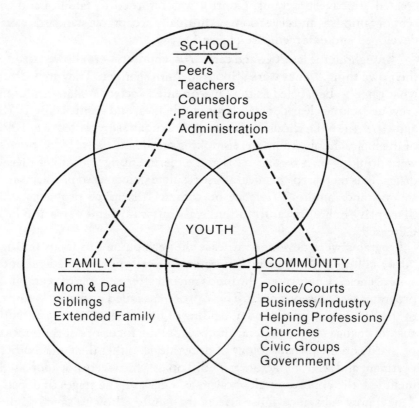

FIGURE I

5. Identification procedures for students with problems;
6. Intervention strategies and techniques;
7. Referral resources available in the community;
8. Treatment programs identified and reviewed.

Developing Community Programs

Successful programs must have clear support from the community, and have adequate and up-to-date materials and resources. Implementation must be performed by knowledgeable professionals.

The following concepts must be presented and accepted when implementation takes place.

1. Chemical use and abuse by an individual affects every individual with whom he/she comes in contact. Therefore, the problem is a "systems" (either family, school or community) problem.
2. To solve the problem, those involved must realize the most effective role they can play, and the limitations of that role.
3. To treat an individual effectively who has a chemical-related problem, the entire family also must be treated.
4. The "no-talk" rule, which characterizes chemically dependent families, also characterizes schools and communities, and it must be broken.
5. The "blame game" must be stopped. Instead of parents blaming the schools, and schools blaming parents about the problems with kids, attention needs to be focused on the problems themselves before behaviors and attitudes can be changed and/or treated in the proper manner.
6. Involved persons must accept equal responsibility for helping to solve the problem—no more, no less.
7. Once responsibility has been accepted, each group must identify areas where change or influence is a reality.
8. Each group must support and facilitate the other in its endeavors.
9. Communication between groups is essential.
10. A common set of goals and standards must be agreed upon.
11. A task force of representatives is mandatory.

With the above serving as a foundation, action can begin. The "no talk" rule can be broken, and open and honest discussion can be achieved at all levels. As community-based programs emerge initially, they should provide parents and community members with factual and accurate information regarding chemical dependence as a disease affecting the entire family. Parents also benefit from programs regarding ways to recognize signs and symptoms of chemical dependence, as well as ways to intervene and how to accomplish intervention in the most appropriate and effective manner. Other community programs can focus on any or all of the following:

1. Parenting skills and techniques
2. Communication skills
3. "Normal" versus "abnormal" adolescent behavior
4. Functional versus dysfunctional families.

Each of the above topics may be expanded for a series of presentations. Development of programs centered on these topics should be in conjunction with the school. The central focus of each program should stress:

1. The importance of developing a solid set of standards for children which are reasonable, fair, and enforced in a consistent and loving manner;
2. Children's need for boundaries and limitations. Children who are in control because they are under control feel better about themselves;
3. The concept of "tough love," i.e., loving children enough to say no, set limits, and enforce rules.

Another area in which community programs can be of benefit is with parents who need to find help for the family. Sometimes, the decision of parents to seek help for their child is a difficult one. When a decision finally is made, the same questions arise in almost every family. How do I know if there is a problem? Where can I go for help? Are there any guarantees that treatment will work? What happens if either during or after treatment my child uses again? The questions, the fears, and concerns are endless. (The following may be excerpted and shared with parents.)

1. How do you know if a problem exists?

The teenage years at best are difficult for both the family and the teenager. This time is characterized by many changes, both physical and emotional. However, when changes are drastic and severe, it is time to find out if what is happening is normal teenage behavior, or is worthy of serious concern. If any of the following signs is apparent, a call for an assessment to determine the seriousness of the problem must be made as soon as possible.

a. Attendance at school is falling off;
b. Increased tardiness;

c. Grades beginning to drop;
d. Physical appearance and dress beginning to change;
e. Friends changing, and increased secrecy regarding activities and friends;
f. Significant increase or decrease in weight;
g. Increased defiance and anger when given direction;
h. Changes in drinking habits;
i. Severe mood swings;
j. Increase in minor illnesses or injuries;
k. Running away from home;
l. Increased behavior problems at school;
m. Use of drugs or alcohol noticeably increasing;
n. Problems with law enforcement;
o. No longer interested in extra-curricular activities at school;
p. Items or money missing from the home;
q. Mention of suicide;
r. Increase in lying;
s. Problems with inter-personal relationships;
t. Problems with family relationships.

Basically, parents must ask themselves whether they are happy and satisfied with the way things are with their families. If the answer is "no" or "sometimes," then the parents need to seek help.

When youngsters become involved with chemicals, the progression of use develops in stages. First, they experiment. Most often, they begin merely to satisfy curiosity and be part of the crowd. Next, they move into a social use period, where they use at parties or on special occasions. Often there are no serious consequences involved. Third, their use pattern changes. They use more frequently; friends and interests begin to change; they schedule activities around the use of chemicals; grades drop; attendance falls off; and sometimes, they begin to violate their value system by doing things they would not have considered prior to using chemicals. At some point, they lose control. They try to stop, but can't. Their usage increases and they get high or intoxicated during the week, at school, or at other "inappropriate" times (there are no appropriate times for teenagers to be intoxicated). The chemical becomes the focal point of their life, to which they constantly return to cope with life's problems and difficulties. If a parent is constantly worried and upset about the child's severe mood swings, inconsistent behavior, refusal to obey, not coming home at night, etc., it is time to ask for help.

2. Where do you go for help?

a. There are several places to begin: (1) Family doctor; (2) School counselor administrator; (3) Drug treatment center/private therapist; (4) Alcoholics/Narcotics Anonymous.

Call someone for a referral to a program which can provide an assessment and evaluation. Some problems may be resolved easily and quickly, if they are addressed early, while others are much more complicated and will require specialized treatment.

b. Once a referral has been made, a call must be made immediately. Don't allow a small change in behavior or a promise made by the youngster to change your mind.

c. Question the agency to which a referral has been made regarding professional credentials. Make sure that the staff members have college degrees and/or professional licenses or certificates.

d. Ask for references. Successful programs have a reputation developed by providing quality care and services to their families. Talk to people who have been involved in the program; talk to several people, rather than just a few.

e. Be aware that quality programs will provide a component of treatment which involves the entire family, not just the identified client. Research on successful treatment programs is consistent in mentioning that successful treatment is in direct proportion to the amount of active family involvement, the development of consistency in dealing with family problems, and the ability of the family to follow through with the entire program.

f. If there is a suspicion that drug and alcohol abuse is involved, make certain that the program or the therapist understands chemical dependence and insists the client remain chemically free as a condition of treatment.

g. If hospitalization is recommended in the first session, always obtain a second opinion.

3. Once treatment is selected, is there a guarantee of success?

a. Very simply, there is never a guarantee that treatment will be successful. However, the rate of success depends on the involvement of the entire family, including mother, father, brother, sister, step-parents, etc.

b. The only guarantee is that treatment will not be successful if the identified client is the only person expected to change.

c. If parents are not satisfied with the amount of family involvement, they must insist on more.

d. While treatment is continuing, it is important to involve the school to some degree. The school can provide positive support to both the family, the client, and the treatment program. This can be accomplished by developing support groups on campus, along with the monitoring of attendance and grades.

When appropriate and when based upon suggestions by the treatment program, attendance at support groups, such as Alcoholics Anonymous, Narcotics Anonymous, Cocaine Anonymous, etc., may be necessary to support those who find it difficult to remain free from chemicals.

4. What happens if the child goes back to drugs after treatment?

a. Parents need to accept that there is always a possibility of a child slipping, and returning to chemical use, even after involvement in a treatment program. Expecting treatment immediately to solve all the problems is not a realistic expectation. Lasting change takes much time and hard work. Should an adolescent "slip," it does not mean the treatment has been unsuccessful or a waste of money.

b. Problems, even in the best of situations, can flare up, go away, and flare up again. Be prepared to face these problems immediately by drawing on the tools developed throughout treatment, and try to avoid falling back into the same behavior patterns which existed prior to treatment.

c. If these "flare ups" cannot be resolved quickly within the family, return immediately to the treatment program for support and direction.

Parents and parent groups can be powerful sources of support and assistance for one another. Programs may be considered which also include parent support groups. These groups can focus on and facilitate much of what is listed above. More importantly, they can provide support for enforcement of standards and follow through when tasks need to be accomplished. Some additional ideas for what parent groups can accomplish are:

1. Developing letters and a statement of concern regarding chemical use/abuse. Send these out to all parents.

2. Publish a set of standards and party rules in local newspapers and newsletters which support school policies.

3. Develop hotlines for students in trouble with drugs or alcohol.

4. Raise money for films or other materials which can be used in school prevention programs.

5. Raise money to pay for teacher training, staff development work-

shops, and student awareness programs.
6. Identify and interview local agencies and resources. The information gathered can be distributed to schools, parents, and other community groups.

Developing A School Program

Schools must also learn and incorporate the concept of "tough love" into the system, and also develop a set of standards consistent with community beliefs. Having policies and procedures either too harsh or too lenient, or inconsistently or unfairly enforced, hinders more than it helps youngsters in need of guidance. Clearly, it is evident that intensive education programs are effective. They can, if properly developed and presented, effect significant changes in attitudes and behavior of adolescents, teachers, staff of the school, parents, and community members. Therefore, effective programs developed within a school system will take much time, energy, commitment, and a great deal of patience. Typically and historically, school programs have been developed which have had limited success (see Figure II). Most traditional substance abuse programs have been focused primarily on prevention, education and awareness. Prevention programs normally are designed to enhance self-esteem, to assist in developing and clarifying values, to teach decision-making skills, and to provide valuable, factual information about drugs and alcohol. The most effective prevention activities are accomplished at grade levels K through sixth grade.

Providing "awareness" programs at the school level is another typical approach to substance abuse. Normally, these programs center around all-school assemblies on drugs, movies about drug/alcohol-related issues, or classroom guest speakers, including representatives from local treatment centers, narcotics officers, and recovering adults/alcoholics. The effects of these programs are short-lived, and are often forgotten until the following year when it is "time" for the "program" to be offered again. Educational programs usually consist of a prescribed unit in the health curriculum. The focus usually is on the pharmacology of drugs, with a few guest speakers and "scare tactic" movies included.

Each of the above programs certainly serves an important purpose and can have a positive and lasting effect on some students. However, these programs seem to have the greatest effect on students who have not begun using drugs, or who are in the stage of early experimentation.

Students who have progressed to frequent misuse/abuse, or to chemical dependence pay very little attention to material and information presented through these means. Many school districts support and enforce very severe disciplinary procedures when students are involved with chemicals on campus or at school activities. By enforcing a well-publicized discipline policy, all students can—and often will—be affected drastically. This approach succeeds in keeping drugs off campus and away from school activities. While accomplishing this, however, the problem only re-emerges elsewhere in the community.

At the other end of the continuum (Figure II), there are approaches which are classified as "crisis intervention." As an adolescent progresses to frequent use, abuse, or active dependency, it is almost certain a crisis will occur. He/she might appear on campus or at an activity under the influence and cause trouble, grades may suddenly drop, attendance may become erratic, interests may change, or values may be compromised or totally disregarded. When this happens, the school is forced into a reactive response, and what results are severe, negative consequences for the student. A parent conference may take place, and the student may be suspended, with a referral to an outside agency for treatment of the adolescent often being made as well. Again, these approaches can be effective for both the individual and the family. Such approaches usually do not serve to identify young people who are in the experimental or social use phase, however, nor do they serve the students who do not use chemicals. For these populations, other approaches are needed.

What Is The Answer? (Figure III)

In developing an effective approach to deal with all aspects of the problem, to impact both the school and the community, and to break through the denial, all of the noted components above must be maintained. However, the scope of each component must be expanded and developed further. The focus has to be on the entire school population, including faculty, staff, students, parents, and the entire community.

Before this new program is developed, the following can be helpful in developing a philosophy and a basis for the program.

1. Students with low self-esteem are likely to become involved with chemicals. They often use drugs to medicate pain and to "feel good." They are highly susceptible to peer pressure.
2. Parents and other family members are role models. In families where

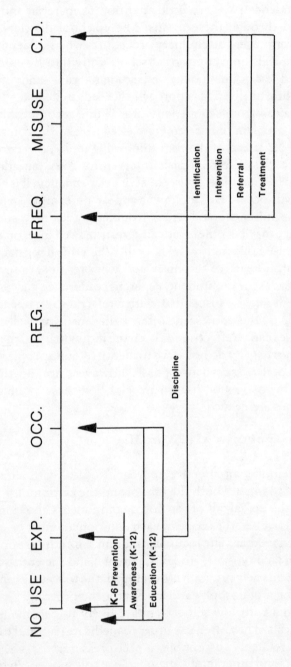

TYPICAL SUBSTANCE ABUSE PROGRAMS

NO USE   EXP.   OCC.   REG.   FREQ.   MISUSE   C.D.

K-6 Prevention
Awareness (K-12)
Education (K-12)

Discipline

Ientification
Intevention
Referral
Treatment

FIGURE II

there are poor relationships, or a great deal of stress, there are likely to be children who will turn to drugs. If children see their parents dealing with the normal stresses of life by turning to drugs, they also will assume that drugs will eliminate any problems in life.

3. Experimentation is directly related to peer pressure. Peer pressure today is less overt than it used to be. Often, it is an individual saying to himself, "I wonder what they will think of me if I say 'no?' They probably will think less of me, so I'll go along." Nonetheless, it remains an important reason why many young people experiment.

4. Use of drugs highly correlates with other negative, self-destructive behaviors, such as truancy, poor grades, problems with the law, depressions, suicide, changes in attitudes, friends, and interests, etc.

5. Kids use drugs for the same reasons adults do—to feel good, to have fun, and because "there is nothing else to do." Boredom is a common reason listed by many young people as a reason for drug use.

6. Many adolescents experience a sense of helplessness and hopelessness, accompanied by a sense of aimlessness and a lack of clear-cut goals.

7. If there is a history of chemical dependency in a family, these children are at a much higher risk than other students.

With this information as a "given," the successful program will address each of the above statements in each and every component of the program (see Figure III).

Another important aspect, pertinent to the creation of a philosophy, is the importance of developing a new awareness regarding adolescent chemical use. An atmosphere of care and concern must be pervasive on a school campus, as well as throughout the community. Adolescent chemical use must not be tolerated, although the school authorities may punish them for their use. Those who experience problems related to use of chemicals should know there also will be an honest effort to provide help and assistance to both the student and the parent.

To expand the traditional prevention, education and awareness program, the following information should be included:

1. Wherever possible, throughout the curriculum, the seven items previously listed must be addressed over and over.

2. Chemical dependency is a disease which is primary, progressive, chronic, and fatal.

3. Accurate and up-to-date information regarding drugs must be presented in a matter-of-fact way, avoiding the "preachy" attitude common in "scare tactic" techniques.

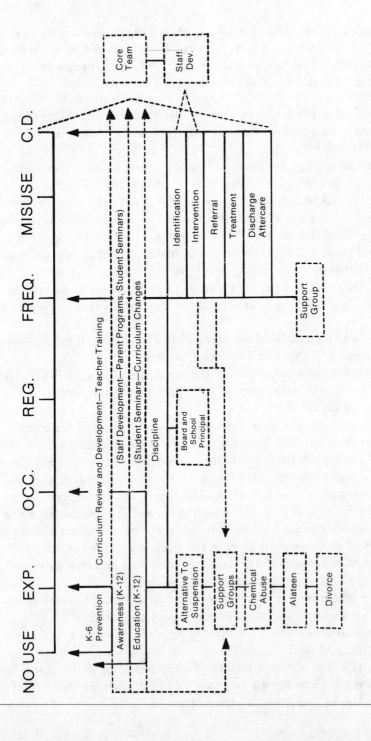

FIGURE III

4. Information on how chemical use and abuse affects the entire family and helps to create roles for family members which may affect all present and future relationships.
5. Specific information regarding children of alcoholics must be presented to all students.

The above information can be taught in many areas of the curriculum. Once faculty and staff have had training conducted by knowledgeable professionals, they can decide easily where appropriately to include the necessary information. Of course, the first curricular areas on which to focus are the health and science programs. Social studies is another area where it is quite easy to include information regarding chemical abuse and dependency issues in the course of study. To reinforce the curriculum, development of support groups for students are extremely important. Once certain issues are addressed in the classroom, and students realize the school will support a request for help, support groups fill up quickly.

Some themes around which support groups for students can be developed are:

1. Young people expressing concern about their own use;
2. Alternatives to suspension for students who have been caught using chemicals at school or school activities;
3. Living in an alcoholic family;
4. Dealing with divorce;
5. Physical or sexual abuse issues;
6. Eating disorders;
7. Self-esteem issues;
8. Dealing with authority;
9. Attendance;
10. Suicide;
11. Students presently involved in treatment, or returning from a treatment center.

Students come to these groups in a variety of ways:

1. Referred by a concerned teacher;
2. Referred by a guidance counselor or nurse;
3. Referred by an administrator;
4. Referred by a parent;
5. Self-referral;
6. Referral by an outside agency.

Groups such as these begin rather small. Typically, they grow rapidly, as participants ask for friends to be included in the groups.

These groups can be publicized through the school bulletin and newspaper, parent newsletter, posters, and by teachers in the classroom. To keep the awareness level high, planned seminars, assemblies, and workshops are critical. These should address not only students, but teachers, other staff members, parents, and community groups. Some topics for these programs may include:

1. How to handle peer pressure;
2. Developing communication skills;
3. Developing human potential (self-esteem);
4. Stages of adolescent chemical dependency;
5. How to know if a problem exists;
6. Enabling behaviors and how to help friends in trouble;
7. Children of alcoholics;
8. Understanding the advertising idustry and alcohol use;
9. Decision-making skills;
10. Positive peer pressure and positive role models.

Note: Once again, each of the above can be developed into a series of programs. This information must be presented in a factual, objective, non-judgmental manner.

Also important in the development of a successful and effective school substance abuse program is the presence of a firm, fair, well-thought-out and consistently implemented discipline policy. The procedure to follow will take time and will necessitate a step-by-step approach:

1. Evaluate effectiveness of present discipline policies and procedures, to ensure they are meeting present needs.
2. Coordinate all policies and procedures throughout the school district.
3. The review of policies and procedures should include staff, parents, students, and community members.
4. Standards of behavior which are acceptable and unacceptable must be agreed upon, written up, distributed, and discussed with those whom they will affect.
5. Policies regarding procedures to be followed when violations occur must be established and implemented in a fair and consistent manner.

When expanding the identification, intervention, referral and treatment aspects of the program, the purpose is to move away from a crisis or "reactive" approach towards a more "primitive" or preventive approach. The strategies needed should be designed to provide for early identification and intervention so referrals and treatment can occur early in the progression of chemical involvement. To do this requires the following steps to be taken:

1. Develop and implement an awareness program for staff and teachers regarding discipline policy, procedures for handling, how to notice problems needing immediate attention, and what to do when those problems are noticed.
2. Develop a means for identification of students exhibiting unacceptable behavior or behavior about which the staff is concerned.
3. Develop a procedure for handling identified students, and ways to track disposition of each referral mode.
4. Develop a plan and procedure for sharing information received with the parents of students.
5. Develop a follow-up plan, and a way to monitor students referred.
6. Develop a system for reporting effectiveness of the program, by tracking the number of students referred, referrals made to outside agencies, disposition, follow-up on grades, attendance, etc.

Once a problem has been identified, it is important that it be handled immediately. Normally, problems with students require a parent conference. Most parent conferences consist of a school person providing the parents with accounts of unacceptable behavior by the student. By gathering data which is factual and observable ("He smelled of alcohol" and "his speech was slurred"), rather than subjective or judgmental ("He was loaded;" "Your son is an alcoholic"), and presenting the information with care and concern, you can make the parent conference into a positive, helping experience, rather than an uncomfortable confrontation. To achieve this, try to accomplish the following steps:

1. Train willing staff members to understand the basic concept of intervention.
2. Identify a team of people who will evaluate information on referrals and who can decide upon the type and extent of the intervention necessary.
3. Have teams (two to three staff members) meet regularly to discuss referrals and the appropriate action to be taken.
4. Develop procedures for the handling of crisis situations such as drug/alcohol overdoses, suicide attempts, physical violence, etc.
5. Have a list of resources available to be presented immediately for families who require referral.

After an intervention has been completed, the family will need to be referred for an evaluation or an assessment. Prior to preparing an intervention, and furnishing a list of providers available to families, you should:

1. Identify and interview several agencies in the community which specialize in chemical dependency.
2. Develop a questionnaire for agencies to complete and return. The questionnaire may include the following: (a) areas of specialization; (b) services provided; (c) amount of family involvement; (d) cost of assessments; (e) time of assessments; (f) expected time lapse between inquiry, call, and appointment; (g) cost of total program; (h) availability of sliding payment plan; (i) type of after-care program; (j) amount and type of follow-up with referral source.

When a student has been referred for treatment, it is important for the parents and the student to know that the school supports their efforts. Both parents and students are likely to feel a lasting stigma attached to hospitalization or psychotherapy, which the school can diffuse in several ways:

1. Identify and assign a staff member to maintain contact with the student while in treatment.
2. Maintain contact with the provider of treatment for the student so efforts to support treatment at the school level are appropriate and not counter-therapeutic.
3. Develop a support group on campus designed for students who currently are in outpatient treatment, or who have returned from an inpatient treatment program.
4. Develop and provide to students and families lists of community resources which provide self-help groups. These may include Alcoholics Anonymous, Narcotics Anonymous, Cocaine Anonymous, Step-Families Anonymous, Families Anonymous, etc.

The development of a successful and lasting program requires the commitment of much time and energy. It requires the education of the entire school staff, from bus drivers to the district superintendent. It requires the support of the community by providing funds to develop staff and purchase materials. It requires public support of standards established by the district. It requires a limited focus on issues that are specific to a particular community and school, and not a global focus. It requires a realization that adolescent chemical use is a problem for everyone, not just for those who have children.

The Schools and the Children of Alcoholics

To this point, the focus of this chapter has been general, but there is one population within the school setting which needs special attention. Children of alcoholics comprise approximately 25% of the school population. With these youngsters at such great risk to be chemically dependent themselves, it is imperative that schools address this issue. Once again, before addressing the problem directly with the identified population, proper information must be provided to the staff by qualified professionals. From the outset, school personnel must realize their limitations and not become involved in treating either the children or their alcoholic parents. Focus needs to be on supporting and validating the children, and involving them in the entire school-based substance abuse program, as well as focusing on other specific areas, either through seminars and curriculum development, or in support groups. Topics may include:

1. The family dynamics of alcoholism, and how children may be affected.
2. How to get in touch with personal feelings, and how to express these appropriately.
3. How to relate to the chemically dependent individual, and how to take care of yourself when closely involved.
4. How to talk about your life without fear that you will not be believed, or that there may be retaliation.
5. How to develop trust in yourself and others.
6. How to make decisions and understand you do have choices in your life.

Working with children of alcoholics as an educator requires a special sensitivity. In the classroom, in support groups, working individually with the CoA, or even as a general school policy, the following tips are always helpful.

1. Create an environment which is psychologically and emotionally safe.
2. Maintain an environment and policies which are predictable and consistent.
3. Accept feelings and help children to express feelings in an appropriate and safe way.
4. Encourage activities which are age-appropriate, fun, and involve much group interaction.
5. Create situations where trust can be developed with peers.

Children of alcoholics need much support and understanding. Teachers and other school personnel must understand that living in an alcoholic environment affects the child's ability to learn and, therefore, hinders the teacher's ability to perform the primary task of teaching. It is important the teachers are provided instruction in this area, carried on by competent and knowledgeable professionals.

Some Cautions and Some Helpful Hints

Developing a program in the schools and the communities is an extremely difficult and time-consuming task. If program developers and participants are not careful, there can be some personal problems which may arise. Chemical dependency is both a family and a systems disease. In the family, the members contract "co-dependency," in which they experience and exhibit many of the symptoms and behaviors of the dependent individual. They experience and exhibit denial; they lose control of themselves while trying to control the dependent's chemical; they develop a tolerance for inappropriate behavior, which they soon perceive as normal; they avoid the problem and minimize the seriousness of the problem; they exhibit sneaky behavior, by hiding or disposing of the alcohol or drugs, or by secretly attending meetings and support groups. Individuals who don't understand the concept of co-dependency often are set up for a tremendous amount of frustration when working with adolescents involved or affected by chemicals. They become caught up in a circle of trying to help, eliciting promises, seeing the promises broken over and over, while new promises are made and no changes noticed.

Most teachers and other helping professionals are interested in seeing people receive help. When working with people affected by their own, or other's chemical use, however, they can become frustrated quickly. The frustration soon leads to anger because the people whom the professional is attempting to help listen attentively, promise change, yet stay as they are. The growing anger leads to attempts to force movement and sometimes ends with statements and behavior which cause a separation and a moving apart, leading to isolation of both parties. When the professional isolates him/herself, the people he/she is trying and hoping to help the most do not get that help. This then leads to guilt, as the professional feels incompetent or ashamed, because of an inability to perform the job. Resentment develops, professional abilities are questioned, feelings of inferiority develop, self-esteem falls, and depression results. This person then becomes a prime candidate for BURNOUT. To avoid these problems, teachers and helping professionals must learn to:

1. Recognize your own limitations when dealing with chemically dependent persons or families.
2. Learn about enabling behaviors and avoid them when working with all types of people.
3. Set limits for yourself and ask for help when feeling overwhelmed by the complexity and frustrations of developing the program.
4. Utilize your own support system and develop a group of people to help with the total program.
5. Recognize and understand that lasting change takes time, and that programs will succeed if based upon sound theory of change.
6. Understand theories of motivation of groups to: (a) develop a set of goals related to the values of the group; (b) make others feel stronger and more powerful; (c) impart a sense of urgency concerning these goals; and, (d) build expectations among people so they can solve their own problems effectively.

Creating Change

When developing a plan for change within a system, the success of the implementation phase will be in direct proportion to the amount of prior effective communication which has occurred. If effective communication has taken place, many objections can be overcome, problems anticipated, and a plan for problem-solving designed. It is essential that plans for communicating throughout the process be made and maintained. For the change to be lasting, there must be a feeling of trust, concern, and confidence that the change taking place is in the best interests of the system and the individuals who are part of that system. To achieve acceptance of the new program, there must be a great deal of information sharing. Results of any needs assessment must be shared and discussed. Goals developed as a result of the needs assessment also must be shared, discussed and changed accordingly. The entire process must be monitored closely and evaluated constantly. Information gained in the evaluation process must be shared openly and honestly with all concerned.

To develop successful and lasting change requires excellent leadership abilities. It takes individuals who are concerned, who understand the system, who understand the theory behind human motivation, and who are willing to commit time, energy, and effort to accomplish a difficult task. People who are successful leaders are able to delegate authority and to trust that the job will be done well. These individuals also understand that any kind of change will take time, with mistakes an inescapable part of the process. For these people, mistakes are opportunities for learning and growth. When developing new programs, successful leaders are constantly communicating with those involved and are committed to a strong staff development program based on the identified needs of the staff. In order to provide quality staff development programs, these individuals keep up with the latest innovations. Their vision is always to the future, and they are always prepared for the unexpected. These people are open to change. Rather than looking back at the past, making excuses for why things can't be done, these people spend their time devising a new way to solve problems. They are creative in their approaches to new problems, and often don't worry about "putting out fires" in the present. Planning for the future takes most of the time, rather than considering the past and the present. The following diagram illustrates the way it should look (see Figure 4).

SUMMARY OF CREATING CHANGE
IN A SCHOOL SYSTEM
PHASE ONE: IDENTIFY GOALS AND DETERMINE NEEDS

A. Identify leader and team.
B. Determine responsibilities of team members.
C. Review current goals and objectives of program (if any).
D. Set new goals for team.
E. Establish time lines.

PHASE TWO: PLANNING AND IMPLEMENTATION

A. Assess individual and team attitudes.
B. Identify groups to be assessed.
C. Develop assessment instrument.
D. Identify problem groups and possible reasons for resistance.
E. Identify support systems.
F. Plan for resistance reduction.
G. Identify necessary resources presently available.
H. Identify necessary resources not presently available.
I. Identify financial needs.
J. Develop strategies for implementation.

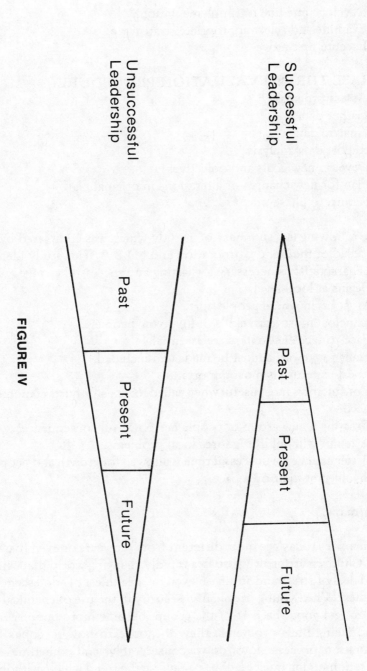

FIGURE IV

K. Develop time line for implementation.
L. Examine and select appropriate strategy.
M. Execute first move.

PHASE THREE: EVALUATION PROCEDURE
A. Assess progress.
B. Gather data.
C. Analyze data.
D. Report data analysis.
E. Develop new goals and objectives.
F. Plan for new changes or alterations in original plan.
G. Return to phase one.

The following is a summary of a study which was completed by John Goodlad of the Rand Corporation and I.D.E.A. This study identified ten characteristics necessary for lasting and successful change.
1. Begins at local level.
2. Must begin where people hurt.
3. Principal must learn skills of involving people.
4. Face-to-face encounters are essential.
5. Plans for rewards must be made and included.
6. Local expertise is most important.
7. Consultant is most useful when called for specific hurts at moment of need.
8. Creating a new group of people has powerful consequences.
9. Attempt will fail if it ignores local problems.
10. Better chance for success if time is allowed for growth and people are involved at their own pace.

Summary

Lifestyles today are quite different from ten years or even five years ago. Children are growing up in a rapidly changing world that causes a good deal of stress and strain on even the healthiest of adolescents and families. When young people find security in the use of chemicals as a way to feel good, be part of the group, become more popular, or to avoid facing life's problems, they do not learn how to cope. Their maturation process slows down considerably, and sometimes even stops. Something must be done to reverse the trend which is leading to the destruction of a generation.

There is hope. The 1984 NIDA Household Survey indicated a continued decline in daily use of marijuana and alcohol. It appears young people are becoming more inclined to take better care of their bodies and to look differently at chemical use, but complacency must be avoided at all costs. Being a teenager in today's world is difficult, and it is even more difficult to be a parent. The pressure is intense to provide a happy, healthy family environment. School programs can help facilitate the strengthening of the families with whom they work, but schools cannot, nor should they, do it alone. Likewise, families cannot, nor should they, "do it alone." Together they can make a difference.

Action is the word for the 1980s. Successful, effective, and lasting programs must be based upon a sound philosophy and solid research. Steps to create the necessary changs must be taken in a slow, meticulous, well-thought-out and planned manner. The excellent quality of the programs based on the model presented here already is helping children, families, schools, and communities to achieve a better quality of life. Schools have developed a more comfortable climate. Children and families have received needed treatment and attention. Communities have gathered resources, materials and energy to effect significant changes in this situation. They have broken the "no talk" rule. We must, however, constantly keep in mind the necessity of keeping up with new and related information. William Blake said it best:

> "Man's desires are limited by his perceptions;
> None can desire what he has not perceived."

Part Four
Adult Children of Alcoholics:
All Grown Up and No Place to Grow

The largest single group of children of alcoholics in the United States today consists of children of alcoholics who are now adults. These people are "adult children" of alcoholics. Part four addresses the many different impacts from their childhoods that carried into their adult lives. Not all adult children of alcoholics have been or are affected in the same way. Adult children of alcoholics may have had common experiences, but not similar outcomes, because of the many intervening variables that affect these different outcomes. For example, the degree of alcoholism in the alcoholic parent, the type and kind of personality of that parent, the gender of the alcoholic and the gender of the child, the age of the child when alcoholism developed in the parent, cultural considerations and the perception of the child about the experience all will affect children of alcoholics differently. However, in chapter fifteen Janet Woititz describes many common characteristics developed by adults who had at least one alcoholic parent. Herbert Gravitz and Julie Bowden, in chapter sixteen, discuss working with children of alcoholics in therapy, and the issues that are likely to be presented. Chapter seventeen, by Joseph Kern, is concerned with the many adult children of alcoholics who now work in the substance abuse treatment field. It addresses the personal and professional issues for the adult child, and discusses the dangers of duplicating the "alcoholic family" environment in the work setting. Suzanne Anderson, in chapter eighteen, offers insights and guidelines for therapists working with black adult children of alcoholics. Finally, in the last chapter of this book, Jane Middelton-Moz and Lorie Dwinell discuss the need for many adult children of alcoholics to work through the many feelings and issues that dominate their adult lives as a result of parental alcoholism during childhood. These issues including working through the feelings of grief, loss, and depression, in order to achieve a healthy adult life.

Chapter Fifteen

Common Characteristics of Adult Children from Alcoholic Families

Janet G. Woititz

The child grows into an adult, and we all know what an adult is . . . until asked to define the word. When we begin to search for the answers, we wonder. What *is* the definition of an adult? It is such a personal definition. Maybe it is that point in life when we sit at the desk where the buck stops. Maybe that is when we become adults . . . the time when we are in charge of our own lives. All people face these questions, which lead to many new questions. We may not even have known what all those questions were, but one thing was clear. We didn't have a lot of answers when we first faced them. The answers came later and slowly.

Living in such uncertainty may shape our adult lives significantly if we experience it during childhood and adolescence, those times when we are forming the values and perspectives with which we will function in the adult world. Emotionally healthy children experience good role models, learn appropriate behavior, and develop a realistic basis for self-esteem and respect for others as they grow through these periods. For children of alcoholics, however, the uncertainty never ends; it extends into and shapes their adult lives in many ways they may not even realize until helped to understand how this has occurred. For them, there exists no clear perspective of reality, no clear role model, no patterns of appropriate behavior, and no consistent basis for developing self-esteem or respect for others. For them, the only

This chapter is based on the author's book, *Adult Children of Alcoholics*. Health Communications, 1983.

certainty is uncertainty.

If you were an adult child of an alcoholic (adult CoA), your entire life would have been shaped by the skewed perspective of life you experienced as a child. If you were an adult CoA, you would have perceived a very different reality on which you based your behavior and your self-image. If you were an adult CoA, you might have lived your entire life without any sense of certainty. What follows is not the result of a scientific study, rather it is a collection of statements adult children of alcoholics [adult CoAs] have made about themselves. All of them are not true of every adult CoA, but all of them are true of adult CoAs as a group, and many of them are true to some extent of all adult CoAs. These statements depict very clearly the extent to which the emotional health of an adult child of an alcoholic is shaped by carryovers from childhood.

1. *Adult children of alcoholics guess at what normal is.*

The significance of this statement cannot be overestimated, as it is their most profound characteristic. Adult children of alcoholics simply have no experience with what is normal.

After all, if you were an adult CoA, how could you have any understanding of normalcy, given your personal history? Your home life varied from slightly mad to extremely bizarre, since this was the only home life you knew. What others would consider "slightly mad" or "extremely bizarre" were usual to you. If there was an occasional day that anyone else would characterize as "normal," it certainly was not typical and therefore could not have had much meaning.

Beyond your chaotic day-to-day life, part of what you did was to live in fantasy. You lived in a world that you created all your own, a world of what life would be like IF . . . what your home would be like IF . . . the way your parents would relate to each other IF . . . the things that would be possible for you IF probably impossible. The unrealistic fantasies about what life would be like if your parent were sober probably helped you survive, but they also added to confusion.

It becomes very clear that even as an adult CoA, you have no frame of reference for what it is like to be in a normal household. You also have no frame of reference for what is okay to say and to feel. In a more typical situation, one does not have to walk on eggs all the time. One doesn't have to question or repress one's feelings all the time. Because you did, you also became confused. Many things from the past contributed to your having to guess at what normal is.

2. *Adult children of alcoholics have difficulty in following a project through from beginning to end.*

The topic one evening in an adult children of alcoholics meeting was procrastination. When I asked the group members to talk about what it meant to them, the opening response was, "I'm the world's biggest procrastinator," or "Somehow I just don't seem to be able to finish anything that I start." These comments are fairly typical, yet it's not too hard to understand why this difficulty exists, because these people are not procrastinators in the usual sense.

In the world of their childhood, the great job was always around the corner. The big deal was always about to be made. The work that needed to be done around the house would be done in no time ... the toy that will be built ... the go-cart ... the doll house ... and on and on. "I'm going to do this, I'm going to do that," but this or that never really happened. Not only did it not happen, but the alcoholic wanted credit for even having had the idea, even for having intending to do it. They grew up in this environment. There were many wonderful ideas, but they were never acted on. If they were, so much time passed that they had forgotten about the original idea.

Who took the time to sit down with them when they had an idea for a project and said, "That's a good idea. How are you going to go about doing it? How long is it going to take? What are the steps involved?" Probably no one. When was it that one of their parents said, "Gee, that idea is terrific! You sure you can do it? Can you break it down into smaller pieces? Can you make it manageable?" Probably never.

This is not to suggest that all parents who do not live with alcohol teach their children how to solve problems, but it is to suggest that at least in a functional family, the child has this behavior and attitude on which to model him/herself. The child observes the process and the child may even ask questions along the way. The learning may be more indirect than direct, but it is present. Since the experience of a CoA is so vastly different, it should be no surprise that they have a problem with following a project through from beginning to end. They have never seen it happen and they don't know how to make it happen. Lack of knowledge is not the same as procrastination.

3. *Adult children of alcoholics lie when it would be just as easy to tell the truth.*

   Lying is basic to the family system affected by alcohol. It masquerades in part as overt denial of unpleasant realities, coverups, broken promises, and inconsistencies. It takes many forms and has many implications. Although it is somewhat different from the kind of lying usually talked about, it certainly is a departure from the truth.

   The first and most basic lie is the family's denial of the problem. So the pretense that everything at home is in order is a lie, and the family rarely discusses the truth openly, even with each other. Perhaps somewhere in their private thoughts there is a recognition of the truth, but there is also the struggle to deny it.

   The next lie, the cover-up, relates to the first. The non-alcoholic family member covers up for the alcoholic member. As the child of an alcoholic, you would have seen your non-alcoholic parent covering up for your alcoholic parent. You would have heard him or her on the phone making excuses for your mother or father for not fulfilling an obligation or for not being on time. That is part of the lie that you would have lived. You also heard a lot of promises from your alcoholic parent. These, too, turned out to be lies.

   Lying as the norm in your house became part of what you knew and what could be useful to you. At times it made life much more comfortable. If you lied about getting your work done, you could get away with being lazy for a while. If you lied about why you couldn't bring a friend home, or why you were late coming home, you could avert unpleasantness. It seemed to make life simpler for everyone. So lying became a habit. That's why the statement, "Adult children of alcoholics lie when it would be just as easy to tell the truth," is relevant. Perhaps it really is not as easy to tell the truth, but lying is what you have heard come so naturally. To admit that "it would be just as easy to tell the truth" would require you to admit that you derive no real benefit from lying, but you have had no experience to confirm such a pattern of behavior.

4. *Adult children of alcoholics judge themselves without mercy.*

   Had you been the child of an alcoholic, there was no way that you were good enough. You were constantly criticized. You believed that your family would be better off without you, because you were the cause of the trouble. You may have been criticized for things that made no sense. "If you weren't such a rotten kid, I wouldn't have to drink." It makes no sense, but if you hear something often enough, for a long-enough period of time, you will end up believing it. As a result, you internalized these criticisms as negative self-feelings, and they persist, even though no one is saying them to you anymore.

Since there is no way for you to meet the standards of perfection that you have internalized from childhood, you are always falling short of the mark you have set for yourself. As a child, whatever you did was not quite good enough. No matter how hard you tried, you should have tried harder. If you got an A it should have been an A+. You were never good enough. A client told me that his mother was so demanding that when he was in basic training, he found the sergeants loose by comparison. So this became a part of you . . . who you are, a part of the way you see yourself. The "shoulds" and "should nots" can become paralyzing after a while.

As an adult CoA, your judgment of others is not nearly as harsh as your judgment of yourself, although it is hard for you to see other people's behavior in terms of a continuum either. Typically you look at things as either black or white, good or bad. Either side presents an awesome responsibility. You know what it feels like to be bad, and how these feelings make you behave. And then, if you are good, there is always the risk that it won't last. So, either way, you set yourself up, either way there is a great amount of pressure on you all of the time. How difficult and stressful life is. How hard it is just to sit back, and relax, and say, "It's okay to be me."

5. *Adult children of alcoholics have difficulty having fun.*
6. *Adult children of alcoholics take themselves very seriously.*

These two characteristics are very closely linked. If you were an adult CoA who had trouble having fun, you would probably be taking yourself very seriously, and if you did not take yourself all that seriously, chances are you could have fun.

Once again, in order to understand this problem you would need to look back at your childhood. How much fun was your childhood? You really would not have to answer that. Children of alcoholics simply do not have much fun. One child of an alcoholic described it as "chronic trauma." You didn't hear your parents laughing and joking and fooling around. Life was a very serious, angry business. You never really learned to play with the other kids. You might have joined in some of the games, but you never were really able to let yourself go and have fun. Even if you could have, it would have been discouraged. The tone around the house put a damper on your fun. Eventually, you just went along with everyone else; having fun just wasn't fun. There was no place for it in your house, you gave it up as an unworkable idea. The spontaneous child within was squashed.

Having fun, being silly, being child-like, is to be foolish. It is no wonder that adult children of alcoholics have difficulty having fun. Life is too serious. Now you have trouble separating yourself from your work, so you take yourself very seriously at whatever job you have to do. You can't take the work seriously and not yourself so you become a prime candidate for burnout. One night a client turned to me with a very angry face and said, "You make me laugh at myself, but I want you to know I don't think it's funny!

7. *Adult children of alcoholics have difficulty with intimate relationships.*

They want very much to have healthy, intimate relationships, but it is extraordinarily difficult for a number of reasons: The first and most obvious is that they have no frame of reference for a healthy, intimate relationship because they have never seen one. The only model they have is their parents, whose relationship was anything but healthy. They also carry with them the experience of "come close, go away," an inconsistency in the loving parent-child relationship. As CoAs, they felt loved one day and rejected the next. The fear of being abandoned was a terrible fear they grew up with. Even if the fear is no longer overwhelming, it certainly gets in the way. Not knowing what it is like to have a consistent, day-to-day, healthy, intimate relationship with another person makes building one very painful and very complicated.

The fear of abandonment gets in the way of developing a relationship. The development of any healthy relationship requires a lot of give and take, and problem-solving. There is always some disagreement and anger which a couple resolves. Any minor disagreement becomes very big quickly for adult children of alcoholics, because the issue of being abandoned takes precedence over the original issue. These overwhelming fears of being abandoned or rejected prevent any ease in the process of developing a relationship. Coupled with a sense of urgency ("This is the only time I have; if I don't do it now, it will never happen.")

this tends to put pressure on the relationship. It makes it much more difficult to evolve slowly, to let two people get to know each other better, and to explore each other's feelings and attitudes in a variety of ways.

This sense of urgency makes the other person feel smothered, even though it is not the intent. I know a couple who have tremendous problems, because whenever they argue she panics and worries that he is now going to leave her. She needs constant reassurance in the middle of the argument that he's not going to leave her, and that he still loves her. When he is in conflict, which is difficult for him as well, he tends to want to withdraw and be by himself. Needless to say, this makes the issue at hand more difficult to resolve than if it were only the issue itself needing to be confronted.

The feelings of being insecure and of having difficulty in trusting, and questions about whether or not you're going to get hurt are not exclusive to adult children of alcoholics. These are problems most people have. Few people enter a relationship fully confident that things are going to work out the way they hope they will. They enter into a relationship hopeful, but with a variety of fears. So, all of the things that cause adult CoAs concern are not unique to them alone. It is simply a matter of degree: being a child of an alcoholic causes the ordinary difficulties to become more severe.

8. *Adult children of alcoholics overreact to changes over which they have no control.*

This is very simple to understand. The young child of the alcoholic was not in control. The alcoholic's life was inflicted on him, as was his environment. In order to survive when growing up, the young CoA needed to turn that around; he needed to begin taking charge of his environment. This became very important as a child and remains so as an adult. The child of the alcoholic learns to trust himself more than anyone else when it is impossible to rely on anyone else's judgment. As a result, they very often are accused of being controlling, rigid, and lacking in spontaneity, which is probably true. It does not come from wanting to do everything your own way. It is not because he is spoiled or unwilling to listen to other ideas. It comes from the fear that if he is not in charge and if a change is made, abruptly, quickly, and without his being able to participate in it, he will lose control of his life. When he looks back on his reactions and his behavior later, he will feel somewhat foolish, but at the time he was simply unable to shift gears.

9. *Adult children of alcoholics constantly seek approval and affirmation.*

We talk about an external and an internal locus of control. When a child is born, the environment pretty much dictates how he is going to feel about himself. The school, the church, and other people all have influence, but the most important influence is what we call "significant others." In the child's world, this usually means his parents. So the child begins to believe who he is by the messages that he gets from his parents, and as he grows older, these messages are internalized and contribute significantly to his self-image. The movement is toward the internal locus of control.

The message that children of alcoholics get is very confused. They do not receive unconditional love. It was not, "I think you're terrific, but I'm not too happy about what you just did." The definitions were not clear, and the messages were mixed. "Yes, no, I love you, go away." So they grow up with some confusion about themselves. The affirmations they do not get on a day-to-day basis as a child, they interpret as negative. Later, when affirmation is offered, they find it very difficult to accept, because accepting the affirmation would be the beginning of changing their self-image, which they may not be prepared to do.

10. *Adult children of alcoholics feel that they are different from other people.*

They also assume that in any group of people, everyone else feels comfortable and they are the only ones who feel awkward. This is not peculiar to them, but the adult CoA never checks it out and discovers that each person has his own way of trying not to look awkward. Interestingly enough, adult CoAs even feel different in a group of adult children of alcoholics. Feeling different is something they have had with them since childhood and, even if the circumstance does not warrant it, the feeling prevails. Other children had an opportunity to be children, but CoAs didn't; they were too concerned with what was going on at home. They could never be completely comfortable playing with other children, never could be fully there. Their concerns about their home problems clouded everything else in their lives.

What happened to them is what happened to the rest of their family—they became isolated. As a result, socializing, being part of any group, became increasingly difficult. They simply did not develop the social skills necessary to feel comfortable or to feel a part of the group. It is difficult for children of alcoholics to believe that they can be accepted because of who they are, and that the acceptance does not have to be earned.

11. *Adult children of alcoholics are either super responsible or super irresponsible.*

If you see an adult CoA, you either take it all on, or you give it all up. There is no middle ground. You tried to please your parents, doing more and more, or you reached the point where you recognized it didn't matter, so you did nothing. You also did not experience a family that cooperated with each other. You didn't have a family that decided on Sunday, "Let's all work in the yard. I will work on this, and you work on that, and then we'll come together."

Not having a sense of being a part of a project, of cooperating with other people, and of letting all the parts come together and become a whole, you either do it all, or you do none of it. You also do not have a good sense of your own limitations. Saying "no" is extraordinarily difficult for you, so you do more and more and more. You do it [1] because you lack a realistic sense of your capacity, or [2] because if you say "no" you are afraid that they will find you out. They will find out that you are incompetent. The quality of the job you do does not seem to influence your feelings about yourself. So you take on more and more and more . . . until you burn out.

12. *Adult children of alcoholics are extremely loyal, even in the face of evidence that their loyalty is undeserved.*

The alcoholic home appears to be a very loyal place. Family members hang in long after reasons dictate that they should leave. The so-called "loyalty" is more the result of fear and insecurity than anything else; nevertheless, the behavior that is modeled is one where no one walks away just because the going gets rough. This sense enables the adult child to remain in involvements that are better dissolved.

Since making a friend or developing a relationship is so difficult and so complicated for an adult CoA, the relationship becomes permanent. If you are an adult CoA and someone cares enough about you to be your friend, your lover, or your spouse, then you feel the obligation to stay with them forever. If you have let them know who you are, if they have discovered who you are and not rejected you, that fact in and of itself is enough to make you sustain the relationship. The fact that they may treat you poorly does not matter. You can rationalize that. Somehow, no matter what they do or say, you can figure out a way to excuse their behavior and find yourself at fault. This reinforces your negative self-image and enables you to stay in the relationship. Your loyalty is unparalleled. Of course, there is also a lot of safety in an established relationship. It is known, and the known is always more secure than the unknown. Change being extremely difficult, you would prefer to stay with what is.

13. *Adult children of alcoholics are impulsive.*

They tend to lock themselves into a course of action without giving serious consideration to alternative behavior or possible consequences. This impulsiveness leads to confusion, self-loathing, and loss of control over their environment. In addition, they spend an excessive amount of energy cleaning up the mess. As children of alcoholics, they could not predict the outcome of any given behavior, so they do not know how to do it as adults. Since there was no consistency at home, they do not have a framework that tells them, "When I behaved impulsively in the past, this happened and that happened, and this person reacted in that way." Sometimes their behavior would be acceptable, and sometimes it would not. Essentially, their behavior really may not have mattered, nor did anyone say to them, "These are the possible consequences of that behavior. Let's talk about other things that you might do." Since there was no consistency in the response and no feedback on the behavior, the CoA is always in a quandary about what might result from any particular form of behavior. Thus, as an adult CoA, he acts impulsively to alleviate the feeling of confusion and indecision he always experiences regarding how to behave, and the results are always unpredictable except in their impulsiveness.

Once the causes for the behavior of adult CoAs are understood, their behavior begins to make much more sense. Adult CoAs live in a world in which nothing is certain, in which someone else determines what is appropriate based on rules that are applied on an apparently random or capricious basis but which are never clearly stated or understood, and in which any apparent affection anyone feels for you may be withdrawn summarily for offenses of which you may be wholly unaware. To remain sane in such an environment, adult CoAs have developed an elaborate set of mechanisms for coping throughout their lifetimes. No one attempting to treat adult CoAs can afford to ignore the "world-view" of the clients whose coping mechanisms he or she may be trying to change. There are real reasons, both valid and invalid, behind the anger of the client who said, "You make me laugh at myself, but I want you to know I don't think it's funny!" Understanding the world view of the adult CoA enables the clinician to help the client develop a more accurate perspective of the world of emotionally healthy people so that they can experience normal consistency of behavior and reasonable certainty. This experience helps enable the adult CoA to accept the affirmation which is the beginning of changing their self-image, and may even result in their being able to laugh at themselves, realize that it is funny, which is the beginning of being able to realize that it is okay to be funny in some situations.

Chapter Sixteen

Therapeutic Issues of Adult Children of Alcoholics: A Continuum of Developmental Stages

Herbert L. Gravitz and Julie D. Bowden

Conservative estimates indicate that there are between 28 and 32 million children of alcoholics in this country. Despite the size of the population, explicit acknowledgement of what issues these children face as they enter adulthood has been quite recent [Black, 1979, 1981, Brown, 1980]. Indeed, those describing the clinical issues that adult children of alcoholics face are explorers, while those working therapeutically with them are pioneers in the true sense of the word. It has taken centuries for the alcoholic to be treated as a human being with a primary, chronic, progressive, and, ultimately, fatal disease. It is taking even longer for the explicit realization that adults who grow up in families where at least one parent is alcoholic are at significant risk of becoming alcoholic, marrying an alcoholic, or developing significant physical or emotional problems themselves [Black, 1979, 1981, Brown, 1980]. The inability of clinicians and practitioners to adequately diagnose and treat the issues presented by adult children of alcoholics will contribute to the multigenerational pattern of alcoholism and to the suffering without meaning of millions of people. Not only is it appropriate at this time that attention be focused on this population, but it is also time to begin to articulate and elaborate upon the clinical issues they face.

In their work with adult children of alcoholics, the current authors have observed a clearly delineated continuum of personal and clinical

Reprinted with authors' permission from *Alcohol Health and Research World*, Vol. 8, No. 4, Summer 1984.

issues. In an earlier work the authors described a number of issues which this population faces. The current chapter presents an expanded view of these issues and groups them into four stages which are seen as unfolding in a sequential manner. Because these issues unfold sequentially, different treatment services and strategies are needed for each stage. Before adult children can deal with the issues of Stage II, they must work through the issues of Stage I. And before there can be true integration [Stage IV], the core issues of Stage III must be dealt with.

STAGE I: SURVIVAL

Initially, adult children of alcoholics expend a great deal of energy in maintaining—at times, regardless of the cost—the survival skills learned in childhood. Stage I is thus The Survival Stage. For a child in a home with an alcoholic lifestyle, life is at best inconsistent, arbitrary, unpredictable, and chaotic. At worst, it is dangerous and terror-filled.

To survive, children of alcoholics learn coping skills founded upon their position of birth [Wegscheider, 1981] and their particular personalities, as well as the personality of the alcoholic parent and the co-alcoholic parent. To compensate for having a mother or father who is not capable of managing the household or taking care of the children, the child learns to control some of the unpredictability of the home. Dinner will be ready at 6:00 p.m. because the child has assumed the responsibility for preparing it. To compensate for the lack of attention and affection received at home, children of alcoholics may become model students and "teachers' pets." In an effort to ease the pain and disappointment of still another promise being broken, the child of an alcoholic will learn not to trust anyone. Because their own view of the family is never validated—the father may routinely physically abuse the child in the evening without any discussion of it the next morning [Stix, 1981]—they learn not to trust themselves. To alleviate some of the feelings of horror and disgust felt toward their parents, the child may "pretend" that everything is fine and proceed to weave incredible tales of life at home. They are not "lying" as the term is commonly defined. Because they live in a home where denial of the truth is the norm, indeed, is a family rule, the children have no model for understanding the concept of "lying" [Wegscheider, 1981]. Thus denial becomes the road to survival.

Unfortunately, the skills so necessary and so assiduously learned in childhood become inappropriate and inadequate as these children "limp into adulthood" [Black, 1981]. Even when ostensibly successful, adult children of alcoholics—much like their primary model, the alcoholic [Stix, 1981]—feel as though their achievements are unwarranted. Many feel particularly fragile, and their defensive structure is highlighted [again, like the alcoholic] by denial both of the problem and of the origin of the problem. Rationalization and projection become secondary defenses used to deal with those issues that cannot be denied. Children may not be able to deny feeling hurt about a broken promise that they would be taken to the zoo, but they may be able to convince themselves that they did not really want to go. Repeatedly and routinely downplaying the importance of a person or an event may alleviate some of the pain these children feel, but it also undermines their own personal sense of importance.

At Stage I adult children of alcoholics are in varying degrees of psychological stress, attributing little, if any, of their suffering to the alcoholism in their family of origin. They feel significant emotional pain, but typically do not know where it is coming from. Literally they are suffering without understanding the source.

STAGE II: EMERGENT AWARENESS

Once aware of their physiological and psychological vulnerabilities, adult children of alcoholics begin to enter the second stage, The Emergent Awareness Stage. The primary issue which signals the beginning of this stage is one the authors have termed "coming out," denoting the process by which adult children begin to identify themselves as the child of an alcoholic. It often occurs as the result of their reading a newspaper story, attending a public lecture, or attending a class designed specifically for adult children of alcoholics. "Coming out" is a paramount step, as it allows the development of a context in which the adult child can begin to process the issues resulting from being reared in an alcoholic family. By espousing the label "adult children of alcoholics," individuals feel permission to accept themselves, to learn a new way, to ask for what they want and to receive what they want. They often were not "children" during childhood.

For many adult children who are just beginning the process of "coming out," breaking the family rule concerning silence is crucial. For the first time the isolation begins to lessen, the stigma is reduced, and a new awareness develops. As they hear other adult children describe their childhoods—with the attendant horrors and disasters—

they listen with astonishment. The isolation experienced as a child leads adult children to believe that their own childhood was more chaotic, more unpredictable, more full of horror than anyone could possibly have imagined. As they continue to listen, they begin to realize the commonality of growing up in an alcoholic household.

The realization that they are not alone and the relief that is gained releases enormous psychic energy that formerly had been used to deny the existence of a problem and to maintain control of emotions and memories. They begin to acknowledge feelings existing from their childhood that of necessity have been denied or repressed. As this energy is released, however, a significant amount of guilt may be experienced by adult children since they are violating a core family rule by breaking the shroud of silence imposed upon them in their childhood [Wegscheider, 1981]. As the process of intrapsychic separation from their family's alcoholism is initiated—through their own acknowledgment of the situation and their identification as children of alcoholics—adult children often feel they are betraying the family. In a family where activity and attention are focused both on the alcoholic and the denial of the alcoholism, to initiate discussion of either subject would invite censure or possible violence. Thus, a child learns early that since a problem does not exist [certainly no one else is talking about it and no one will validate the child's perceptions], the feelings regarding the problem must not exist either.

Because adult children emerge from their families feeling and being isolated from others, Stage II offers a different and new identity, i.e. as an adult child of an alcoholic. These adult children realize, often for the first time, that there are legitimate and external reasons for their suffering. The isolation is reduced as they continue to realize that others have lived through childhoods similar to their own—and survived. Sharing the experience begins to alleviate some of the pain associated with being the child of an alcoholic.

STAGE III: CORE ISSUES

Once adult children can acknowledge and accept the influence of their past, they are ready to examine the patterns of feelings, thoughts and behaviors that have beset them as adults and that may have initially prompted their seeking help. Stage III is thus termed The Core Issues. From their work with adult children of alcoholics at the Stanford

Medical Center Alcohol Clinic, Brown and Cermak [1980] described five central issues that adult children faced. It was their contention that the issue of control—control of environment, others, and self—was so pervasive that it dominated the four other issues of mistrusting, ignoring personal needs, denying feelings, and being unable to define or limit responsibility, particularly with regard to the alcoholic parent[s]. The current authors have seen these five issues repeatedly and believe they indeed are core issues at this developmental stage.

Just as Brown and Cermak contended that the issue of control permeated all other issues, the current authors believe that the issue of "all-or-none" behavior is equally important and is so crucial that it too pervades all other issues. The "all-or-none" phenomenon is the tendency for adult children of alcoholics to think in mutually exclusive terms: things are either "black or white," "all wrong or all right." Many adult children are also "myopic": not only are they prone to use denial as a defense mechanism, but often they cannot see their own strengths and assets. In effect, they become disassociated from their own resources. They look inside, but because of their "all-or-none" behavior, they perceive only their weaknesses.

It is because the "all-or-none" behavior is so ingrained and so frequently used that adult children experience such difficulties with other issues. Thus, trust is either present or absent, and, if present, present to an unrealistic degree. Similarly, if there is a lack of trust, it is total. As children of alcoholics, errors were cast in terms of "You made a mistake. You are bad," instead of "You made a mistake, and I still love you." Without the qualifying statement "and I still love you," a mistake becomes a judgment on the child's character, one that might be heard repeatedly. Hence, the child is either "good" or "bad;" not only has it never been explained that there is a gray area between those two terms, but the concept of a mistake as value free is unknown by the child of an alcoholic.

This inability to think in terms of degrees invariably exposes adult children to failure: very few people can be totally trusted, while few should be totally distrusted. The "all-or-none" characteristic also significantly precludes the adult child's ability to define and categorize problems into smaller and thus more attainable steps or pieces. Therefore, they typically perceive themselves as continually failing, which further exacerbates already existing feelings of low self-esteem.

The same "all-or-none" characteristic also colors the way adult children of alcoholics deal with feelings. They tend to equate feeling with behaving and are, consequently, very reluctant to deal directly with their feelings. If anger is expressed, the adult child of an alcoholic may typically experience fear or severe panic, convinced that violence will follow or that the relationship will be severed. And in their experience, this may have been true. Furthermore, because adult children of alcoholics generally have an over-developed sense of responsibility, they often believe that they are the cause of others' emotions. Thus — because of another's anger they feel they should have been able to control — they have once again failed. In fact, the equating of feeling with behaving is so strong that specific therapeutic strategies, e.g., explicitly giving permission to do nothing or emphasizing the option of choosing not to answer a question, must be utilized to prevent the adult child from over-exposure or premature exposure to feelings.

The "all-or-none" issue can also result in adult children of alcoholics experiencing severe difficulties in establishing adequate and useful boundaries between themselves and others. Brown and Cermak [1980] found this to be particularly true with regard to the adult child's alcoholic parent[s]. As they leave their family of origin, these children may become involved in a relationship with an alcoholic partner, confusing the feeling of smothering for that of love, or because they have not had an appropriate role model for intimacy as children, they may be left out of relationships altogether and become even more isolated. The adult child of an alcoholic is likely to bounce back and forth between the two states: they may demand such fierce devotion and loyalty as to be totally rejected [a self-fulfilling prophecy for some] or they will be afraid to ask someone to drive them to the airport for fear of being forever indebted and dependent—or once again rejected.

These issues culminate in the adult child's inability to develop a sense of personal rights [Whitfield, 1981]. They are continually apologizing, feeling that any discord must be because of them. The anticipation of expressing a need or want may produce extreme anxiety and subsequent rationalization, e.g., "I won't ask for help because I'm not a good person," further exacerbating feelings of failure and low self-esteem. The lack of an appropriate belief system in this area must be dealt with before significant further progress can be made.

STAGE IV: INTEGRATION

The authors view the "all-or-none" phenomenon as so central that they believe Stage IV in the developmental continuum begins as the "all-or-none" behavior fades. The Integrative Stage is ushered in as the breakdown of the "all-or-none" phenomenon begins to facilitate the development of a belief system which legitimizes self-acceptance. When the concept of a belief system which establishes personal rights is understood and adopted, adult children of alcoholics are ready to confront the final therapeutic issue, taking care of themselves. Characteristically, they have learned to take care of family members [the alcoholic, the co-alcoholic spouse, siblings] while learning to ignore their own needs and wants. As adults, they no longer know what to ask for or even believe they have the right to ask.

As the concept of taking care of one's self becomes more and more inculcated into the adult child's emerging repertoire of new behaviors, they begin to make qualitative changes. Stage IV can be seen, for example, when adult children of alcoholics begin to play and have fun without feeling overwhelmed by feelings of guilt. It is marked by limit setting, where adult children establish appropriate boundaries between themselves and others, particularly their parents. They become appropriately trusting, open to feelings, and are able to make long-term as well as short-term commitments. In group therapy for adult children of alcoholics, for example, Stage IV is seen when the adult child no longer apologizes for utilizing the group's time. The adult child experiences the freedom—or "personal right"—to answer or not answer another's question, particularly that of the group leaders. Adult children of alcoholics may choose to confront their parents and reconcile the love-hate dichotomy of feelings that exists. They can accept their parents' alcoholism and recognize that it is not their problem or fault. As they allow themselves to be who they are, they can allow others to be who they are.

One adult child's final group session illustrates cogently the integrative stage. All her adult life she had felt compelled to participate in family rituals which had left her feeling used and abused. She stated,

> "I have spent my entire life being the good daughter so that my parents would not be upset by my behavior."

She went on to say:

> "Group has brought me freedom from living for them. Last weekend, I refused to participate in a family activity that

included the potential for a drunken scene by my alcoholic parents."

Another simply stated, "I became an adult."

CURE OR RECOVERY?

It has become increasingly clear to the authors that there is no "cure" for adult children of alcoholics. Much as alcoholics must continuously live with their alcoholism, adult children of alcoholics must continuously live with their own history and vulnerability. However, this need not preclude a satisfying and enjoyable life. The ability to efficiently run a household at age nine may have been an asset, but at age 30 it might be a liability. The discipline and self-control necessary for a child to develop good study habits is invaluable in the work force. With appropriate therapy, followed by self-monitoring and periodic consultation, the childhood survival skills so disruptive to an adult child of an alcoholic can be effectively utilized for personal growth and an enjoyable life.

CONCLUSIONS

The authors believe there are specific clinical issues which typify the population of approximately 30 million children of alcoholics, and these issues emerge, unfold, and must be dealt with in a sequential manner. It is believed that the lack of a coherent developmental scheme for working therapeutically with this population has hindered effective, and particularly efficient, interventions because services appropriate for adult children at Stage I are highly inappropriate for those dealing with the issues of Stage IV, and vice-versa.

The inability of practitioners in the helping professions to adequately diagnose and deal with the issues of an adult child of an alcoholic may mean that, for the adult child, the next stop will be an alcohol treatment detoxification center. Clearly not all adult children of alcoholics will be able to avoid becoming even more enmeshed in the disease of alcoholism. The National Institute on Alcohol Abuse and Alcoholism estimates that only 5% of the children of alcoholics are receiving the clinical services they need [Whitfield, 1981].

The emergence of a developmental continuum has significant implications for treatment. To be most effective, a broad range of intervention services—ranging from an article in the newspaper to intensive psychotherapy—is needed. Help begins with information and education. Psychotherapy cannot be maximally effective until connections are made between the past and the present. Appropriate treatment is contingent upon the adult child's stage along the developmental continuum herein described. Continued work and research in this area will not only mean satisfying and productive lives for the adult children of alcoholics, but will also be a major step toward preventive work in breaking the cycle of generational alcoholism and in alleviating the suffering without meaning of millions of people.

With the "all-or-none" phenomenon in mind, we present this developmental continuum not as a definitive statement of the issues adult children of alcoholics face, but rather as a statement meant to stimulate others into thinking conceptually about a population of approximately 30 million Americans in need of clinical services. As the authors have seen over and over, no one survives unscathed in an alcoholic family.

REFERENCES

Black, C. "Children of Alcoholics," *Alcohol Health and Research World*. 4 [1]: 23-27, 1979.

Black, C. "Innocent Bystanders at Risk: The Children of Alcoholics." *Alcoholism* 1 [3]: 22-26, 1981.

Brown, S. and Cermak, T. "Group Therapy With Adult Children of Alcoholics." *California Society for the Treatment of Alcoholism and Other Chemical Dependencies Newsletter*. 7 [7]: 1-6, 1980.

Stix, H. "The Troubled Children of Alcoholics." *The Los Angeles Times*. V:2, March 12, 1981.

Wegscheider, S. *Another Chance: Hope and Health For Alcoholic Families*. Palo Alto. California. Science and Behavior Books, Inc., 1981.

Whitfield, C. "Children of Alcoholics: Treatment Issues," in: *National Institute on Alcohol Abuse and Alcoholism Research Monograph Number 4—Services for Children of Alcoholics*. Washington, D.C.: U.S. Government Printing Office [DHHS Publication Number (ADM) 81-1007], 1981.

Chapter Seventeen

Adult Children of Alcoholics as Professionals in the Alcoholism Field

Joseph C. Kern

Purpose

The purpose of this chapter is to draw a parallel between the dysfunctional aspect of the alcoholic family and the alcoholism field. Alcoholism treatment agencies and constituency groups are at high risk for incorporating certain dysfunctional aspects of the alcoholic family system within their structures. This is in part due to the large numbers of untreated adult children of alcoholics who are service providers and in leadership roles in the field. As Woititz (1983) has shown, untreated adult children of alcoholics tend to recreate the dysfunctional aspects of their family of origin; seek relationship settings that perpetuate these aspects, and remain isolated from new learning experiences.

Woitiz (1983) and Cermak (1982) have shown how this occurs with an interpersonal and intrapsychic clinical setting. Here we shall demonstrate how identical dynamics can occur in addiction professional, constitutency, and advocacy areas. In addition, several case studies will be presented along with treatment and prevention recommendations.

Background

Janis (1982) has shown how the chemistry or Gestalt of a working group can have a dramatic impact on product outcomes. He has identified several aspects of a phenomenon called GROUPTHINK which is characterized by a single-minded rigidity or purpose which defies corrective feedback; a closed information system; a system demanding loyalty and avoiding internal and external criticism and one which only adds new members who will conform to the existing belief system and norms of the group. This phenomena can have a devastating, negative impact on decision making, since the group avoids new information and contact with reality. Hence, their decisions become less appropriate to problem-solving and more invested with preserving the group's norms and belief systems. Janis (1982) has shown how this arrogance of insulation resulted in faulty decision-making in such areas as Watergate and in prolonging the Vietnam conflict.

Berne (1964) has taken the GROUPTHINK phenomena beyond the descriptive state and has developed techniques for exposing and correcting its potentially destructive features. Some business and management firms have been receptive to examining these process issues, understanding that their resolution will result in healthier decision making, and hence, more appropriate outcomes.

The addictions field, however, has been slow to be introspective about its own internal dynamics. This is due, at least in part, to the youth of the addictions field and the pressing need to focus on service delivery to alcoholic people and their families. Another factor is the prevalence of denial in the addictions field. Service providers are quick to identify this defense as a major obstacle at the treatment site, yet believe that they are immune to its influence within a professional and constituency context. In short, the addictions field can become as dysfunctional as a diseased alcoholic family, and our systems of care are at high risk for the disease of the attitudes.

Problem Definition

In order to better understand the relevance of GROUPTHINK to the addictions field, we will use Wegscheider's (1981) "Rules In The Alcoholic Family" as an orienting framework. Table 1 lists said rules, their relevance to the addictions field, and the potential consequences.

Rule 1 - The alcoholic's use of alcohol is the most important thing in the family's life. This "rule" by which alcoholic families operate, can easily be transformed into a single-minded belief that one's own agency or advocacy issue is the only and most vital concern in the field. Compulsive devotion to an agency or advocacy issue necessarily implies that other agencies or issues are of less importance, and that they require fewer

TABLE ONE "RULES IN THE ALCOHOLIC FAMILY"	MANIFESTATION IN UNTREATED ALCOHOLISM SERVICE DELIVERY AND ADVOCACY FIELD	CONSEQUENCES
1. The dependent's use of alcohol is the most important thing in the family's life.	My agency or constituency is the most important thing; to the exclusion of others.	*Competition rather than cooperation. *Compulsive dedication to a single issue. *Winners and losers orientation—if another group is successful, then "I lose." *Perception of limited and shrinking resources.
2. Alcohol is not the cause of the family's problem.	Our agency or constituency group is not the cause of problems in the Addictions Field.	*Lack of ability to be to be introspective. *Self-righteous - arrogance. *Insulation from corrective feedback. *Rigidity.
3. Someone or some thing else caused the alcoholic's dependency; he is not responsible.	The other agencies and constituency groups are at fault—they have to change in order for things to improve.	*Projection of responsibility. *Dependent on others to change. *Playing the role of the victim.
4. The status quo must be maintained at all cost.	The other agencies and constituency cannot and will never change; hence, our position is justified.	*Isolation. *Retaining old distorted perception of the "other." *Fear of change. *Fear of sharing and loss of control.
5. Everyone in the family must be an "enabler."	Everyone in my agency or group must be loyal only to this agency or cause; covering up mistakes.	*Enabling of incompetents. *Accepting a high level of errors. *Rescuing and excusing those who cannot meet expectations.
6. No one may discuss what is really going on in the family, either with one another or with outsiders.	Buiding of insular agency or constituency group which is isolated.	*Secret keeping. *Vow of loyalty. *Poor networking. *Isolation.
7. No one may say what he is really feeling.	Lack of clear, honest dialogue between agencies and constituency groups.	*Smile and gossip, but don't confront. *Store up anger at the "other" and feed off the resentment. *Negative bonding outside of one's own constituency group.

(1) SEE WEGSCHEIDER (1981), P. 80.

resources.

The consequences of this viewpoint foster competition rather than cooperation. Agencies and constituency groups see themselves in competition for resources; that there is a limited and possibly shrinking set of resources, and that the world consists of winners and losers. Hence, if any agency or issue gains, it is at the expense of some other group. Just as in the dysfunctional alcoholic family, there are winners and losers; the possibility of everyone winning is inconceivable. Hence, competition results internally in the field, rather than a joint cooperative effort to gain more resources and to advocate for all constituency groups to win. This is a direct reflection of the dysfunctional alcoholic family system which remains internally competitive with a belief that emotional energy is limited and shrinking, rather than expanding and limitless.

Rule 2 — Alcohol is not the cause of the family's problem. Public support for alcoholism programs has been slow to develop in the United States; public awareness of the disease and lingering stigmatized views of the alcoholic person both remain. These and other problems in the addictions field are often responded to in much the same manner as the alcoholic family does to alcoholism. The typical response of agencies and constituency groups is to assume that one's actions are above reproach and to find other reasons why such problems exist. The consequences of this response is a lack of ability to be introspective about how one's agency or constituency group may be adding to the problem partly. The all-or-none thinking of dysfunctional alcoholic families (Woititz, 1983) is used to assert that one's group is perfect and in no way contributes to the problems in the addiction field. Obviously, this rigidity of thinking blocks new information from being received which could result in internal changes within one's group. Corrective feedback is continuously turned away in favor of a self-righteous reaffirmation of a group's high-sounding principles and motives.

Rule 3 — Someone or somebody else caused the alcoholic's dependency; he is not responsible. The analog to the addictions field is clearly apparent in the field's tendency to blame other agencies and groups for problems, and to imply that the other agencies must change in order for things to improve. As in the dysfunctional alcoholic family, members wait for others to change in order that they may live; the field often waits for the "other" (e.g., government, public attitudes) to change before things will improve.

The consequences for the addictions field is the presence of agencies and constituency groups that project blame onto each other; they feel and act victimized by the success of others and they avoid action, waiting for the other agency or group to change. One result is external "finger pointing," which serves the dual purpose of avoiding internal change and preserving one's own position of being flawless. The final view is that no change is required on my part, whereas the "other" has to do all the changing a position destined to keep all groups frozen in inaction.

Rule 4 — The status quo must be maintained at all costs. The resistance of the alcoholic family to change and its tendency to return to old, destructive patterns of behavior are well known.

Likewise, the addictions field has a strong tendency to maintain images of the "other." For example, the medical and mental health fields historically have been insensitive to the needs of alcoholic people. Recent attempts by them to change to a point of greater awareness are sometimes met with a cynical attitude by the addictions field that "they will never change." This attitude maintains the status quo of the addictions field as outside the mainstream of health services; it continues isolation and avoids change.

Loss of control is an important factor at work here. Sharing of responsibility for the care of alcoholic people with other professions necessitates that the addictions field would not be in complete and total control of the treatment process. The arrogance of isolation serves to hold rigidly onto control over the treatment of alcoholic people, and to perpetuate secret-keeping by not sharing addiction-specific knowledge with other professions, all in the service of maintaining the "status quo."

Rule 5 — Everyone in the family must be an enabler. The closed alcoholic family system is often characterized by family members pretending to be normal and covering up for the inadequacies of others. Hence, the denial of the alcoholic person grows as family members protect him from the consequences of his behavior.

Likewise, the alcoholism field often demands a high level of loyalty from its members and healthy criticism is interpreted as disloyalty and not being a "true believer." A total and complete commitment is demanded from agency staff or members of constituency groups; limited involvement is not tolerated. In addiction, involvement with several causes (e.g., children of alcoholics, the elderly, etc.) often is seen as a sign of disloyalty, and involvement with the "enemy," (e.g., distillery industry) is considered being a traitor.

Errors in judgment will always occur. Instead of evaluating them dispassionately, there is a frenzied attempt to justify them and to "enable" the continuance of the error. The result is a closed information system dedicated to resisting change.

Rule 6 — No one may discuss what is really going on in the family, either with one another, or with outsiders. The dysfunctional alcoholic family is noted for the irony of denying the presence of alcoholism, despite overwhelming evidence to the contrary. The secret-keeping continues both within and outside the family system, keeping the family protected from intervention. The shared secret-keeping and denial is often the single uniting principle that the family shares.

Systems of care are also high risks for becoming isolated and insular. Secret-keeping, both within the group (e.g., "cliques") and towards outsiders, is common. It is startling to observe agencies and groups that coexist in the same community, yet know little of each other's activities and skills. Resolution of conflict is also relevant here. Imitating the dysfunctional alcoholic family system, inter-agency conflict is often not resolved in a direct, honest manner; instead, the system recoils with isolation, reaffirming the shared bond of loyalty to the group. The result is poor networking and communication, both within and outside the addiction's field, which slows the overall progress of the addictions field.

Rule 7 — No one may say what he is really feeling. There is a strong message in alcoholic homes—don't feel! This dictum is so strong that it results in family members being unable to identify feeling states and, hence, unable to access them. The prohibition against the healthy expression of anger is particularly apparent.

The addictions field also has problems with the clear, honest, and mature expression of feelings. Being dominated by adult children of alcoholics, the field is at high risk for rumors and "gossip" and the attendant result of building resentment. Without resolution, the pool of resentment at other agencies and groups grows and builds a wall designed to avoid change. The net result is a field of care that itself perpetuates the illness of nurturing resentments, inappropriate and sometimes public expressions of anger at others, and a tendency to avoid working at relationship building.

As with alcoholic families, the above characterization is the extreme case of the disease process. We know that the disease comes in varying intensities and forms. The general principle is that the addictions field will gradually slide into the above process unless safeguards are taken at prevention and systems treatment applied when it does occur.

Case Materials:

What follows is a description of two illustrative cases: One from a treatment agency and the other from a typical state.

Treatment Agency — The initial presenting problem of New City's Alcoholism Treatment Agency were: the low number of referrals both into the clinic and from the clinic to other providers; chronic complaints from other agencies (i.e., Probation Dept.) that they had difficulty obtaining information on clients referred to the agency; high dropout rate of clients (i.e., over 50% did not complete the treatment contract); and the lack of a comprehensive treatment program, including co-equal services to alcoholic people, co-dependents, and children.

These were viewed as possible symptoms of a systems breakdown. The staff was interviewed, records reviewed, and outside agencies contacted as to their view and experience with the New City Clinic.* What emerged was the picture of a clinic which was more than 10 years old that had gradually slipped into becoming a diseased alcoholic treatment system. Immediately apparent was the division between staff along professional versus paraprofessional lines. The recovering staff did not view the disease as a family one, and believed that the entire staff should be devoted to treating alcoholics. They also felt that professionals (e.g., social workers) could not help alcoholic people because they were not alcoholics. This conflict was always subclinical and never surfaced in a direct way. Instead, staff grouped into cliques: family workers together versus recovering staff.

The Clinic Director was manipulated by each faction for preferential treatment, but she** never openly discussed the issue with all staff present. Instead, she met privately with each faction and simply listened to their complaints without resolving the conflict through healthy communication. The tenured staff tended to isolate new staff members and kept secrets as to the clinic's operation so that the new staff could not easily learn their job. Hence, the clinic had one grouping of tenured

---

*Fictitious name
**Generic use of he or she

staff, who held the secret of the clinic's operation to themselves, and newer staff, who tended to turn over at a rapid rate.

When confronted with the low number of out-of-clinic referrals for needed services [e.g., detoxification], the clinic staff said that they had few clients who need these and other services. This tendency toward isolation was further evident by the staff's absence from regional meetings, in-service education, and other opportunities to share with other colleagues and agencies. They blamed the Probation Department, their parent organization, and other outside agencies for the clinic's problems and showed little ability to be introspective. Information flow was through "gossip." When official announcements of policy were made, they were met with sarcasm and disbelief. Finally, the clinic staff took on the roles Wegscheider [1982] has presented as characteristic of the dysfunctional alcoholic family. The New City Clinic Director was the "lost child" very weak and ineffective. Staff generally enabled her weakness by covering up for her inability to make clear and forceful decisions. Easily manipulated, she had problems in tolerating negative feelings expressed by staff and provided superficial supervision. Clinic problems were blamed on outsiders, and the Director presented herself as a victim of a large insensitive bureaucratic structure, hence eliciting sympathy from staff.

The senior family counselor was the "scapegoat," who was constantly blamed for clinic problems. At staff meetings, she raised issues of staff resistance in engaging families at intake and other process issues and was regularly either ignored or criticized.

One alcoholism counselor was the "mascot" who, although a middle aged woman, dressed as a youth, defied clinic rules in a jocular manner, and was very hyperactive.

The clinic senior secretary was the unit's "hero," who tried to fix mistakes [e.g., missing or late correspondence] and who presented a smiling image to outside agencies. The net result was a clinic which was not family treatment focused and which had poor staff morale, was isolated from other treatment resources, and nurtured long past resentment held towards outsiders; in short, it was clear diagnosis of alcoholism within the clinic structure!

Constituency Group—Most states have statewide chapters of various alcoholism constituency groups to represent special interests: labor-management; children of alcoholics; women; minorities; council[s] on alcoholism, and public and private sector treatment agencies. One particular state was observed to have symptoms of systems breakdown: in-fighting between the various groups; secret keeping accompanied by lack of sharing among them; a public show of cooperation but a deeper level of competition; and insistence of loyalty of members to each group and cause—multi-group involvement was considered disloyal and re-telling of past problems between the groups nurtured resentments.

The net result was the lack of a clear, agreed upon agenda for alcoholism services in the state which all groups could support. Each group independently sought financial and membership support for their cause, hence alcoholism concerns in the state had a low visibility, with the resulting lack of private and public support.

SOLUTIONS—Treating a dysfunctional alcoholic system bears a strong resemblance to treating the same disease within an alcoholic family. The following systems treatment strategies are recommended:

1. Diagnosis by outside consultants—As with the dysfunctional alcoholic family, outside intervention is required to begin the process of recovery. For the alcoholic, it is often an employer or the criminal justice system. For a dysfunctional alcoholic system, it can be the parent organization to which the clinic reports or an outside regulatory/licensing agency. In short, self-diagnosis by the dysfunctional alcoholic system is rare; outside forces are needed to confront the problems.

After outsiders have identified the symptoms [See Table 1], the next critical step is to diagnose correctly the symptoms as reflective of the disease of alcoholism. This is an essential component to begin recovery, since it begins to remove blame and guilt and to substitute identification with a diseased process. Again, this is best done by an outside charge agent who can be objective and dispassionate.

2. Socio-Therapy—We have found the use of socio-therapy [Goldstein, 1973] to be very useful in helping a dysfunctional system to begin change. Briefly, staff of the treatment agency or constituency group plays the role of some other service provider and is assigned a specific dysfunctional task [e.g., a secret keeper[s]; scapegoat, blamer, etc.] and the group is confronted with a crisis [e.g., increase clinic census or lose funding, etc.]. The group is directed to come up with a consensus solution within a limited time frame [e.g. 20 mins.]. The net result is that the group cannot solve the problem because of the dysfunctional nature of the structure. There can be an extensive discussion of feelings generated in the role play, and reflection on the consequences of their dysfunctional behavior [i.e., clinic closes, etc.], both of which produce negative results. Parallels to the feelings and dysfunctional behavioral patterns in the alcoholic home are drawn in order to enhance identification with the disease model of systems illness.

The use of humor and exaggeration are important in helping participants overcome initial resistance. Following these steps, the facilitator then outlines the aspects of healthy family system [e.g., communication, etc.]. Role playing resumes with the facilitator acting as a role model to enhance healthy communication patterns. Feelings and behavioral outcomes are again explored, which typically generate support and cooperation. The facilitator can then help the group to reflect on outlining concrete achievable steps to produce a healthier system of care and advocacy. A socio-therapy session can last from as brief a meeting as two hours to an entire day. One critical feature is to repeat the sessions frequently in order to enhance growth.

3. Producing an Open-Communication System—As with the family, permanent structural changes are required in order to promote health. One such change is to open up and revitalize communication networks both within and outside the current structure. This can take the form of weekly meetings with referral agencies, regional meetings within other services providers, mandated in-service education for staff which is outside the agency structures and the rotating of staff into and through other systems of care. We have found that these steps, taken together, can form the basis for the recovery of an alcoholic system. As with the alcoholic family system, in the treatment and constituency area, there are still some who do not respond to these efforts. In particular, we have seen untreated adult children of alcoholics in these systems seek treatment for their co-dependency, and occasionally some staff leave who cannot tolerate the change.

A FINAL NOTE ON PREVENTION—Knowing that the addictions field is a high risk for the disease, we can take various steps to minimize or prevent the above destructive processes from occurring. These include:

A. Establishing an open communication system by scheduling regular contact with outsiders.
B. Scheduling regular socio-drama sessions to focus on process and relationship issues.
C. Frequent discussion of systems breakdown symptoms and char-

acteristics of adult children of alcoholics.

D. Establishing a mixed working group that includes helpers who have not been personally affected by the disease.

E. Regular in-service education designed to bring in new ideas and generate excitement and bonding.

Our systems of care and advocacy require the same nurturing and attention as the alcoholic family.

REFERENCES

Cermak, T.L. and Brown, S., Interactional Group Therapy with the Adult Children of Alcoholics. *Interactional Journal of Group Psychotherapy*, 1982, 32 [3], 375-389.

Berne, Eric, *Games People Play*. Grove Press, Inc. 1964.

Goldstein, Arnold P., *Structured Learning Therapy*. Academic Press, Inc., New York, 1973.

Janis, Irving L., GROUPTHINK. Houghton Mifflin, Co., Boston, 1982.

Wegscheider, Sharon. *Another Chance: Hope and Health For The Alcoholic Family*. Science and Behavior Books, Palo Alto, California 1981.

Woititz, Janet G., *Adult Children of Alcoholics*. Health Communication, Inc., Hollywood, Florida 1983.

Chapter Eighteen
Working with Black Adult Children of Alcoholics

Suzanne E. Anderson

When examining the issues of black adult children of alcoholics [ACoAs], we must consider a number of factors. Since their racial identity cannot be isolated from the examination of their characteristics as ACoAs, it is critical to connect with the realities of the Black Experience. This Experience involves history, society's view of blacks, black self-concept, racial identity, the civil rights movement, socioeconomic factors, and racism. In light of this, the issues of black adult children of alcoholics cannot be compared to white adult children of alcoholics, but rather can be viewed in relation to:

1. Parenting styles of blacks and their effect on children,
2. Black child personality development,
3. The black community and its view of alcoholism,
4. Characteristics of adult children of alcoholics,
5. The development of black psychology, and
6. Counseling techniques appropriate for black people.

In this chapter, we will examine how these contributing factors affect the personality, behavior, assessment, and treatment of black adult children of alcoholics. Then we can begin to appreciate their denial and resistance in admitting to alcoholism as a problem in their family and in getting involved in traditional therapy. For them, the alcoholism becomes relative to the Black Experience, and consequently, both need to be incorporated into their clinical picture.

Review of Literature

In reviewing the literature on blacks and their family life, it was disturbing to find a great deal of biased, unreliable information that depicted all blacks in a negative manner. Contrary to some researchers' approaches, all black people do not have the same experience, background, or issues. There are many subcultures within the Black Experience. For example, different characteristics and dynamics are exhibited by northern, southern, immigrant, inner city, and rural blacks, as well as those in the low and middle income groups. Furthermore, education and mobility contribute to the cultural variations. This diversity skews research that does not take these differences into account.

The research of the '60s and '70s was primarily comparative to whites, assuming white as the norm, and inferred that blacks were pathological. In recent years, however, many social scientists are beginning to study black families from a perspective that recognizes the cultural variations, functionality, and validity of black family lifestyles [Peters-McAdoo, 1981].

Black adult children of alcoholics then must be considered from this enlightened perceptive where their issues are seen as not more pathological then their white counterparts. The contributing variables of the Black Experience previously noted help to determine a clinical picture.

Black Parenting

Inherent in black parenting is the responsibility to prepare the children to survive as competent adults while dealing with racism, economic distress, and oppression. This function can be traced back to the slave family that was expected to prepare its children to accept exploitation and abuse [Comer-Fantani, Cardenas, 1980]. Low self-esteem and passive/aggressive behavior were ways of adapting to slavery. [Interestingly, the same two characteristics are used repeatedly in studies to describe adult children of alcoholics.] Recent research findings of ecologically oriented studies have reported black families to be strong, functional, and flexible [Peter-McAdoo, 1981]. There is a high priority on self-esteem as a way of coping both with racism and with the special environmental stress of living simultaneously in two worlds—the black community and the world of mainstream society. According to Peters and Massey, "Black parents recognize that their children must be accepted in the Black community in order to have friends and they must be accepted in the white community in order to survive. . . They want their children to grow up being and feeling equal, comfortable, responsible, effective, and at home in the world they live in . . ." [Harrison-

Rossy, Wyden, 1973]. Black parents have developed patterns of coping with racial oppression internally, strategies proven to be effective in the past that are incorporated into their own socialization process" [Peters-McAdoo, 1981]. Therefore, these parents work at striking a balance between protecting their children from the negative messages of society and developing a strong racial identity.

This partially explains the bond between all black children and their parents. Black children intuitively know that their parents function in this capacity and have a sense that it is a very stressful responsibility. Therefore, they reciprocate the caring by protecting their parents from those they perceive as oppressors and by excusing inappropriate behavior. This can set up denial for the black adult children of alcoholics.

Generally, it is the mother to whom male and female black children feel the closest. Traditionally, black fathers have been more likely to provide material assistance, whereas black mothers give advice and encouragement [Staples, Ebony, 1984]. Black mothers often teach their children to honor and respect their father even when he is not able to provide for the needs of the family [Comer-Fantini, Cardenas, 1980]. This implies that a dysfunctional, alcoholic mother would be protected by the child and an alcoholic father would continue to be respected. Hence, talking about or to either parent in a negative manner is viewed as a serious sign of disrespect that warrants discipline. Even when the child becomes an adult, doing so [as in discussing parental alcoholism or behavior] evokes a great sense of guilt.

Discipline in the black family is generally described as direct and physical. Most black parents emphasize obedience which they equate with respect, love, and achievement. Black fathers of lower socioeconomic status "describe themselves as strict, using physical as opposed to verbal punishment liberally." Middle-income black fathers in McAdoo's 1979 study "expected their child to respond immediately to their commands, would almost never allow angry temper tantrums from their child, and perceived themselves and their attitudes toward child rearing as moderate to very strict." Rarely was withdrawal of love practiced by the black parents. This strict type of discipline of black parents has been shown to be "functional, appropriate discipline of caring parents" [Peters-McAdoo, 1981].

This may explain why many black adult children of alcoholics deny parental physical abuse. When one is considered to have been abused, it is usually because the physical punishment was more severe than for the other siblings or because other family members or the community perceive it as such. Note that the victim's personal feeling is not the standard that determines validity. Typical black parenting, however, involves physical discipline accompanied with love, low tolerance for the expression of anger, preparation to deal with racism and oppression, and development of racial identity.

Self-Concept

In that upward mobility and education are affecting the values and attitudes of many of today's blacks, parenting styles among blacks may be in a state of flux. Nevertheless, most of today's black adults were raised prior to or during the civil rights movement of the '60s that raised black consciousness and black self-concept. Regardless of what was happening in the family, the self-esteem of all blacks was influenced by and part of a larger movement that made a statement—Black is Beautiful. A variety of adults, older children, and friends also influence the self-concept and personality development of any one black child. When the male parent is absent, male children can identify with other male figures in his environment, i.e. uncles, grandfathers, etc. School teachers and ministers have been found to be primary socio-emotional and psychological support systems, providing time, communication, solace, support, and comfort [Scanzoni, 1977]. This factor alone can help to offset the detrimental effects of familial alcoholism.

The black family supports friendships in childhood, partly because they help counteract feelings which result from racism. Each black adult has approximately ten others he considers to be significant others [Manns-McAdoo, 1981]. These "outsiders" make up a kind of extended family and thus become part of the family system. Consequently, they are aware of family problems. When alcoholism is present, as in any addicted family system, they help to enable and to deny the problem. The significant others also influence the way black adult children of alcoholics perceive their experience. Therefore, they can support or sabotage the realization of the effects of familial alcoholism.

Black Community and Self-Concept

Black communities differ vastly throughout the United States. Such variables as local politics, zoning, and unemployment will affect community attitudes and behavior [Wheeler, 1977]. The various subgroups within the community often add to the conflicts and pain. The black self-concept, which needs group identification for development of its racial identity, can house these feelings of conflict. Because of group identification, black people who do not live in the black community neighborhood still can identify with and influence the values. This is especially evident with black role models as Jesse Jackson, Shirley Chisholm, and others.

Despite the conflicts, it is possible for black children to develop positive, actualizing self-concepts in this society. Black communities containing children and their families must be characterized by a sense of peoplehood, group identification, black consciousness, or pride. The family must be able to identify with or experience a sense of belonging to the community. When these conditions prevail, the black community acts as a filter against harmful inputs of the white community [Barnes-Jones, 1980].

The Black Community's View of Alcoholism

Blacks, having strong fundamentalist traditions, either abstain from or abuse chemicals. Black churches hold a highly moralistic view on drinking alcohol. Black communities, in general, tend to deny alcoholism as a primary disease. Instead, they make excuses by blaming conditions and racism as justification for excessive alcohol use (NIAAA, 1978). These conflicts and extremes in thinking go without resolution. Consequently, the community does not clearly define standards for acceptable and unacceptable chemical use. Denial becomes a part of group identification. Hence, blacks are allowed to develop sophisticated defense systems which delay their getting into treatment. Only when their health or employment has deteriorated do they seek help. Some use religion to stop on their own; others fall back on the African tradition of seeking help from a family member.

Since black families also deny the alcoholism, they do not accept that it has had a serious effect on them. Although they verbally support the chemically dependent individual's recovery and pray for him/her, they do little to get involved in the process themselves, and often sabotage it. For example, Marsha, a 26-year-old, black, female adult child of two alcoholic parents was admitted to the hospital for a drug overdose/suicide attempt. Her parents were long-standing, active members of the community in which she lived. They visited her at the hospital numerous times and consulted with her psychiatrist. Upon discharge, the family and community gave her a "Welcome Home" party with, as they stated, all the alcohol and drugs she wanted to help her out of her depression! Needless to say, this began a series of hospitalizations with the same diagnosis.

With both the community and family accepting this kind of thinking, the black alcoholic and the black adult child of the alcoholic risk alienation from their signficant others when they admit to alcohol related/mental health problems. Consequently, the presenting problem for which they seek help may not, on the surface, appear to be connected with alcoholism, i.e. depression, job problems, relationship problems.

Co-Dependency

Unknowingly, co-dependent behavior is encouraged in many black families and becomes part of the Black Experience. In addition to learning repressed feelings, attitudes around food, alcohol, gambling, work, and religion border on compulsiveness as a way of coping and living. For example, workaholism is encouraged and seen as a sign of upward mobility; excessive eating and drinking is equated with relaxation and pride; gambling is a way of making money. Similar rules to those that support co-dependent behavior, such as don't trust and don't rock the boat, exist as a way of dealing with racism. As there is a stigma attached to being alcoholic, so is there to being a person of color in this country. Oppressed black families who do not feel the possibility of upward mobility and feel stigmatized will tolerate alcoholism without question. Their feelings of victimization override their desire to understand alcoholism as a primary disease.

Counseling Black Adult Children of Alcoholics

Counseling black adult children of alcoholics presents a challenge. The clinician, in order to make valid assessments, has to connect the Black Experience and black psychology—a perspective for understanding black functioning [Tounsel-Jones, 1980]—with the dynamics and treatment of the addicted family system. In implementing the treatment plan, the techniques the therapist chooses to employ must be applicable to both black clients and adult children of alcoholics. These techniques must facilitate an examination of individual personal issues such as self-concept, racial identity, and adult children of alcoholics issues, as well as issues of the larger society such as discrimination, political policies, and alcoholism in the community. Thus, some goals of treatment include:

1. Develop a realistic self-concept,
2. Stimulate the feelings of blackness,
3. Develop a sense of collective selfhood,
4. Retrieve the child within,
5. Gain understanding of alcoholism and its effect on the individual
6. Connect with personal needs, and
7. Develop a plan to work on changing the system or community.

The Clinician

Clinicians who work with ACoAs carry a responsibility to identify and work on any personal chemical dependency and co-dependency issues. When black clients are involved, the clinician, black or white, needs to examine his/her own racial attitudes and sense of the Black Experience. Hence, a broad understanding of the political realities of black American existence and an awareness of the continued survival of black life are necessary [Tounsel, A. Jones-Jones, 1980].

When a black client gets in touch with conflictive feelings about his blackness, it may be necessary to refer him to a black therapist. "Conflicts about blackness are almost impossible for the white therapist to deal with sufficiently" [F. Jones-Jones, 1980.] "Many white counselors have expressed the feeling of inadequacy in coping with racial pain" [Taylor, Bell-*Focus on Family*, March/April, 1984.]

Trouble accepting a black therapist is an indication of poor self-concept in regards to blackness. It can be traced to the history of black-white relationships in this society, where many blacks have viewed the white professional as likely to be better trained and more competent [F. Jones-Jones, 1980]. Developing a relationship with a black therapist, however, can be used to help the client gain a better sense of self while also working on ACoA issues.

CLINICAL PICTURE

Denial/Resistance

In view of the larger picture of society's and the community's influences on black life, it is understandable that many black ACoAs do not perceive that their life has been different from that of most black people. So one cannot assume that black adult children of alcoholics will relate to what we already know about ACoAs and co-dependency. Many have commented "That is not me!" when presented with the information. With the high level of denial prevalent in this population, some resistance may be their sense of the Black Experience. Let us examine some examples.

—Generally, it is agreed that ACoAs have experienced degrees of trauma in their homes and, thus, are acutely aware of family tension.

Some black ACoAs perceive themselves as having experienced more trauma outside the family, in society, than inside it. Their tension antennae extend beyond the family to their communities and society. Their understanding of the racism and discrimination their parents have had to deal with in society helps them to rationalize the alcoholism and alcoholic behavior.

—Many ACoAs have a lot of anger about the poor parenting they received. They have a desire to express this anger to their parent, but since a symptom of their co-dependency is repressed feelings, they are unable to do so.

Black families generally do not tolerate expression of anger toward one's parents. The high value placed on respecting and obeying parents may contribute to the depth of black ACoAs' repressed anger. Thus they do not think or feel that it is within their ability or right ever to express their anger to their parent. On the other hand, a certain level of anger with society is allowed expression in the home, but there is the fear that one will be persecuted in society if it is expressed openly. Consequently, black ACoAs receive a strong message that "anger equals fear" from both the family and society.

—With the emergence of the ACoA movement across the country, information about the issues is being promoted by white role models in films, conferences, and literature. As a result, ACoAs are identifying their issues and seeking help.

Many black ACoAs do not identify with or even know about the movement. And they have no role models. Many black families have strong fundamentalist/religious beliefs and use the church as a coping mechanism. Therefore, when black ACoAs find themselves having difficulty coping, they go to the church for help. Although they may find some relief, their issues are not really being addressed. Many feel guilty about their parent's alcoholism, and the church with its moralistic view of alcoholism may feed into and strengthen their hidden guilt feelings.

Some black ACoAs do get help in treatment centers because they become addicted themselves and seek help for their own chemical dependence, but they are subject to the same familial denial. Some admit to parental alcoholism after they admit to their own, but continue to deny its contribution to their lives. In other words, they continue to protect/"respect" their parent. They are acutely aware of their community's opinion of their parent's alcoholism and now of their own. The clinician's awareness of black ACoAs denial systems can allow him to support and accept the clients from a holistic point of view. He can also facilitate the actualization of the identity as black ACoAs. Those clients who do come to terms with the fact that their parent are alcoholic may have a very powerful experience. These black ACoAs are often highly motivated to address their issues, and are in need of immediate attention and support.

Assessment

In order to make valid assessments that determine treatment methods, the clinician has to examine the problems in the context of the black client's environment. Some of the factors that contribute to the differences include:

1. Community background:
   native American or immigrant
   neighborhood of origin, i.e.
   black, integrated, white
   north, south
   innercity, rural, suburban
   community attitudes about drugs, alcohol, getting help
   community resources
2. Family background:
   type of parenting

family attitudes and values about work, education, getting help
mobility of family
perception of both parents and sibling
alcohol/drug use
dynamics between them

3. Other influences:
significant others in past and present life
church
role models—Do they have any? Are there any in their
 community with whom they could connect?
experience with racism
economics

4. Present life:
personal drug/alcohol use
social lifestyle
type of community they presently live in
 attitudes
 resources
their perception of present problems
self-concept
racial identity development

Thus, the implication is that the clinician must evaluate each person's dysfunctioning within the realm of their Black Experience.

Treatment Approaches/Framework

Now we can take what we have discussed about black families and black ACoAs and integrate it with black psychology to develop a framework for treatment. The following is a suggested list of treatment techniques and approaches.

1. USE THE RELATIONSHIPS OF SIGNIFICANT OTHERS IN BLACK ACoAs LIVES IN THERAPY.

Black ACoAs need to connect with people who were there with them during their childhoods in order to validate their reality.

Since the black family supports childhood friends, more than likely these friends experienced some of the alcoholism in that family; they can be used in adulthood to validate feelings and may need to work through some of their own feelings about the issue.

Since siblings may continue to deny, friends are valuable. These friends can support and validate the work being done in therapy.

If the alcoholic has stopped drinking on his own, the black ACoA may feel proud and question his/her perception that alcoholism existed. His pride may interfere with his own need to address his anger. Validation allows the space for his own needs.

2. USE TECHNIQUES THAT ENCOURAGE ACTIVITY RATHER THAN PASSIVITY.

Blacks and ACoAs have mastered passive/aggressive behavior. Active techniques allow ventilation of feelings and acceptance of going against the norm. Furthermore, they tap into the black ACoA's sense of drama.

Just as traditional verbal therapy is ineffective with ACoA's, so it is with black clients.

3. USE GROUP THERAPY—IT IS IMPORTANT TO HAVE OTHER BLACKS IN THE GROUP.

Group support allows black ACoAs to express their anger and have others there who are not intimidated by it. Often, whites are intimidated by "Black Anger." A racially mixed group allows black ACoAs to deal with both the familial and societal messages around anger. [See case study.]

In addition, the isolation ACoAs experience in their lives and racial group identification can be addressed.

4. ADDRESS THEIR OWN CHEMICAL USAGE.

ACoAs tend to compare their own chemical usage and behavior to that of their parents. This action can either support that they have a problem, or enable them to continue denying their own addiction.

If it is determined that they have a chemical addiction, this must be the primary treatment focus.

Nevertheless, discussing these comparisons to the parents allows the addicted black ACoAs to work through their own denial and to relieve guilt. Attention should be given to comparing community attitudes and resources as well.

5. ADDRESS RACIAL AND PERSONALITY DEVELOPMENT ISSUES.

ACoAs have unresolved problems that were not worked through during appropriate developmental stages. Thus, retrieving the child within and working through these problems so the ACoA can mature and nurture self is a goal.

6. USE SHORT TERM TREATMENT.

Blacks generally do not stay in therapy long, so close-ended ACoA groups with specific goals are appropriate.

7. GIVE FOCUS TO THE PRESENTING PROBLEM AND BE CONCRETE.

By the time black ACoAs get into treatment, they have searched for answers elsewhere and failed. They may need some crisis counseling.

8. DO NOT BE AFRAID TO BE DIRECT AND USE CONFRONTATION SKILLS.

Black clients tend to respect someone who will be out front with the issues and with whom they can be honest. Practicing honesty is important for ACoAs.

9. DO NOT CRITICIZE THE PARENT.

Black ACoAs will react to this by not trusting. They will protect their parents. However, allow them to do the criticizing.

10. HELP BLACK ACoAS TO EXAMINE THE LARGER PICTURE.

They need to examine alcoholism realistically, family dynamics, generational issues, society's attitudes and political realities concerning discrimination, and legal issues.

11. SUGGEST WAYS OF CHANGING THE SYSTEM.

This may seem strange to address in therapy, but black clients need not to feel impotent. They are part of a community and need to examine ways they can remain in their community while changing themselves.

Involvement in setting up Al-Anon meetings for black ACoAs, establishing alcoholism education, and being politically active are important to developing some role models for recovery in the black community.

Accomplishment in this area connects with the characteristics of development of a positive self-concept [see section on black community self-concept.]

A CASE EXAMPLE

The following case was chosen not because it was typical of black ACoAs, but because it particularly involved many of the dynamics previously discussed. Some details have been deleted because of space limitations, and the name has been changed.

Judy, a 30-year-old, black, mother of two pre-school female children sought inpatient treatment for her heroin addiction. She had been detoxed from heroin two months previously when her alcoholic father died of cancer, but she continued to drink alcohol. She complained of feeling depressed and excessively fearful, and expressed wanting help with anger, grief, and anxiety. She also complained of having difficulty parenting. Judy presented as an attractive, competent, congenial but pensive woman with conflicting values.

Judy was the youngest of four children. Her oldest sister, ten years her senior, and her aunt raised her from age ten. At that time, her father was found guilty of shooting and killing her mother while under the influence of alcohol. He spent five years in prison. Judy said the family never talked about this. Throughout her early adulthood, she repeatedly tried to leave her community, but she always returned. Her father also returned to their black community and was generally accepted. Judy made contact with him a couple of years before his death. She was presently living with two men, continuing her pattern of involvement in distant relationships with invalidating men.

Judy's reaction to her father was complex. She loved and wanted her father, but was not allowed to express her anger toward him. Her anger was as connected to him as to the community and society. Her clinical picture indicated both chemical and co-dependency issues, in that the repressed fears, anger, and anxiety precipitated her chemical usage, but there were also issues of the larger society, community, and family.

Was her mother's life only worth five years? If he had shot a white woman, would he have gotten more prison time? What does this say to her about her value as a black woman? What messages does the community's acceptance of her father give to her about her feelings? In that the family never talked about the incident and their feelings, who could Judy go to about her conflicting feelings? How could she deal with her female children?

In treatment, Judy was placed in a racially mixed group led by a white, male therapist. In that she had so many issues, priorities had to be set in her treatment plan. The primary focus was on her recovery from her chemical dependency, with attention given to her co-dependency. The racial identity and self-concept as a black woman and addict were addressed by her connecting with a black female therapist and black role models in her community.

Judy, identifying herself as an ACoA, chose involvement in an ACoA group led by the black female therapist. Here, she drew a picture of her father shooting her mother as her primary childhood memory. As her feelings were explored, Judy's anger surfaced in a powerfully intense manner, her anger with her father exploded in conjunction with the conflict about her self-concept as a black woman and addict. Whites in the group were intimidated and froze, even though they wanted to support her. The black members and therapist, identifying with her, supported her. Judy was guided through her emotions and was allowed to express some repressed feelings. The blacks in the group related similar feelings with her, thus developing a sense of collective selfhood. They also confronted one another about addictive behavior and the realities of their Black Experience.

As her therapy continued, Judy expressed feeling relief and support. She strongly connected with the other black group members, and felt warmth for the white members who allowed her to be herself. They were still experiencing the power of Judy's life drama, however, and needed much staff support. Judy was introduced to some sober, black addicts in her community who remained in close contact with her on her return home. Judy's sister was contacted via phone, but did not participate in the sessions. The therapists' impression was that this woman was very controlling and angry and directed her anger at Judy's treatment of her children. The children were involved in treatment.

Judy immediately got involved in Narcotics Anonymous in her community, and has been chemically free for one year.

Recovery, however, has been a struggle for her. Judy has more unfinished business to deal with in her life, but she did not follow through with more extensive therapy. More than likely she will not do so until she is in crisis, but her present connection with blacks in Narcotics Anonymous allows her some group identification and community support.

In this case, Judy's self-concept as a black woman was affected by the racism of American society, the community's attitude and acceptance of deviant alcoholic behavior, familial alcoholism and denial of feelings, and her own chemical dependency. Her motivation to address her issues allowed her to get in touch with their power within her. She responded positively to supportive, active therapy, and had to be confronted in treatment about some of her negative behaviors. A racially mixed group and therapy team were key factors in addressing societal and familial messages. Her connection with her community was redirected by developing relationships with healthy role models. She has sporadically maintained contact with the black female therapist.

SUMMARY

Of course, not all black ACoAs have been affected the same way or to the same degree, therefore discretion and creativity must be utilized by the clinician. This chapter is not meant to be a comprehensive study of black ACoAs; much more research is needed in this area. I have simply used a review of literature and my clinical experience to point out some dynamics and observations, in the hope that you have understood some of the complexities facing clinicians and black clients. The intricacies of their issues must be thought through in order to offer hope and help.

REFERENCES

Banks, James A. and Brambs, Jean D., *Black Self-Cponcept*. New York: McGraw-Hill, 1972.

Barnes, Edward J. The black community as the source of positive self-concept for black children: A theoretical perspeptive." In R.L. Jones, [ed.] *Black Psychology*, New York: Harper and Row, 1980.

Billingsley, Andrew. *Black Families in White America*. New Jersey: Prentice-Hall, 1968.

Comer, James P. The black family: An adaptive perspective." In M.D. Fantini and Rene Cardenas, [ed.] *Parenting in a Multicultural Society*, New York: Longman, 1980.

Dunmore, Charlotte J. [compiler] Black Children and their Families: A Bibliography. San Francisco: R. and E. Associates, 1976.

Fantini, Mario D. and Cardenas, Rener, [ed.] *Parenting in a Multicultural Society*, New York: Longman, 1980.

Harrison-Ross, Phyllis. Parenting the black child. *Pediatric Annals*, Vol. VI: 9 [1977], 84-94.

Hill, Robert B. *The Strengths of Black Families*. New York: National Urban League, 1972.

Jackson, Gerald G. The emergence of a black perspective in counseling. In R.L. Jones, [ed] *Black Psychology*, New York: Harper and Row, 1980.

Jackson James S. et al. Group identity psychologist as consultant and therapist." In R.L. Jones, [ed.] *Black Psychology*, New York: Harper and Row, 1980.

Jones, Reginald L. *Black Psychology. New York: Harper and Row, 1980.*

Manns, Wilhelmina. Support systems of significant others in black families. In H.P. McAdoo, [ed.] Black Families, Beverly Hills: Sage, 1981.

McAdoo, Harriette Pipes, [ed.] *Black Families*. Beverly Hills; Sage, 1981.

Myers, Hector, et. al. *Black Child Development in America: 1927-1977—An Annotated Bibliography*. Westport, Conn.: Greenwood Press, 1979.

Peters, Marie Fe. "Parenting in black families with young children: A historical perspective. In H.P. McAddo, [ed.] *Black Families*, Beverly Hills: Sage, 1981.

Scanzoni, John H. *The Black Family in Modern Society*. Chicago: University of Chicago Press, 1977.

Skolnick, Arlene and Skolnick, Jerome H. *Family in Transition*. Boston: Little, Brown and Company, 1980.

Staples, Robert, Ph.D. "The mother-son-relationship in the black family." *Ebony*, 39:74, October, 1984.

Taylor, Pat and Bell, Peter. Alcoholism and black families." *FOCUS on Family and Chemical Dependency*, U.S. Journal, Vol. 7, No. 2:34, April, 1984.

The Unseen Crisis: Blacks and Alcohol. NIAAA, 1978.

Tounsel, Patricia L. and Jones, Arthur C. Theoretical considerations for psychotherapy with black clients. In R.L. Jones. [ed.] *Black Psychology*, New York: Harper and Row, 1980

Upsher, Curtis, Jr. "The Development of Black Self Esteem: Theory and Review." Unpublished, University of Pittsburgh, 1978.

Wheeler, William H., Ph.D. *Counseling from a Cultural Perspective*. Trainee/Resource Manual, Atlanta, Georgia, 1977.

White, Joseph. Toward a black psychology. In: R.L. Jones, (ed). *Black Psychology*, New York: Harper and Row, 1980.

Willie, Charles V. *The Family Life of Black People*. Columbus, Ohio: Charles E. Merrill Publishing Co., 1980.

Chapter Nineteen
After the Tears: Working Through Grief, Loss and Depression with Adult Children of Alcoholics

Jane Middelton-Moz and Lorie Dwinell

Joan sat in a chair in our office. She had been crying for about 15 minutes, and her eyes were swollen and red. Unlike other times, however, she made no effort to hide her tears or to stop crying. After a time had passed she said, "What is there after the tears? It's funny. When I first came here, I worried about myself because I never felt anything, never cried. Now I wonder if I'll ever stop." Joan had been in therapy for approximately a year and a half. Initially she had entered therapy because she had read an article Jane had written on children of alcoholics and had recognized in herself many of the characteristics, including frequent depressions, difficulty in intimate relationships, overpowering feelings of guilt and shame, difficulty expressing feelings, and poor self-esteem. She was a dance instructor, had a lot of students and yet experienced feelings of failure in her occupation. She states that she often felt like an observer in life, numb, not knowing what she felt in many situations. She was afraid of conflict and spent a good deal of time pleasing other people, yet not knowing what she believed about anything. During her first year of therapy, she talked a lot about what it was like growing up in an alcoholic family. She often talked about extremely painful situations in her childhood without connecting to her own emotions. Joan often talked to me about feeling that there were many different parts of her at war with each other. She was an extremely creative person, and Jane asked her to draw herself. She drew three pictures. The first was of a tiny little girl huddled in the corner, afraid and shaking with tears in her eyes. The second was a picture of a very angry girl, furious at the first and trying to hurt her. The third was a picture of a very calm and beautiful ballerina with very slight smile. When Jane asked who was the strongest of these three, she said, "Well, it must be the girl that's angry at the other one, or the ballerina. It certainly wouldn't be that terrified child because I have been trying to get rid of her all of my life."

Joan creatively depicted through her art what many children of alcoholics feel: a part inside that is a child who never went through developmental stages, a child who very early felt fear and sadness in her/his alcoholic home, a child who never cried the tears nor told anyone the fear because of the unspoken loyalty in the family. The angry child represented depression, that punitive part of adult children that feels deeply and profoundly unlovable, the part that will not allow them to experience their own fear, the part that feels extremely guilty and responsible for their parents' problems. They think the alcoholism in the family is their fault. The ballerina represents the fifty-year-old, five-year-old: the survivor, the perfectionist, the constantly hypervigilant part of the self, the person who remains constantly in control, the compulsive striver, the overachiever, the workaholic, the adaptive part of self that presents to the world a picture of stability, pleasing, and achievement.

Like Joan, many adult CoAs are admired, are envied, are successful, and yet, no matter how many rewards or how much applause is given, they never feel a sense of self-worth. Inside they experience emptiness and a powerful self-alienation. Children of alcoholics tend to have great empathy for other people and feel deeply the pain of others, and yet display very little compassion for the child within themselves. It was important in the therapeutic process for Joan to realize that behind the mask of strength was the stronger self, the child of the past. It was important for her to get to know that child, to cry with that child, to attain for herself again a freedom and spontaneity through the process of mourning, and to end what Alice Miller called, "the courtship between grandiosity and depression"; to experience, through the mourning process, the deep pain of abandonment that was once felt; and to attain again, rather than emotional constriction, the freedom to experience a full range of emotions. Perfectionism, overachievement, compulsive caretaking and pleasing in the adult child is often a defense against the intense pain of childhood loss. Often that loss consists of whole developmental periods—loss of childhood, loss of self. There is a great deal of pain in the realization that an alcoholic family is a battlefield that makes a child "afraid to walk without stilts" [Miller.]

George Vaillant, in his book, *The Natural History of Alcoholism*, states that often living with alcoholism is second only in stress to being in prisoner camps in World War II [Vaillant]. When an individual lives with an air raid a day, chronic stress becomes normal. In order to protect the ego from the disintegration resulting from that degree of trauma, individuals have to adapt with massive uses of denial and repression. It is difficult for an adult, but if that person is a child living with the constant unpredictability of an alcoholic family, he/she has to put so much energy into just surviving that the developmental process is put on hold. The child survives through the use of denial, hypervigilance, and psychic numbing. Because so many adult children from alcoholic homes show survival skills and characteristics similar to individuals who have survived the trauma of war, clinicians in the field, such as Timmen Cermak, M.D., see the survival characteristics of adult children as a variant of post-traumatic stress disorder [Cermak].

A clinician in Seattle, Jean Burgan, created a story which helps us understand the necessity for the development of hypervigilance, denial, and repression in children from alcoholic homes. This is the story of one day in the life of a little girl from an alcoholic home. The little girl gets up in the morning at a normal time. For most five-year-old children, that is about seven or eight o'clock. Her mother had been up drinking late the night before and is still in bed when the child wakes up. The little girl waits patiently downstairs. Her mother wakes up at around eleven o'clock and comes into the kitchen. Because she drank heavily the night before, the little girl's mother has a hangover. She is feeling sick and irritable. The last thing in the world she wants to contend with upon arising are the needs of a little girl. The little girl walks into the kitchen and says, "Good morning, mommy, I've been waiting for you to get up. I'm hungry, can I have some lunch?" The mother pushes her away and tells her that she does not want to be bothered. The little girl walks away feeling that she has done something wrong. Five-year-olds do not understand hangovers. They believe they are magicians and responsible for what goes on around them. The child feels that she has done something wrong. Mother reaches for the vodka bottle, then the tomato juice and makes herself a Bloody Mary. She drinks it and makes another.

A little while later, the little girl returns to the kitchen and tries again. "Good morning mother. You look beautiful this morning. I don't want to bother you, but I'm really hungry. I'd like some lunch." Because mother has had a couple of drinks, she now reaches a stable blood alcohol level. She is no longer irritable. She no longer has a headache, and she is feeling normal. She turns to her daughter and says, "Good morning honey. Certainly you may have a sandwich. What would you like? Bologna and cheese, peanut butter and jelly, liverwurst?" It does not occur to the little girl that mother's new behavior is because she has had something to drink. Instead she feels that she must have done it right this time. She leaves the kitchen knowing that her sandwich will be made and feels happy. Mother continues to drink. When she returns to the kitchen a little while later, her sandwich has been made and is on the table. Her mother has now had enough to drink to be on the rising side of a blood alcohol level. She is at what is called "star time": she is feeling high and on top of the world. The little girl goes to sit down at the table and the mother runs and picks her up and covers her with wet, slobbery kisses. She says to her daughter, "You're the best little girl in the world. This afternoon, I'm going to take you downtown and buy you a 10-speed bike."

The little girl doesn't understand that her mother's new behavior is because of further drinking. She feels a vague discomfort because of the wet, slobbery kisses. She doesn't understand why. What she thinks is that she has done something right. She has pleased her mother, and she is going to be rewarded with a brand new bike. After she has eaten her lunch, she goes out to play while her mother continues drinking in the kitchen. When she goes back into the kitchen later in the afternoon, mother has had enough alcohol to be on the falling side of an alcohol curve. She is at this point, snarly, angry, drunk. The little girl runs up to kiss her mother and says, "Mommy, mommy, are you ready to go and get the bike?" Her mother pushes her away saying, "What are you talking about, you little brat. You're always asking me for things, Get out of my sight." The little girl still does not understand that her mother's change in behavior is because of alcohol. She feels that she had done something terribly wrong to disappoint her mother. She feels sad and leaves the kitchen, crying. The little girl sits on the porch, trying to understand what it is she has done wrong, trying to figure out what she is going to say, trying to figure out how to make her mommy happy. Mother continues to drink, and when the little girl comes back into the house an hour later, she finds her mother passed-out on the kitchen floor. Most adult children of alcoholics that we have treated, remember the first time they found their parent passed-out. They report the terror of that first occasion, because they thought they had found their parent dead.

This little girl is not living in a safe and consistent home. She is living in a war zone where her mother changes constantly from hour-to-hour, depending on the amount of alcohol she had ingested. The little girl does not relate to a stable mother. She relates to five, depending on the degree of inebriation. She learns very early to stay out of her mother's way during that hangover state and to get reasonable needs met when her mother is not drinking or has a stable blood alcohol level. She learns to get unreasonable needs met when her mother is at "star time", and she learns to stay out of her way when she is snarly, angry, and drunk. When she is an adolescent, she might take her mother's keys or steal money out of her purse when she has passed out. What she learns most is that there is something wrong with herself, and she learns to be afraid of her environment. She represses the first time she saw her mother drunk on the kitchen floor because it is too painful to remember. She develops a fantasy mother in her mind who shows her love, because developing children cannot tolerate abandonment. She learns to be hypervigilant and constantly aware, in order to survive. The massive life energy that is necessary to maintain this hypervigilance and denial causes an arrest in emotional development. She becomes fifty at five, and her own development is put on hold. Like a soldier in a war zone, she learns that chronic trauma is normal, and in order to survive, she learns to repress emotionally and to deny what is experienced as constant danger. She detaches emotionally and develops emotional constriction, rather than spontaneity. She learns either to stay out of her mother's way or to constantly take care of her mother and always be good. She feels deeply and profoundly unlovable, and learns like the ballerina, that she is only acceptable when performing or doing. The price children pay in an alcoholic home for being thirty at five, is often to feel developmentally that they are five years old at age thirty.

The family is the arena for both growth and healing of its members. One of the most important and vital tasks of the family is to provide a haven from the stressors of the outside world. If the boundaries that separate the family from the world are either too rigid or too lax, the family within those boundaries will become impoverished and devitalized. In an alcoholic home there is often little interaction between members and the outside world.

In a healthy family, each parent is an individual, and the parents together are the sources of nurturing, protection, and learning for the children. The parents have a boundary around their relationship which allows the child the freedom to develop normally and allows children in the family to form their own unit of support. In an alcoholic family, because of the constant need for survival and hypervigilance on the part of the children, normal development does not occur, because the focus of the parents is not on the developing needs of children. The focus is on alcohol. The children learn that their needs cannot be met and so alter their needs accordingly, which leads to a consistent over-control of self. Because the child has to constantly be aware of the parent's needs, feelings, and behavior in order to survive, the child loses concept of self and develops chronic over-responsibility for others. The parent's needs become the children's needs. The parent's wishes become their wishes. The parent's sadness and grief become their sadness and grief. Rather than fostering the development of healthy individuals, the alcoholic family fosters enmeshment or extreme detachment.

Children from alcoholic homes learn very early that they cannot trust their environment. They learn to control their needs, and they learn to trust only themselves. They become chronically counter-dependent because dependency means pain and feared loss of self. This rigid counter-dependence was dramatically exemplified by this adult-child story. "I was at a picnic with a group of friends on a hot July afternoon. One of my friends had a Siberian Husky, and I noticed the dog was hot, so I gave him a partially full carton of ice cream. A few minutes later, I inadvertently stepped on the ice cream carton on my way to the picnic table. The dog growled and bit my bare foot. I looked down to see my foot covered with blood. I became temporarily confused and didn't know what to do. I walked into the house, turned on the cold water in the bath tub and tried to stop the blooding. I watched the icy cold water run over the wound, but the blood didn't stop. I tried to think of how I was going to get myself to the hospital. A friend had followed me into the house, and I looked up at her perplexedly and said, 'I don't know how I'm going to drive myself to the hospital.' She was shocked at my reaction. She said, 'There are 20 people here. Somebody will drive you to the hospital.' What was most shocking to me was that it had never occurred to me to ask for help. It wasn't that I thought about it and decided not to. It just never occurred to me."

Children from alcoholic families never learned the ABC's of feeling. The only way they could survive was to constrict themselves emotionally. Because the focus was on alcohol, there was no network in the family that supported affect or communication. There was no place where it was safe enough to work through feelings. The permission to feel and the degree of allowable catharsis is always directly proportional to the amount of support to work through feelings. Children of alcoholics do not begin to work through delayed grief and loss until they feel safe enough and have enough support to do so. They need to feel safe enough in the therapeutic setting to go back and walk through the trauma. it takes a long time (in the therapeutic setting) for the adult child to feel safe enough to begin the grieving process and it is absured to talk about short-term treatment with adult children of alcoholics. For adults, who as children learned not to trust, it takes time to develop a trusting relationship. The first year or year-and-a-half of therapy often focuses on relationship building. The adult child needs to test the safety of the therapeutic relationship, and to develop the sense of supportive environment necessary to begin the grieving process.

Those therapists who talk about treating children of alcoholics in ten sessions are actually talking about education. They provide an intellectual framework and cognitive understanding of what has happened, but not the structure of a safe environment to work through long-term grief. Alice Miller states, "The opposite of depression is not joy, but spontaneity" (Miller). Spontaneity is the ability to experience the full range of emotions, and in order for this to occur, adult children need to work through the grieving process. Working through grief allows for the independence of mastery of the self. The process of grief work in therapy is as Freud called it, the process of "remembering, repeating and working-through" (Freud—remembering, with the support of the therapist, the day the child found mom on the kitchen floor, waling through the trauma, experiencing the feelings, developing empathy and connection with that child of the past.

It is important for adult children of alcoholics to recognize that their defenses were once friends that protected their ego from the devastating pain that could not be experienced in childhood, but that those defenses later became barriers to their experiencing the fullest range of emotional relationships as adults. The by-product of delayed grief is emotional constriction, and the reward for working through the grief process is the freedom of choice, spontaneity, and the ability to experience the rainbow of emotions between the stark black and white that they have learned to feel as children. Chronic, unresolved grief shows itself in many forms:

1] Compulsive caring for other. "The compulsive caregiver seems to attribute to the one cared-for, all the sadness and neediness that he is unable or unwilling to recognize in himself [Bowlby].

2] Fixed rage. A wall of anger that serves as a barrier to the outside world.

3] Persistent numbing, or detachment from one's self and one's life. These persons feel like observers constantly, they never feel that they are truly experiencing the world in which they live.

4] Constant undoing to tendency to recreate similar events to those experience in early childhood along with the attempt to undo the pain that was done. They are actors playing a role in a play that has the same beginning and ending over and over again. This often accounts for repetitive relationship patterns in adult children of alcoholics which delayed grief.

5] Avoidance of any stimulus that reminds one of the pain that was felt. This leads to isolation in life and restriction of activities.

6] Drug and alcohol abuse.

7] Chronic, recurring depressions.

8] Re-occurring nightmares.

9] Consistent, oppressive guilt.

10] Constant somatic complaints, including headaches, stomach aches, ulcers, lower bowel dysfunction, difficulties with blood pressure.

Stages in recovery for adult children involve acceptance, grief, and integration which leads to behavior change. One of the mistakes that is made in programs designed to give education only, is the expectation of behavior change before the mourning or grieving process. Many adult children whom we have treated have gone through many programs like Assertiveness Training repeatedly and experience consistent failure because they cannot operationalize in their lives the skills that they have been taught. Behavior change occurs only after the trauma has been repeatedly walked through and the grief has been fully experienced. Education concerning the characteristics of adult children of alcoholics is important in the therapeutic process, because it normalizes what is often considered abnormal. It allows adult children to see themselves as survivors who developed defenses to protect themselves in an abnormal family. Cognitive understanding provides a framework and structure to work through the grieving process, but education alone is not an end in itself. Education is instead a "life raft" to retreat to an occasion when the pain and sadness feels like "too much." Education is an aid in pacing grief, not a replacement for mourning.

The freedom that is gained through the process of mourning is the freedom of choice. Many adult children of alcoholics suffering from delayed grief have lived in the prison of a never-ending cycle of disappointment, repression of pain, depression, workaholism, frantic push towards success, and disappointment again. The applause and rewards are never enough, never felt. Alice Miller talks about the emptiness and loneliness of the illusion of touch through achievement:

"Narcissus was in love with his idealized picture of himself but neither the grandiose nor the depressed Narcissus could love himself. His passion for his false self only made object love impossible, but also love for the one person who was fully entrusted to his care—he, himself" [Miller].

Through the process of mourning, adult children of alcoholics experience the pain of the illusion of the "happy child of the past" while also reclaiming the empathy for the child inside that really was. If the therapeutic environment is supportive to the process, the adult child will enter into the full experience of mourning which will eventually lead to integration and the freedom to reconstruct their life rather than to a life controlled by the pain of the past. For many, the repression of unresolved grief has not only meant denial of self, frequent depressions, and massive guilt, but also the illusion of control. Many have repetitively entered relationships that are punitive and lack nurturing, yet feel helpless to separate from them because of a sense of desperation they could not understand. Many have worked around the clock, becoming "stimulous junkies" who could not relax and live their lives except through mazes of deadlines and goals. They exprienced the feelings of loneliness even when surrounded by others. They have developed caseloads rather than friendships and allowed relaxation only through illness. They constantly confronted, in attempts to relax, the rigidity of that master inside, depression.

There are no shortcuts in the treatment of delayed grief. Grief can be experienced only by an individual in therapy when the relationship with the therapist is experienced as safe and supportive; only then can the process of remembering begin, walking with direction back through the trauma and working it through. Grief is the pain that heals itself if the individual experiencing it or others do not get in the way.

"What is there after the tears?" The experience of grief allows for the reclaiming of history, of family, of the child of the past. It allows for the ability to reclaim the choices of the present, the memories of the past, and the dreams of the future. It allows the freedom spontaneously to experience joy, sadness, anger, success, loving and being loved, and to live a life of balance and of choices with the freedom to say "yes" or "no" without the terror of feared abandonment. Through grief comes the realization that the pain of abandonment took place in the past, and there is nothing that can be done in the present that will change that loss. After the tears comes the freedom to experience the rainbow of emotions which exist between the painful world of darkness and the illusion of a bright fantasy world that never was.

REFERENCES

Bergman, Martin S. and Jucovy, Milton E., Ed., *Generations of the Holocaust*. New York, N.Y.: Basic Books, Inc., 1982.

Burgan, Jean, Bellevue, WA: Jean Burgan, Inc.

Bowlby, John. *Attachment and Loss, Vol. III: Loss*. New York, N.Y.: Basic Books, Inc., 1980.

Cermak, Timmen L., M.D. Conference Presentation, First Northwest Regional Conference, Seattle, WA, June, 1984.

Freud, Sigmund, "Remembering, Repeating, and Working Through" in The Standard Edition of the Complete Psychological Works of Sigmund Freud. London: Hogarth Press, Vol. XIII.

Lipton, Robert J. in Mischerlich, Alexander and Margarete, *The Inability to Mourn*. New York, N.Y.: Grove Press, 1975.

Miller, Alice, *Drama of the Gifted Child*. New York, N.Y.: Basic Books, Inc., 1981.

Vaillant, George. *The Natural History of Alcoholism*. Cambridge, Mass.: Harvard University Press, 1983.